# Kicking at the Darkness

## Bruce Cockburn and the Christian Imagination

## BRIAN J. WALSH

**Brazos**Press

*a division of Baker Publishing Group*
Grand Rapids, Michigan

© 2011 by Brian J. Walsh

Published by Brazos Press
a division of Baker Publishing Group
P.O. Box 6287, Grand Rapids, MI 49516-6287
www.brazospress.com

Printed in the United States of America

Library of Congress Cataloging-in-Publication Data

Walsh, Brian J., 1953–
    Kicking at the darkness : Bruce Cockburn and the Christian imagination / Brian J. Walsh.
        p.  cm.
    Includes bibliographical references and indexes.
    ISBN 978-1-58743-253-8 (pbk.)
    1. Cockburn, Bruce—Criticism and interpretation. 2. Popular music—Religious aspects—Christianity. I. Title.
    ML420.C6116W35  2011
    781.64092—dc23                                                                                2011025056

Unless otherwise indicated, Scripture quotations are from the New Revised Standard Version of the Bible, copyright © 1989, by the Division of Christian Education of the National Council of the Churches of Christ in the United States of America. Used by permission. All rights reserved.

Scripture quotations labeled RSV are from the Revised Standard Version of the Bible, copyright 1952 [2nd edition, 1971] by the Division of Christian Education of the National Council of the Churches of Christ in the United States of America. Used by permission. All rights reserved.

All lyrics by Bruce Cockburn have been quoted with permission. © Golden Mountain Music Corp.

11   12   13   14   15   16   17          7   6   5   4   3   2   1

for Jubal, Madeleine, and Lydia

*... with pain the world paves us over*
*Lord, let us not betray*
*God bless the children with*
*vision of the Day*

# Contents

# Preface

The stage of Toronto's Massey Hall was full of a "who's who" of Canadian musicians who had come together to honor the forty-year contribution of one of their most esteemed colleagues. The word *iconic* was used frequently. And no wonder. Consider the man's résumé: thirty-one albums (twenty of which went gold or platinum), a reputation as one of the finest guitarists in the world, numerous Juno Awards, induction into the Canadian Music Hall of Fame, and recipient of the Order of Canada. Now add in all of the honorary doctoral degrees in music or letters from Memorial University of Newfoundland, St. Thomas University, University of Victoria, York University, and McMaster University, *and* an honorary doctor of divinity from Queen's University. Not bad for a music school dropout. And that music school—the Berklee College of Music in Boston—also conferred an honorary degree on this artist in 1997.

We are talking about Bruce Cockburn.

With Cockburn playing with a right hand influenced by the likes of Mississippi John Hurt and the left hand of an accomplished jazz guitarist, it is no surprise that this guitar virtuoso is placed in the company of Andrés Segovia, Bill Frisell, and Django Reinhardt by *Acoustic Guitar* magazine. Blending modal jazz, classic blues, folk, rock—and sometimes even reggae, punk, and rap—with a fine ear for world music influences, Cockburn's music is simply unclassifiable.

Cockburn songs have been covered by artists as diverse as Jerry Garcia, the Barenaked Ladies, Jimmy Buffett, Anne Murray, Maria Muldaur, The Rankins, Dan Fogelberg, Steve Bell, Michael Occhipinti, Holly Near, Chet Atkins, Elbow, Judy Collins, the Skydiggers, Third World, Blackie and the Rodeo Kings, and k.d. lang. U2 refer to Cockburn in "God Part 2" on the *Rattle and Hum* album when Bono sings,

> *I heard a singer on the radio*
> *Late last night*
> *Says he's gonna kick the darkness*
> *Till it bleeds daylight.*

The artists that gathered that evening in Massey Hall did so under that evocative Cockburn metaphor—"kicking at the darkness." And it was clear from both the performances and the testimonies from the stage that these musicians understood this kicking at the darkness to be a deeply spiritual discipline. Repeatedly throughout the show, comments were made about Cockburn's spirituality. Perhaps this perspective on Cockburn came to its poignant and humorous height in some onstage banter between host Jian Ghomeshi and Barenaked Ladies lead singer Ed Robertson. Having launched his career with a cover of Cockburn's "Lovers in a Dangerous Time" (in which we meet that metaphor "kick at the darkness till it bleeds daylight"), Robertson was asked if this was his favorite Cockburn song. No, was the reply. And in the banter that followed it took a while to learn that the early song "One Day I Walk" was Robertson's favorite. A good choice. But in the midst of the dialogue Robertson said, "Actually I like his 'Jesusy' songs the best." The coining of the term "Jesusy" occasioned laughter from the audience and then some further joking around about whether this might have crossed some kind of line of religious propriety. But in the midst of it all Robertson still made his point clear: "I'm not really a 'Jesusy' kind of guy. But I love Bruce's 'Jesusy' songs."

"Jesusy" songs. In an industry that has been uneasy, at best, with anything that is overtly "Christian" in content, a non-Jesusy artist like Robertson is drawn to Cockburn's songs about Jesus.

Jesusy songs. While Cockburn wisely steered clear of the "Contemporary Christian Music" scene early in his career and has intentionally avoided being labeled a "Christian artist," his Jesusy songs are noted as some of his best at a concert celebrating his forty-year contribution. And no one in the audience was embarrassed or confused. Everyone knew what Robertson was talking about, and my hunch is that many people in the hall agreed with him, whether they were Jesusy kinds of people or not.

Now, I need to come clean from the outset. I am a Jesusy kind of guy. A profound sense of shared Christian faith is one of the things that have drawn me to Cockburn's music over the last four decades. Like many other Christians, I have found that Cockburn's art has resonated deeply with my own life and with how I understand myself to be a Christian. As we will see, Cockburn is uncomfortable and often disgusted with much that passes as Christian in our culture. I share that discomfort. And you will have to keep reading to discern just what kind of a Christian I might be. But it is clear that you don't have to be a Christian of any sort to find yourself deeply moved by the music and lyrics of Bruce Cockburn. His audience is decidedly pluralistic. Christian, secularist, New Age, Jewish, Eastern spiritualist, you name it, and you will find folks from these various worldviews at a Bruce Cockburn concert. And maybe you don't even need to have any interest at all in spirituality to love a good Cockburn song. But the word on the stage that night was that Cockburn's spirituality is at the heart of his art. You can appreciate his music without paying much attention to the spiritual foundation of it all, but you just might be missing something.

So, is this book about Bruce Cockburn's spirituality? Well, yes and no. Yes, this book takes as its point of departure the deeply Christian spirituality that we meet in Cockburn's music. But this is not an attempt to explain Cockburn's spirituality. As you will see in the opening chapters, there is a sense in which this book isn't so much *on* Bruce Cockburn as it is a conversation *with* his art. Nor is this book a biography. Rather, I am more interested in seeing what happens when Cockburn's songs, interpreted in the context of the whole body of his work, are brought into creative dialogue with biblical faith. Biblical metaphors, images, and references are ubiquitous in his writing. So the issue isn't a matter of imposing biblical faith on the lyrics. But I also will not limit the discussion to Cockburn's use of biblical imagery. Nor is the intention to offer an explication of something like "the theology of Bruce Cockburn." If there is a theology that emerges in these pages, then it is a theology of my own construction. Cockburn may or may not agree with the theology on offer here. But whether or not he agrees—or, for that matter, whether or not you, the reader, agree—my hope is that you can see that these ideas have emerged through a respectful interaction with Cockburn's work.

This book had its origins in an earlier, coauthored project that never came to completion. In the early nineties I began writing a book on Cockburn with my friend Richard Middleton. Other projects came along, however, and we let that manuscript move to the back burner and then off the stove altogether. This book bears little resemblance to that earlier project, but I would be remiss if I did not acknowledge my debt to Richard Middleton for many of my interpretations of Cockburn's work. Some of my most enjoyable memories are of sitting around with Richard, listening intently to a new vinyl record (remember them?) by Cockburn.

A number of people have read this manuscript at various stages of its development and offered helpful comment and encouragement. I especially want to thank Byron Borger, Rob Crosby-Shearer, and Steve Bouma-Prediger. As always, my wife, Sylvia Keesmaat, has been my closest reader and editor. Thank you. I am also indebted to my students, who have often met Cockburn's music for the first time in my classes at the University of Toronto and the Toronto School of Theology. A special thank-you goes out to those who have taken my "Music, Culture, and Prophecy" course. You have read much of this book in its various incarnations over the years.

Place is important for writing. That is true for Cockburn, and it is certainly true for me. I wrote most of this book at Russet House Farm in Cameron, Ontario. This is my home, and I am just beginning to sense how this place is shaping me in all kinds of ways, not least in my writing. Jim and Kathy Armstrong's house on Balsam Lake has also been a wonderful place to write while watching migrating ducks on the water just outside the window. And finally, I had an incredibly fruitful week of writing at Camp Fowler in the Adirondacks during the summer of 2009. My gratitude to Kent Busman for his hospitality and enthusiasm for this project.

This book was written with the financial support of the Priscilla and Stanford Reid Foundation. While I can say with some certainty that Mrs. and Dr. Reid were not fans of Bruce Cockburn, they were people of deep Christian commitment and broad vision. The foundation that carries on their legacy generously supported my writing of this book during a sabbatical that I was granted from my work as the Christian Reformed campus minister to the University of Toronto.

That campus ministry, especially the Wine Before Breakfast community, has also been integral to this project. Many of Cockburn's best songs are prayers. In the context of Christian worship at the University of Toronto, we have allowed those songs to take their place within the context of prayer. A special thanks to the "bandhood of all believers" over the years at Wine Before Breakfast.

Books need publishers. When I told my publishers at Brazos Press that I had decided to write this book, there were shrieks of joy around the table. You see, they are all huge Cockburn fans. Special thanks to Rodney Clapp and Bobbi Jo Heyboer for supporting this book and being patient waiting for it. I hope it didn't feel like you were waiting for a miracle. And thanks to Lisa Ann Cockrel, Lisa Williams, Derek R. Keefe, and Jeffrey Reimer for fine editing work on this book.

I also would like to express my gratitude to Bruce's manager, Bernie Finkelstein. Bernie has always been gracious and encouraging in his response to my previous publications about Cockburn, as well as this project. Thank you.

And finally thank you to Bruce Cockburn himself. Like Bernie, Bruce has also been very gracious, if not bemused, by my theological interest in his art. In private correspondence Bruce said that while reading this book he found himself "deeply affected by the feeling of having been understood. Doesn't happen every day." That is pretty much what most Cockburn fans feel when they listen closely to every new album. Somehow by sharing his experiences, his perspectives, and his feelings in his art, we feel understood. That's what great art does.

My children all heard the music of Bruce Cockburn when they were still in the womb. They have all had the opportunity to hear Bruce play live. They know that if their dad throws a provocative line their way in the middle of a conversation, it is likely a quote from Bruce Cockburn. Bruce once sang, "God bless the children with visions of the Day." My prayer is that my children would be such visionaries. And so I dedicate this book to Jubal, Madeleine, and Lydia.

At the end of the fortieth-anniversary concert at Massey Hall, all the performers came back on stage with Bruce for the final encore. Of course, they sang "Mystery," from the 2006 *Life Short Call Now* album:

> *You can't tell me there is no mystery*
> *Mystery*
> *Mystery*
> *You can't tell me there is no mystery*
> *It's everywhere I turn.*

There they were. Some of the best singers, songwriters, and musicians in the country, singing a hymn to the mysterious character of things. And there we were, a near-capacity crowd all singing along. You can't tell us there is no mystery. You can't reduce things to their scientific explanation or their price tag in the marketplace. We know better. We even experienced something deeper at Massey Hall that night. Something that we have tasted almost every time we have listened to Bruce Cockburn. There is a depth of mystery to the world, in the intimacy of our relationships, in our hopes and our fears, in our laughter and our tears. And Cockburn has helped us to get a glimpse of that mystery. And when we all sang, "This feast of beauty can intoxicate / just like the finest wine," we knew that in many ways, Cockburn's songs had invited us to that feast. Then came the final verse:

> *So all you stumblers who believe love rules*
> *Believe love rules*
> *Believe love rules*
> *Come all you stumblers who believe love rules*
> *Stand up and let it shine*
> *Stand up and let it shine.*

That's us. Stumblers who believe love rules. And in Cockburn we recognize a fellow stumbler. But somehow, listening to his music helps us to believe and gives us the courage to stand up and let it shine.

# God,
# Friendship,
# and Art

The seats couldn't have been better. The Trailf Music Hall in Buffalo, New York, was packed with devoted fans. And while there were no reserved seats, I walked in with a group of twenty students to the best tables in the house, held for us by the manager. We had traveled from Toronto for the show as a "field trip" from a course that I was teaching at the University of Toronto called "Music, Culture, and Prophecy." A phone call to the venue with a special request for some block seating resulted in these wonderful seats, much to the envy of everyone around us. Two six-string guitars, one twelve-string, one resonator guitar, and one amazing performer. That's all it took to transform that space into a place of profound meeting. Bruce Cockburn was in town. And he did not disappoint.

One fan posted a review that said the show "transcended the expected extraordinary experience into the realm of sacred."[1] There was something deeply spiritual about that evening, and so many other evenings, in the company of Bruce Cockburn. And nowhere was that more poignantly experienced than in the very last song of the show. Indeed, the very last lyrics to be sung were, "God's too big to fit in a book / But nothing's too big to fit in my heart."[2] The song, "To Fit in My Heart," was an odd choice to conclude his second encore. Nothing catchy about this tune. No immediate familiarity with the audience. Not a song to send the fans home humming the tune or singing the chorus. Yet these are also the closing lines on the album that Cockburn was showcasing on this tour, *Life Short Call Now*.[3] This is a song of deep humility.

In an earlier song, "Understanding Nothing," Cockburn confessed that as he stands before a world in which "patterns shift too fast to be discerned," he finds himself brought up short and is forced to conclude that "all these years of thinking / ended up like this / in front of all this beauty / understanding nothing."[4] So again in this more recent song the artist is deeply aware of the limitations of his understanding. Yet in this song, "To Fit in My Heart," it isn't the world's beauty that puts the artist in his place, so much as it is the world's vastness. The first verse meditates on the sea of "endless silver / wave forms crash in." And it would appear that the artist has a camera in his hands, because he concludes that the "sea's too big to fit in the frame." Or maybe this isn't just a reference to a photograph. Maybe he is suggesting that there is something about the vastness of the sea and all that it represents that goes beyond any "frame," any attempt to grasp and control, any attempt at complete understanding, any framework.

The second verse of the song only deepens the mystery. "Seas come, seas go / where they stood deserts flow." Even the vast space of the sea is bound by time. Seas come and go. Not even the sea is eternal. And so Cockburn sings, "time's too big to fit in the brain."

But it is the third verse that brings it all together. "Spacetime strings bend / world without end." "Spacetime" combines the first two verses—the space of the sea and the time that bounds it—and yet this is a "world without end." Anyone familiar with religious language would not be surprised that this phrase "world without end" will lead us to talking about God. Where else but in religious liturgy do we talk about something, or someone, who exists and is faithful "world without end"? This is a God-allusion to be sure. But if the artist is to refer to God in the face of a space that is too big to fit in a frame or a time that is too big to fit in a brain, then this will have to be a God who is "too big to fit in a book." The God of such a world, the God who has created such a world, indeed, the God that Bruce Cockburn continues to believe in and meditate upon, is not a God who can fit in a book.

However, none of these things—the vastness of space, the infinity of time, or the God who has created both—is "too big to fit in my heart." The recurring concluding line of each verse of this song quietly, yet confidently, proclaims that "nothing's too big to fit in my heart." Don't try to control, manipulate, or master the world of space and time, and don't try to bind God by any book—even the Bible—the artist is saying. But that doesn't mean that we are left without any knowledge. You see, all of these things—even God—can fit in the heart.

After the show, Bruce had graciously agreed to meet with my twenty students and me. When I commented on the oddness of the choice of "To Fit in My Heart" as a concluding song for the show, Bruce acknowledged that it wasn't a typical show-closer but then said, "I was thinking about you guys when I chose the song." A little bit of theological advice from the artist to the students? Perhaps a little bit of cautionary advice to a theologian who is about to write a book of theological reflections in response to Cockburn's body of work?

The world is too big to fit in a frame or even in a brain. And God is definitely too big to fit in a book. How about Cockburn? Can Cockburn fit in a book? Well . . . no. But it isn't just the sheer size of the Cockburn catalog (now spanning some forty years and thirty-one albums), nor even the breadth of themes, motifs, issues, and images that characterize his work, that makes it impossible to fit Cockburn in a book. Cockburn's work, thought, beliefs, poetry, music, and songs can't fit in a book because he won't allow it. Or perhaps it would be better to say that attempting to "fit" Cockburn into a book would necessarily do violence both to the man and to his art. As we will see later in this book, Cockburn understands his life and his art more in terms of journey than of destination. And so the only thing a book that engages Cockburn's art can do, if it is to honor this artist and not violate his artistic integrity, is join him on his journey, explore whether there are resonances with our own journeys, and see if there is wisdom to be found in his reports from the road that will help us navigate our own path forward.

God is too big to fit in a book, and if anyone dares to write theology (including the authors of Scripture), then they must do so with considerable caution and humility. Bruce Cockburn isn't God, but a theological engagement with his body of work also requires caution and humility. And so this book makes no claim to have come to any definitive understanding and explanation of the thought of Bruce Cockburn. This is not a book on the "theology of Bruce Cockburn." Nor is this a book of biography. The issue before us is not the life of Bruce Cockburn per se (though we will have occasion to refer to various events as they prove to be helpful to our larger project), but the body of work that Cockburn has produced for us.

Cockburn once said, "Dogma sucks," and therefore he feels "obliged to resist the need for orthodoxy in [himself] and in the world at large."[5] Orthodoxy—that is, the presumption of having achieved correct beliefs—is inherently dangerous, suggests Cockburn. Once you believe that you have come to final truth, once you are convinced that your interpretation of the world has divine sanction and a sense of absolute finality, then, says Cockburn, you end up with "shutters in the mind" that close you down to the voices of other people and to the possibility of truth and even revelation coming from other sources.[6] So it is not surprising that in one of his most recent songs he confesses, "I've mostly dodged the dogmas our life is all about."[7] Concluding that "dogma is the real spiritual enemy," Cockburn says that he "began to move toward a spirituality that was about freedom and openness and love."[8]

It is in a similar spirit of openness that I write this book interpreting the lyrics of Bruce Cockburn. So I make no claim to definitive interpretations in this book. Other interpretations of particular songs and even of the whole body of work are possible, and while this book is indeed an exploration into a Christian worldview, a Christian imagination, I do not presume to expound "the worldview of Bruce Cockburn."[9] Rather, the worldview that will emerge in these pages is "in dialogue" with Cockburn's work and has been deepened, expanded, sometimes corrected, often disturbed, questioned, and, at times, confirmed through that dialogue. If there is anyone's worldview in this book, then it is my own. But I'm also not so sure that my own worldview is well served if it gets captured in a book. At best, a book (like a song) can only bear witness to a worldview.

I am not trying to put Cockburn's worldview "in a book." In fact, I'm not trying to put *any* worldview in a book. Rather, I am offering an exploratory, suggestive, and hopefully creative appropriation of a biblically rooted worldview that is in playful dialogue with Cockburn's body of work. It seems to me that playing evokes playing. If you see a bunch of kids kicking a ball around, then you want to join in. The same thing happens with the best art. Cockburn "plays" for us. We come to a concert, and he plays onstage. We purchase his music, and we play it in the privacy of our own lives or in the company of others. Such art is played and it evokes play. A good song may make us move our bodies in dance. Sometimes it makes us want to sing along, and other times it inspires us, makes us wonder, or raises deep issues for us as the images of the lyrics and the movement of the music play in our imaginations. This book is about such playing. I am playing around with the images, themes, motifs, and ideas that we meet in the significant body of work that Bruce Cockburn has produced for us.

The songs, I say, are "for us." If Cockburn wanted to write music for himself, then he would never have released a recording or gone on tour. "Writing music, for me," Cockburn once said, "is about touching something deep in someone else from a real place in yourself."[10] There is, in this relation between artist and listener, a beautiful intimacy. We find ourselves touched in a deep and real place when we allow Cockburn's music to go there for us. And if we don't allow the art to touch us deeply, then we are likely missing the point. But again, the art is "for us." While Bruce Cockburn, his record company, and his manager may own the intellectual property rights to the songs, the songs are, nonetheless, "for us."

Cockburn describes the relation between artist and audience in this way:

> My job is to try and trap the spirit of things in the scratches of pen on paper, in the pulling of notes out of metal. These become songs and the songs become fuel. They can be fuel for romance, for protest, for spiritual discovery, or for complacency. That's where you all come in. *You* decide how a song will be heard and felt.[11]

There is something wonderfully gracious about that. *We* decide how a song will be heard and felt. The songs are gifts. "The gift / keeps moving— / never know / where it's going to land. / You must stand / back and let it / keep on changing hands."[12] And so in this book the gift has been received, the gift of Bruce Cockburn's prodigious body of work. This is a gift that has offered us interpretations, meanings, images, visions, and truths. It is a gift that has explored (and continues to explore) life in its ecstasy and sorrow, joy and grief, hope and despair. Through the gift of words and sounds, lyrics and rhythms, poetry and music, Cockburn constructs worlds of meaning and invites us into those worlds.

What I want to do in this book is to receive that gift in all of its richness and keep it moving. Rather than "trying to stay static" and put Cockburn in a book, I want to pass the gift on by playing with the images that Cockburn offers us and allow new meanings to emerge.

When it comes right down to it, it's all about meaning. U2 front man Bono puts it this way: "The world demands to be described, and so, painters, poets, journalists, pornographers, and sitcom writers, by accident or design, are just following orders, whether from high or low, to describe the world we're in."[13] Artists are in the world-description business, says Bono, whether they know it or not, and whether they are taking their orders from above or below. But Bono also says that "as much as we need to describe the world we do live in, we need to *dream up the kind of world we want to live in.*" We paint our pictures, write our poetry, and compose our songs "above all *to glimpse another way of being.*" And "in the case of a rock-and-roll band," says Bono, glimpsing another way of being "is to dream out loud, at high volume, to turn it up to eleven. Because we have fallen asleep in the comfort of our freedom."[14]

Cockburn doesn't always turn it up to eleven, but his music is decidedly about waking us up out of any culture-induced slumber that might be lulling us into numbness. However, Cockburn doesn't wake us up simply by condemning the present order of things. Rather, he dreams up another world and offers us, through both his art and his advocacy work, a glimpse of another way of being.

## Cockburn among the Psalmists

When Bruce Cockburn was inducted into the Canadian Music Hall of Fame at the thirtieth annual Juno Awards, the taped testimonials from Midnight Oil's Peter Garrett, Cowboy Junkies' Margo Timmins, and Jackson Browne all bore witness to the esteem in which Cockburn is held among other artists.[15] But it was, characteristically enough, Bono who offered the most apt description of Cockburn's artistry. At the end of a list of superlatives, Bono summed it all up by calling Bruce Cockburn a "psalmist." From Bono there is no higher praise than that.[16]

Bono has called the psalmists the rock-and-roll artists of ancient Israel. They gave voice both to the secured vision of the community and to the pain and disappointment when that vision was so devastatingly left unrealized and the hopes unfulfilled. Old Testament scholar Walter Brueggemann argues that the psalms are bold acts of poetic "world-making" and "re-symbolizing" in a context of contested symbols, contested worldviews. Psalms, writes Brueggemann, "create, evoke, suggest, and propose a network of symbols, metaphors, images, memories and hopes so that 'the world' in each successive generation, is perceived, experienced and practiced in a specific way."[17] And Brueggemann elucidates that specificity by saying, "*The world enacted by these Psalms . . . is intergenerational, covenantally shaped, morally serious, dialogically open, and politically demanding.*"[18] Is Bruce Cockburn among the psalmists in this sense? I believe he is. Not only will I argue that Cockburn's songs invite us into a "world" that is evoked, suggested, and proposed through a wonderfully rich network of symbols, metaphors, images, and memories, but I also hope to show how that "world" is intergenerational, covenantally shaped, morally serious, dialogically open, and politically demanding. Anyone who has even a passing acquaintance with Cockburn's work will know that his vision is politically demanding and morally serious. The fact that the man is now in his sixties and that his concerts attract teens to people in their seventies bears witness to the intergenerational scope of his reach. Look a little closer and you begin to see that this is a dialogically open worldview. Cockburn is always on the move—musically, lyrically, geographically, culturally, and spiritually. As we proceed I hope it will become clear that God is at the heart of his vision of life, the God that we also find in the "covenantal" vision of Israel's psalmists.

## On Worldviews

Perhaps it is time to explain what I mean when I talk about a worldview. Worldviews are both visions *of* and visions *for* life. They are descriptive *of* the world, providing a lens, an angle, a perspective through which we understand and interpret the world; and they are also prescriptive *for* the world, providing us with our most foundational values and norms. As such, worldviews tell us both what the world *is* and what it *ought to be.*[19] A worldview is not a "system of thought," but rather an implicit orientation, a fundamental way of leaning into life, of experiencing and living in the world. It is less a matter of thought than a way of imagining life.[20] As a vision both *of* and *for* the world, there is a reciprocal relationship between one's interpretive or symbolic framework and how one actually engages the world and lives one's life. There is always a give-and-take between experience and perspective, between lived life and interpretation. We act in certain ways because we see the world through a certain lens. Our vision *of* the world is always a vision *for* the world that takes on flesh in our day-to-day lives. A storied vision of life becomes a "lived narrative"; it results in a certain lived practice.[21] And, in turn, those lived practices shape, confirm, transform, and sometimes undermine our interpretations of the world, our worldview, our grounding stories.

My assumption in this engagement with Cockburn's work is that Cockburn interprets the world from a certain storied perspective. While that perspective is informed through many experiences and has necessarily grown, changed, and been questioned and further developed through those experiences, it is also clearly rooted in a particular story, namely, the story of Jesus and of God, whom we meet in the Hebrew and Christian Scriptures. While Cockburn's work employs an incredibly rich array of metaphors, narratives, and images, it seems to me that we do well to interpret his work as a whole through the symbolic horizon of a broadly Christian worldview. Cockburn is indeed on a journey, but that journey has an unmistakably Christian shape and direction.

Again, let me be clear that while I am engaging in interpreting Cockburn's art through the lens of a Christian worldview, and while I am even bold enough to suggest that this is an important and illuminating lens through which to interpret Cockburn's body of work, in this book I do not presume to have definitively uncovered Bruce Cockburn's worldview. In an important sense, Cockburn is not really the subject of this study. What I'm really striving for is the renewal of a Christian imagination. And I invite you to enter into the imaginary world that Cockburn constructs for us in his songs, precisely because I find that entering this world is so helpful in the shaping of such a Christian imagination.

I have said that worldviews answer ultimate questions. There are certain kinds of issues that seem to reside at the mythic-symbolic foundation of human life. These are questions that have no universal answer, but I'm willing to wager that they are universal in being asked. Everyone, I'm suggesting, answers, usually implicitly and seldom explicitly, at least four such questions.[22] All great myths, all foundational stories, can be interpreted as answering these kinds of questions. First, Where are we? What is the nature of the world in which we find ourselves? Second, Who are we? What does it mean to be human? Third, What's wrong? What is the source of brokenness, violence, hatred, and evil in life? Fourth, What's the remedy? How do we find a path through this brokenness to healing? Where is the resolution to the evil in which we find ourselves?

In this book I will use these four questions to structure our exploration of Cockburn's work and a Christian worldview. Again, the point is not to systematize Cockburn's "answers" to these questions. Rather, I offer these questions, these foundational and ultimate human issues, as an interpretive window into both the Cockburn corpus and a renewed Christian imagination.

## An Aesthetics of Generosity

I've said that we need to receive Cockburn's songs as gifts and that we are called to a responsible stewardship of these gifts. Interpretation is one part of that stewardship, one way in which we honor the gift. Gifts are to be passed on. If there is light to be received in a song, then that light mustn't be snuffed out or hidden away. It is a light for sharing.

In that spirit, I'd like to conclude this short introduction with a few comments on one more song that gives us a window into Cockburn's aesthetic, his approach to his art. On the 1999 album, *Breakfast in New Orleans, Dinner in Timbuktu,* we hear a beautiful song called "Isn't That What Friends Are For?" In spoken verses and a sung chorus, Cockburn confronts us with a "heavy autumn sky," an impending winter, and a "frail sun" that is setting and leaving us in darkness. All of this is to tell us that "the world is full of seasons; of / anguish, of laughter."

This song is addressed to someone whose season is winter, whose season is one of anguish. It may well be that "love's supposed to heal, but it / breaks my heart to feel / the pain in your voice." Healing doesn't seem to be at hand, so the artist professes, "I would crush my heart and / throw it in the street / if I could pay for your choice." That such a sentiment echoes a Christian understanding of what Christ does on the cross, we only note here. As far as the artist can see, "Isn't that what friends are for?" Isn't a willingness to sacrifice yourself in the face of the anguish of another person precisely what friendship is all about? If a friend, a true friend, could somehow pay for the bad choices that you have made, choices that have resulted in pain and brokenness, wouldn't a friend do such a thing?

In the second verse the artist assures his friend that "you're as loved as you were / before the strangeness swept / through our bodies, our / houses, our streets." Do you remember what it was like before things went so terribly wrong? Back "when we could speak without codes," when we felt at home with ourselves, with each other, with the world? Do you remember that before this debilitating disorientation took over, you felt loved? Well, my friend, you are still loved. Nothing that has happened, nothing that has got so messed up and so confused, can take that away from you.

And then the song comes to its denouement with these incredible lines:

> I've been scraping
> little shavings off my
> ration of light
> and I formed it into a
> ball, and each time I
> pack a bit more onto it.
>
> I make a bowl of my hands and I
> scoop it from its secret cache
> under a loose board in the floor
> and I blow across it and I send
> it to you
> against those moments when
> the darkness blows under your door.
>
> Isn't that what friends are for?
> Isn't that what friends are for?

The sun may be frail and it may be setting. Winter may be approaching and the daylight will decrease. This may well be a season of darkness in all kinds of ways, but the artist has been saving up scrapings of his ration of light. He's been hiding it away so that he could scoop it from its secret cache and blow across it, sending it to his friend "against those moments when / the darkness blows under your door. Isn't that what friends are for?"

I do not pretend to know anything about Bruce Cockburn as a friend. But I have lived with his art for all of my adult life. And in these lines I find a testimony to his aesthetic. He hasn't got any more light than the rest of us. But he scrapes a little off each night, and when he writes a song, he blows that light across the guitar strings and over and through the lyrics so that what little light he may have can come to us against the moments when the darkness is blowing under our door. This is an aesthetics of generosity. This is an artistry suffused with grace. In short, I think that Bono is right. Bruce Cockburn is a postmodern psalmist.

Before exploring this contemporary psalmist's contribution in terms of the four worldview questions, however, we need to reflect further on the nature of this investigation and sketch out the overall shape of his vision. So in the next chapter I will offer some further methodological reflections, allowing the two songs "Wondering Where the Lions Are" and "Lovers in a Dangerous Time" to imaginatively frame the discussion. Then, in chapter 3, we will sketch out the bigger picture of Cockburn's body of work through the metaphor of windows.

# Ecstatic Wonderings and Dangerous Kicking

## Imagination and Method

*the world survives into another day
and I'm thinking about eternity
some kind of ecstasy got a hold on me.*

Those words from "Wondering Where the Lions Are" came to mind this morning as I watched the sunrise over the fields at my farm home. I wasn't up that early to feed the cows—my ladies don't mind sleeping in a little. No, I was up early to pray. Don't get me wrong, this is not my general pattern. I am not the kind of guy who has a tight and rigorous schedule of spiritual practices. It's just that this morning, and the mornings of the last week, and the mornings for who knows how much longer, I have made a commitment to pray for a young single mom who is on her deathbed, her body wracked with cancer. A host of us around the world have formed a "prayer quilt" to surround and cover this woman, her two kids, and the rest of her family with prayer.

So, with death on my mind and sorrow in my heart, I watched the sunrise and thought of these words, "Sun's up, uh huh, looks okay / the world survives into another day." And you are probably humming the tune in your head right now, aren't you? If you have picked up this book, then you might not know all that much about Bruce Cockburn, but you will almost certainly know this song, "Wondering Where the Lions Are" from his 1979 album, *Dancing in the Dragon's Jaws*.[1] The eminently sing-along tune and the playfully suggestive lyrics of this song sent it to the twenty-first spot on the Billboard Hot 100 list in June of 1980, and it has remained a mainstay in Cockburn's live performances.

The sun came up this morning, and while I was accompanying my friend in the valley of the shadow of death, this song by Bruce Cockburn was accompanying me. The sun came up, and this world, "this bluegreen ball in black space / Filled with beauty even now / battered and abused and lovely,"[2] has survived into another day. Whether my friend has survived, I don't know. I know that she will never read this book in this life. I suspect that before this chapter is finished, I will have attended her funeral.[3]

And that sun coming up this morning got me thinking about eternity. Now, I don't know if I would have found my imagination moving in the direction of eternity anyway, given the fact that I was praying for someone about to face the eternal. But I'm pretty certain that this morning's sunrise, eternity, and ecstasy would not have all come into my imagination without Bruce Cockburn's song "Wondering Where the Lions Are." So I am grateful to Cockburn. Grateful that writing in a very different context, some thirty years ago, he put together words and music that could resonate with me this morning. I suspect that most people reading this book have similar experiences of Cockburn's songs (and the songs of many other artists as well). The artist engages the world, sees something there, and finds just the right words and music to put that experience into a three-minute moment that somehow captures things for us, somehow gives voice to what we had intuited but didn't quite have the words for. The artist opens our eyes so that we see and experience the world anew, more deeply, and maybe in a way that brings some kind of healing for us.

Cockburn's "Wondering Where the Lions Are" wasn't about a single mom dying of cancer. In fact, it's about a whole host of things. As he tells the story, Cockburn had been up late having a disturbing conversation about the buildup of tension between Russia and China, two nuclear powers at the end of the 1970s. And the problem was that while the West knew something about how détente and deterrence worked when dealing with the Russians, the Chinese were a wild card.[4] Might they actually employ nuclear weapons, thereby setting off a worldwide nuclear holocaust? Not very pleasant images to take to bed with you.

The next morning Cockburn was driving along the highway in his truck, and with his right hand (Cockburn is left-handed) he scribbled down in his notebook, "Sun's up, looks okay, the world survives into another day." Another day of survival. Another day when the most horrendous weapons ever created by humankind have not been deployed. And all of this seems to grab the artist with some kind of ecstasy and leads him to thinking about eternity.[5]

The song evolved over a number of months. More moments of ecstasy, more premonitions of eternity—the experience of communion with another person ("you be in me and i'll be in you"), hikes in the woods, visions of a flying boat rising off a lake (is that an airplane or maybe a metaphor for another sunrise?), an image of military personnel in formation, Vancouver Bay full of freighters about to sail away—everyday experiences of a rich life that pays attention, all embraced with some kind of ecstasy, all occasioning meditations about eternity. Temporal moments that, for some reason, point beyond themselves.

And . . . all bound up somehow with lions. "I'm wondering where the lions are." While the cover art on the 1975 album, *Joy Will Find a Way*, depicting a little girl with a very large lion, conjures up images of Lucy and the Great Lion, Aslan, in C. S. Lewis's *Chronicles of Narnia*, the metaphor in the song seems to be a little different. Not a singular lion or a lion of salvific significance, but multiple lions at the door, which appear in a dream and are not as frightening as they were before. Lions as threat, yet somehow declawed. Lions that ought to inspire fearful panic, and yet the artist is experiencing some kind of ecstasy. So as he entertains ecstatic visions of eternity, he finds himself "wondering where the lions are." Where are those mythic forces of evil and destruction? They were so real just last night. They were so real anticipating a nuclear war. They were so real contemplating a young woman on morphine dying in front of her children.

## Theological Criticism

It seems to me that Cockburn's "Wondering Where the Lions Are" is inescapably theological. There is something deeply spiritual about this ecstasy. T. S. Eliot would say that this isn't really all that remarkable, because all great art is deeply spiritual. That is why Eliot wrote that "literary criticism should be completed by criticism from a definite ethical and theological standpoint."[6] The point is not that one finally judges a work of art from one's own ethical and religious perspective without regard to the aesthetic value of the work itself; but rather, any art that merits serious attention, any art that will tell us something of the truth of the world and our place in it, will disclose something of the ultimate character of things. Or to use the metaphor from "Wondering Where the Lions Are," any art that gets us "thinking about eternity" is an art that calls forth theological dialogue and reflection.

It is clear that Cockburn himself has a similar understanding of his own art. In conversation with Mike Rimmer in 2003, Cockburn said,

> My job is to translate what I understand of the human experience into some
> sort of communicable form, that then becomes a vehicle for the sharing of
> experience with whoever is interested enough to listen. So that allows the
> field to be extremely broad. Although there are some songs that deal directly
> with spiritual experiences, most of what I write is an observation, informed
> by my particular interest in spirituality.[7]

While *some* songs are explicitly addressing spiritual experiences, *most* of Cockburn's songs are informed by his interest in spirituality. I would modify this slightly and suggest that while some of Cockburn's songs are explicitly concerned with helping us to get thinking about eternity, all of his writing is rooted in his own emerging and changing understanding of eternity, his own emerging and changing understanding of the nature of spiritual life.

It is important that we do not attempt to freeze Cockburn's spirituality at a particular point in time or from a particular "theological" perspective. In a 1986 interview for *Nerve* magazine, Cockburn said, "The fact that I'm a Christian has an obvious effect on how I see the world, which in turn shows up in the songs."[8] But both the association of the word *Christian* with the religious Right in America and Cockburn's own deep distaste for all "dogma" that ends up functioning as a violent weapon with which to attack others have led him to "rely on oblique imagery to get at the real things."[9] While he has a profound and deep sense of "walking with God," he also knows that such language is almost totally inexplicable to most people, precisely because such pious talk has been co-opted and defiled by a religious fundamentalism that has been at the heart of so much evil in the last few decades. Yet, Cockburn can't help himself. He has a decidedly Christian-shaped experience of God that is caught in mere "glimpses." Those glimpses, however, "are strong and tantalizing." And so he confesses that the "sense of being in the company of God is continually growing. And I like it!"[10]

## "Just Beyond the Range of Normal Sight"

In Cockburn's music we catch some glimpses of the divine. These glimpses are often oblique and seldom dogmatic. And at their best, these songs give us a glimpse of what lies "just beyond the range of normal sight." This brings us to another morning, another sunrise, another day in which the world survived. But this is a morning characterized more by an ominous uneasiness than by ecstasy, more a sense of danger than relief. Staying with that 1979 album, *Dancing in the Dragon's Jaws*, where we first heard "Wondering Where the Lions Are," let's consider what was effectively the album's title track, "Hills of Morning."[11]

It is morning. We are "underneath the mask of the sulphur sky," and "a bunch of us were busy waiting." A pause between the words "busy" and "waiting" literally leaves us waiting for a moment. Something is about to dawn; the morning brings with it an expectation. We are waiting and we are watching. We are "watching the people looking ill-at-ease / watching the fraying rope get closer to breaking." Perhaps this is the fraying rope of the false images of who we are. Perhaps it is the untenable rope that holds our culture together. But whatever it is, the life of those who are ill at ease, the life of those who live in the tenuousness of this fraying-rope reality is patently "normal." These people move "back and forth /

in between effect and cause." There is a normality to living with a fraying rope, a normality to being ill at ease, a normality to the debilitating brokenness of life, a normality to having a sense that it is all about to fall apart. And while we will have to wait for a later song for Cockburn to tell us that "the trouble with normal / is it always gets worse," on this morning the artist offers us a vision beyond such constricting normality.[12] You see, "just beyond the range of normal sight / this glittering joker was dancing in the dragon's jaws."

If we want to break free from this constricting vision of normality, then we will need a new vision. We will need a new perspective, a way of seeing that goes beyond the normal. This fraying rope is getting closer to breaking. There is something fundamentally untenable and precarious about our situation. And what the artist invites us to see on this morning is not a vision of eternity, but a vision of someone who has embraced the precariousness of our situation. This glittering joker responds to our ill-at-ease condition with a playful, ecstatic, and perhaps mocking dance right in the very jaws of danger, in the dragon's jaws.

Who is this joker? While medieval imagery often employed the character of the joker or jester as a symbol for the Christ, Cockburn appeals to the shroud of mystery and even secrecy that we meet in the Gospels (especially the Gospel of Mark). "The only sign you gave of who you were / when you first came walking down the road / was the way the dust motes danced around / your feet in a cloud of gold." While you constantly confused people and left them befuddled with your cryptic teachings and blasphemous behavior, the dust motes, the very dust of creation, recognized who you were. Creation danced in response to your presence, and now, through the eyes of this artist, we see you dancing . . . in the dragon's jaws.[13]

The real tip-off that this peculiar joker is Jesus is that in his wake things get turned on their head. "But everything you see's not the way it seems / tears can sing and joy shed tears." Wasn't it Jesus who said, "Blessed are you who weep now, for you will laugh," and, "Woe to you who are laughing now, for you will mourn and weep"?[14] And doesn't this Jesus stand in the tradition of the Hebrew psalmists, who could sing, "You have turned my mourning into dancing"?[15] Isn't this Jesus among the prophets of Israel who proclaimed that because God "will wipe away the tears from all faces," "turn their mourning into joy," and give them "gladness for sorrow," the people will therefore "rejoice in the dance"?[16] This theme of sorrow being turned to joy, tears giving way to laughter, and all of this breaking out into celebratory dance is common in Israel's Scriptures. And it all comes together in Jesus, the glittering joker dancing in the dragon's jaws.

So if we can see just beyond the range of normal sight, if we can see through Cockburn's eyes, and through the imagery and music of this song, something that goes to the heart of our uneasy fraying-rope state of being, something that breaks the stultifying normality of living between effect and cause, if we can see the possibility of redemptive reversals through the agency of this glittering joker, then what? What do we do in response to this dance? Cockburn wants to join in. In fact, he not only wants to join the Christ in this dance, but he also wants to be so close to the dance that he actually participates in both the dance and the dancer.

> Let me be a little of your breath
> Moving over the face of the deep—
> I want to be a particle of your light
> Flowing over the hills of morning.

Now, what is all this about? If we take our cue from the chorus, then we need to go back to the beginning. If we want to play with these evocative images, then we need to allow our interpretation of this song to be informed by the biblical metaphors upon which Cockburn draws. There is in this chorus a clear allusion to the very beginning of the Bible, the very beginning of the biblical story. Where was it that we first met a "breath" "moving over the face of the deep"? At the beginning. At the dawn of creation, at the dawn of that first morning, we read that "the Spirit [or "breath" or "wind"] of God was moving over the face of the waters."[17] And where was it that we first met a light flowing over that creational morning, but in the voice of the Creator, who says, as the first word, "Let there be light."[18]

The ill-at-ease morning that dawns "underneath the mask of a sulphur sky" meets the light-filled and Spirit-endowed morning of the dawn of creation through a vision of the Christ dancing in the dragon's jaws. These are theologically rich and spiritually evocative images that simply cry out for biblically informed interpretation. And while the artist sings of a longing to be so close to this joker's redemptive dance that he is actually a little of the Christ's breath and a particle of his light, Cockburn will offer a prophetic warning of his own at the end of the song. The concluding lines of the last verse tell us that "you can take the wisdom of this world / and give it to the ones who think it all ends here!" If you can't see just beyond the range of normal sight, if you can't see beyond this fraying-rope world and catch a glimpse of something incredibly redemptive going on, if you don't have the imagination to embrace a world born of the Spirit and suffused with light, if you think that "it all ends here," and that tears will always have the last word, never to be turned into joy, then you can have the wisdom of this world. But you will remain caught in the anxious treadmill of a culture in crisis, moving "back and forth / in between effect and cause." You will find yourself debilitated by a dehydrated imagination that does not drink from the depths of spirituality on offer from biblical faith, and you will have no ability to see "just beyond the range of normal sight."

In this early, explicitly Christian song, Cockburn offers an evocative discernment of a culture in crisis together with a biblically suggestive vision of Christ rooted in rich allusions to the most foundational images of the Hebrew and Christian Scriptures. And while he offers a spirituality of participation in Christ through the metaphor of dancing, this is a dancing with eyes wide open, a dancing in the dragon's jaws. The point is not to avert our gaze from this sulphur-sky world, or to dismiss those who are ill at ease, or to ignore the real dangers of a fraying rope getting closer to breaking. Cockburn has a profound sense of the danger of our times, the unsustainability of our way of life, the vulnerability of a world in crisis, and the desperateness of the human condition. There is no escapism in this song, precisely because the very one whose breath was over the face of the deep is the one that Cockburn now sees dancing in the dragon's jaws.[19] There are dragons out there! The sense of dread, the paralyzing fear of it all falling apart, is well captured in those mythical creatures of violence and chaos. Yet that is precisely where the Christ is to be found. In the jaws of the dragon. And if we are to be a particle of his light, if we are to put on our dancing shoes and join this Lord of the dance, then it is into the dragon's jaws that we too must go.

## Catching Ourselves in the Act of Interpretation

Perhaps this interpretation of "Hills of Morning" is met with an incredulous question: "You found all that in a four-minute, thirty-two-second song consisting of two verses and a repeated chorus?" Is all of that really "there" in this song? Or might I be reading into it a little? Might I be offering an interpretation that maybe Cockburn himself might not recognize? Let me answer with a fourfold "yes." Yes, I found all of that in this short song. Yes, it is all really there. But also, yes, I am undoubtedly reading into the song, because I can't imagine any other kind of reading. And yes, it may well be that the composer of this song wouldn't recognize or even agree with everything that I've just said about the song, but this doesn't overly worry me.

I have just engaged in an act of interpretation. I have discussed this song and suggested a particular way of interpreting its meaning. And I have engaged in an act of appropriation. I have begun to take the meaning of this song as my own, made some beginning moves toward an application of that meaning to life in a culture that is interpreted as in crisis, and even allowed the song to begin to suggest new meanings and interpretations of some of my own most foundational beliefs. For example, while the image of Christ as a joker has been part of the Christian imagination for centuries, the idea of this joker "dancing in the dragon's jaws" begins to open up the meaning of what happened on the cross and what happens at the heart of Christian "cross-bearing" discipleship in new ways for me. Indeed, if the reference back to the first chapter of Genesis proves to be a fruitful path of interpretation, then even more vistas of interpretation open up. Interpreting the first chapter of Genesis as a rhetorical alternative to the dominant Babylonian mythology of exilic Israel, and recognizing the mythically powerful role of the sea goddess Tiamat as the force of chaos and destruction within that mythology, begins to set the mind wondering about whether Cockburn's "dragon" and Babylon's Tiamat might be closely related.[20]

Was Bruce Cockburn thinking of Tiamat when he wrote these lines? I don't know. But the mythical place of dragons can be traced back to Tiamat and other ancient sea monsters with little difficulty. Did he have Genesis in mind when he referenced "the face of the deep"? Was he talking about Jesus when he saw that glittering joker? Did he have in mind words of Jesus and perhaps words from psalmists and prophets when wrote that "tears can sing and joy shed tears"? Given his own biblical literacy, and given where he was on his own spiritual journey when he wrote this song, it seems quite reasonable to think that he both knew the allusions he was making and intended to make them.

But does it matter? Does it matter whether the artist intended everything that can be interpreted in his work, or even that he would see it all there if an interpreter brought it to his attention? Yes and no. Let me put it this way: while I wouldn't give the artist the final word on any matter of interpretation of his own work, I am interested in knowing what I can about what the artist might think about a piece of his own work. So yes, the artist has some interpretive authority over his work. But not final or exhaustive authority. Artists can say more than they mean. They can make allusions without intending to do so.[21] But the allusions are "really there"! Or at least they are there if you have eyes to see.

Let me be clear that I am not saying that "anything goes" when it comes to my interpretations of Bruce Cockburn's songs. Any interpretation needs to have merit in relation to the work being interpreted. Interpretation needs to be faithful to the art under discussion. We could say that interpretation is itself an act of performance. Think of the artwork as the score of a symphony, and the interpretation as the performance of that symphony by an orchestra under the direction of a conductor. Each performance is different, because each performance is an interpretation of the score. There is, therefore, freedom and creativity in the interpretation but also a requirement to be faithful to the score. Without fidelity, this is not a performance of this particular symphony. But without creative freedom the performance is wooden, uninspired, and the music would have been better off left on the page and not imposed upon a listening audience.[22]

Note that fidelity here is to the artwork, not necessarily to the artist. In fact, the only way that one can respect the artist is by respecting the art. And we cannot be cavalier in our interpretations. To do interpretive violence to a work of art is to do violence to the artist. Nonetheless, it seems to me that the greatest compliment that you can give to an artist is to take his or her art seriously and to engage in creative interpretation and appropriation of the work.

Songs create meaning and suggest further meaning. The meaning of a song like "Hills of Morning" isn't final and fixed when Cockburn completes the composition. Not only can the song change in meaning as the artist performs it in different contexts and at different times, but it also takes on meaning as it is interpreted by another person or even a community of people in a different context and at a different time. What a song "means" is constantly emerging and negotiated in the dialogue between the work itself and the audience, listener, or interpreter.

## Some Interpretive Assumptions

I said in chapter 1 that this book would engage in exploratory, creative interpretation and free appropriation of the meanings to be gleaned from Bruce Cockburn's
songs. I also said that this was a book of theology, and in the discussion of "Hills of
Morning" I hope that I have at least begun to demonstrate that Cockburn's songs
call forth theological discussion and interpretation. But if we "catch ourselves in
the act of interpretation,"[23] if we stop and inquire into just exactly what was going
on in that discourse occasioned by Cockburn's "Hills of Morning," then was there
any interpretive "method" at work there? Are there any criteria that might govern
such interpretation? While I will not offer a fully worked-out interpretive method
here, there are at least four criteria that I bring to my interpretation.

First, any theological engagement with a work of art must be faithful to the work
itself. The work, the song, needs to be taken seriously "on its own terms" before
any interpretation of its meaning is either rejected or employed for theological
reflection. Writing about film, Robert Johnston rightly insists that "theologizing
should follow, not precede, the aesthetic experience."[24] I don't listen to a Cockburn
album first and foremost because I am looking for theological material. I listen
to this music because it is beautiful and powerful and touches me deeply. Out of
that aesthetic experience theological reflection may arise. But for that to happen,
I need to catch the allusions, make the connections, listen between the lines, allow
the song to question me, allow my faith to question the song, and enter into a
deep dialogue with the song.

Second, if this is a "theological" engagement with Cockburn's work, then the
artwork is one voice, even the first voice, but not the only voice in the engagement.
Scripture is also an important voice in this dialogue. Sometimes I will allow a song's
scriptural allusions to spark my imagination, and then I'll run with those images
for a while. Other times I will allow the images, themes, tensions, and struggles
of a song to send me back to biblical faith with new eyes, reinterpreting biblical
texts in light of the song. And I will always attempt to hear a song in a broader
cultural context and allow the artwork, together with the Scriptures, to engage
that cultural context.

This concern with biblical themes is certainly not alien to Cockburn's understanding of his own work. Reflecting in 1979 on the serious responsibility of the
artist, Cockburn said that "an artist, especially an artist with religious convictions,
has to pay . . . close attention to what it is they are saying in their art." The artist
needs to seriously consider "whether or not . . . what's being said is true. And
'true' for me has a lot to do with whether it coincides . . . , at least in some subtle
way, with scripture. I don't see myself as particularly involved with, writing gospel
songs, as such. But when I do write a song I . . . [ask], 'well is that right or isn't
it?' "[25] Whether a song is true or not will hang at least partially, and usually subtly,
on Scripture. Undoubtedly, Cockburn wouldn't quite put it this way today, some
thirty years later. Nonetheless, it seems to me that we can continue to discern such

biblical resonance throughout his body of work. Moreover, such resonance will be essential for any fruitful theological engagement with these songs.[26]

Third, a theological engagement with Cockburn's art must bear the fruit of cultural discernment. While this kind of theological reflection must maintain a double fidelity—both to the art on its own terms and to the Scriptures—neither the art nor the Scriptures are really taken seriously if the interpretation goes no further than personal enjoyment or even a deepening of one's religious experience. To take Cockburn's art on "its own terms" is to engage his art in terms of its politically demanding and morally serious message. While there is all kinds of room for introspection when listening to a Cockburn song, and that is quite appropriate, we miss both the breadth and the depth of his vision if we do not attend to the mystery and violence, wonder and oppression, love and injustice of what he sees. Cockburn chronicles in his songs the full range of human experience and emotion. A theological engagement with that chronicle will want to learn how to see the world through this art. Seeing the world through these songs, I am assuming, will result in a more profound discernment of our cultural context. And without such discernment, any theological reflection is reduced to disconnected and irrelevant intellectual game playing. Theology, like music, is something we play. But the stakes are too high for this to be a mere game.

Finally, I offer this exploration of Bruce Cockburn's songs in service of the awakening of the imagination. Walter Brueggemann has said that "the key pathology of our time, which seduces us all, is the reduction of the imagination so that we are too numbed, satiated and co-opted to do serious imaginative work."[27] I come to these works of imagination for the reawakening of the imagination, and such reawakening is so necessary, I suggest, precisely because of the pathology that Brueggemann identifies. Philosopher Paul Ricoeur has argued that people live their lives more by what they can imagine than by the supposed beliefs that they conceptually hold.[28] And the crisis of our time is that we live in a culture of captive imaginations. Indeed, it is a tell-tale characteristic of imperial ideology that the imaginations of the population are monopolized by the dominant sociocultural and politico-economic forces. No wonder "every totalitarian regime is afraid of the artist."[29] The artist insists on seeing beyond the range of normal sight, not allowing our imaginations to be limited by a sense of the inevitability of the present state of things. The artist, or at least an artist who will reawaken our imaginations from our culturally imposed slumber, will offer alternative metaphors, images, and symbols through a porous, open, and elusive language that awakens an alternative imagination.[30] Seeing through the artist's eyes, feeling through the musician's rhythms and tonalities, and finding ourselves playing in a world that is mediated to us through the images of the singer's lyrics, we have the opportunity to experience and imagine the world anew.

C. S. Lewis once wrote, "The poet is not a man who asks me to look at *him*; he is a man who says 'look at that' and points."[31] Or, as Cockburn puts it, "It is the artist's job to mirror or reflect everyone's experience through the artist's experience."[32] This, however, is not a matter of simple aesthetic enjoyment. It is potentially a matter of life and death. Clearly alluding to St. Paul's contention that in Christ there is neither male nor female, slave nor free,[33] Cockburn has sung:

> *male female slave or free*
> *peaceful or disorderly*
> *maybe you and he will not agree*
> *but you need him to show you new ways to see*
>
> *don't let the system fool you*
> *all it wants to do is rule you*
> *pay attention to the poet*
> *you need him and you know it.*[34]

While these rhyming couplets might not be Cockburn at his most allusive, the point is clear. We need the poet for renewed and liberated vision precisely because the dominant cultural system is deceptive and hegemonic.

## Cockburn among the Prophets

In the Hebrew Scriptures such poetry was primarily the art of the prophets. Walter Brueggemann argues, "*The task of prophetic ministry is to nurture, nourish, and evoke a consciousness and perception alternative to the consciousness and perception of the dominant culture around us.*"[35] Similarly, Cockburn has said, "I think if you're an artist, you're immediately put in a position of opposition to mainstream society, because you are trying to tell the truth."[36] The prophet breaks through the deceptive captivity of the dominant imagination by bringing to public expression the pain, oppression, and terror that have been denied and covered up in the service of life as normal. That is why the prophet insists that "the trouble with normal / is it always gets worse."[37] Numbness is pierced with pathos. Cutting through numbness to penetrate self-deception, the prophet must "offer symbols that are adequate to confront the horror and massiveness of the experience that evokes numbness and requires denial" and "speak metaphorically but concretely about the real deathliness that hovers over us and gnaws within us . . . neither in rage nor with cheap grace, but with the candor born of anguish and passion."[38]

A prophetic ministry does not nurture, nourish, and evoke an alternative consciousness and imagination simply through passionate critique of the prevailing imagination, however. That critique is itself rooted in an alternative vision of the way things ought to be and will one day be. Prophetic utterance occurs in the context of a conflict of imaginations, and the prophet both offers a criticism of the ruling order and energizes the community with an alternative vision of a different future. The prophet announces to the forces of oppression that "people see through you,"[39] while also giving voice to a hope that is still "working and waiting for a miracle."[40] Subversion and hope go hand in hand.

Artist and art theorist Wassily Kandinsky argued that art must never be only the child of its time. Art that is "only the child of the age," he wrote, "is not germinative" and is therefore "unable to become the mother of the future." This, he contended, "is a castrated art. It is transitory; it dies morally the moment the atmosphere that nourishes it alters."[41] In contrast to this kind of castrated art, Kandinsky described "another art capable of further developments which also springs from contemporary feeling." Such art is simultaneously the "echo and mirror" of contemporary experience, "but it also possesses an awakening prophetic power which can have far-reaching and profound effect."[42] This is an art that is clearly rooted in and a reflection of contemporary experience while also possessing an *awakening prophetic power*, a power of awakening in the midst of our slumber, a prophetic power that will nurture, nourish, and evoke an alternative vision and way of life. Prophetic art is a subversive genre that "cracks the pavement of the status quo."[43] This, I contend, describes the art of Bruce Cockburn.

But the subversive nature of prophetic literature must not be confused with the dominating character of propaganda. Yes, the prophet has a word to say. Yes, this literature and this art offer a vision of life with specificity and direction. But the generative and transformative power of prophetic art is cheapened and stripped of integrity when it becomes a power play by the artist, imposing beliefs and worldviews upon his or her audience for intellectual assent and self-justification. Authentically prophetic art leaves space for free interpretation. Indeed, any art that is profoundly and truthfully revelatory, any art that has the potential to unveil reality for us, and any art that has apocalyptic applicability achieves its meanings precisely in the freedom of its interpreters. Anything else falls prey to the temptation of propaganda.

It is not surprising, then, that David Dark should list Cockburn among the artists that he turns to for such prophetic vision. Speaking more generally he writes, "I am grateful for and in dire need of whatever art can keep me awake and alive to the mystery, whatever keeps me paying attention, whatever reminds me that none of us (and no ideology) are possessors of the final say. Art that doesn't bear witness to the opaque, the mysterious, or even allow any ambiguity is propaganda at best and, at worst, a ministry of death, an exercise in sentimentalizing, self-congratulatory delusion."[44] While Cockburn can write a touching and tender love song, there is no room for sentimentality in his art. And while he can find himself railing against what people "call democracy," he resists the temptation to propagandize in his art.[45]

We can illustrate Cockburn's prophetic art that eschews all cheap sentimentality by considering his most well-known love song, "Lovers in a Dangerous Time."[46] But we'll get there by first reflecting on Cockburn's discernment of the times.

## "Lovers in a Dangerous Time"

Prophets are visionaries who discern the times. Prophetic vision is always tied to time. What time is it? How can we know what to do if we don't know what time it is? How can we discern a path forward if we can't discern the times? Discerning time is essential to cultural discernment. If we are to know where we are, how we got here, and where we are going, then we will need to know what time it is. "Every culture is, to a great extent, a reflection of the temporal orientation it adopts."[47] A temporal orientation addresses itself to the larger, ultimate questions of history: its overall goals, where history is going. Our temporal orientation gives us a vision for the future that functions as a foundation from which we evaluate history and our participation in it. As a storied vision of and for life, a worldview is always a temporal perspective. We interpret the events around us and discern which events are history-making and who are the history makers in terms of some understanding of the nature of time, the goal of history, and where we are in the unfolding of history.

For example, whether a worldwide economic recession is a time for renewed vigilance to realize our dreams of prosperity or a time to seriously question those very dreams depends on one's worldview. Is an economic crisis a time of painful "market correction" or a time of inevitable market collapse? Is it time to "not apologize for our way of life," as President Obama said at his inauguration, or is it time for some pretty serious apologies and redirection? It depends on how you tell the time.

True to a prophetic calling, Cockburn has always been a time teller. Here's how he told the time in his 1978 song "Feast of Fools."[48]

> It's time for the silent criers to be held in love
> it's time for the ones who dig graves for them to get that final shove
> it's time for the horizons of the universe to be glimpsed
>     even by the faceless kings of corporations
> it's time for chaos to win and walk off with the prize
>     that turns out to be nothing (fooled you, fooled you).

Cockburn's reading of the times is one of passionate love and prophetic reversals. What time is it? "It's time for the silent criers to be held in love." It's time for those who have been deeply broken or brutally oppressed to be embraced, held in security and hope. But if it is time for the silent criers to be held in love, then it is also time for those "who dig graves for them"—the abusers, the oppressors, the ignorers—"to get that final shove." Cockburn's reversal is deeply biblical, because those who gain the world will lose it.[49] Prophetic blessings are always accompanied by prophetic woes.[50] Your time is up, says Cockburn. You "faceless kings of corporations," living in your world of illusion, will finally get a glimpse of the way the universe really is before chaos (not your self-interested, imposed world of economic order) wins and walks off with the prize that in the end turns out to be empty, vacuous, "nothing." "Fooled you, fooled you."

What time is it for Bruce Cockburn? It is time for radical reversals. This is a vision of historical discontinuity, where the status quo is *not* accepted as normal, precisely because "the trouble with normal is it always gets worse." What time is it? It is the time of "the grinding devolution of the democratic dream."[51] It is ending time; it is a time of cultural closure; it is a time of cultural dissolution. And as such, it is an extremely dangerous time.

What time is it? Cockburn answers that question evocatively in "Lovers in a Dangerous Time." In the opening lines we hear that the hours seem to "grow shorter as the day goes by." There is a shortening of time. So short, in fact, "that you never get to stop and open your eyes." Perhaps this is a reference similar to the impending winter of "Isn't That What Friends Are For?": a shortening of the day and an extension of the darkness of night.[52] But, whatever it is, the zeitgeist leaves us with no time to stop and look, no time to take it all in and get our bearings. What time is it? Couldn't tell you, I don't have enough time to even figure it out.

And in this shortening of the time, in this sense that perhaps time is running out on this experiment in civilizational culture, we find ourselves caught between anxiety and wonder. "One day you're waiting for the sky to fall / the next you're dazzled by the beauty of it all." That is where a prophetic imagination takes us. We find ourselves caught between dread and joy, between a sense of impending disaster and delight. One day it feels like the sky is about to fall. The whole civilizational edifice is going to collapse along with the very ecological foundations of life that have been so compromised, so assaulted by our industrially fueled way of life. And yet this world of wonders can still dazzle us with its unspeakable beauty.

And somehow, living in the tension of destruction and beauty, between apocalyptic dread and creational delight, we still fall in love. We still embrace each other in intimacy. We are still lovers. But if this love is not to be reduced to the cheap sentimentality of a Valentine's Day card, then it will need to be a love with its eyes wide open to the context in which we will be lovers. We need to see that we are "lovers in a dangerous time."

What time is it? It is a dangerous time. It is a time of endings, a time of threat and violence. Yes, we come together as "fragile bodies of touch and taste / this vibrant skin—this hair like lace." Yes, we come together in all the richness and bodily sensitivities of sensuality. Indeed, in this very sensuality, Cockburn discerns nothing less than "spirits open to the thrust of grace." Our sexuality has sacramental meaning. Sexual intimacy is, at its best, an openness to grace, a medium of divine presence in our lives. And yet, if the time is short, if "you never get to stop and open your eyes," then you also never have "a breath you can afford to waste." Who knows?—this might be your last breath. This might be the last moment that you and your lover have for touch and taste. This might be the last chance you've got for that thrust of grace. Because, you see, "you're lovers in a dangerous time."

The time is dangerous for lovers not just because the time is short but because it has no time for love. "When you're lovers in a dangerous time / sometimes you're made to feel as if your love's a crime." Who's got time for love in such a precarious time? Who's got time for love when cynicism would strip us of all such sensitivities? What are you doing wasting time on love when there is money to be made, economies to be saved, wars to be fought, and civilizations to be rebuilt? These are dangerous times: don't waste any time on something as inefficient, frivolous, and unproductive as love! So what does the artist do in the face of such "criminal" activity? If the prophet has discerned well and we are indeed living in a dangerous time, an exhausting time of shortening hours and shortened breath, an anxious time of impending collapse, what are we called to do? We are called to realize that "nothing worth having comes without some kind of fight / got to kick at the darkness 'til it bleeds daylight." If the "beauty of it all" is worth saving, if "fragile bodies of touch and taste" are something that we can't imagine life without, if love is something worth fighting for against all the odds, then, sings Cockburn, we've "got to kick at the darkness 'til it bleeds daylight." If Cockburn is a psalmist, then this is a psalm of lament, in which the psalmist is not going to let go until God answers his prayer. If Cockburn is a prophet, then this is an oracle in the darkness of exile that knows the exile will be long, but he will not give up on the hope of return, the hope of light shining in the midst of the darkness.

There is nothing passive about such prayers and such hopes. And there is nothing passive about the powerful imagery of this song. We've got to "kick at the darkness." In the words of Mary Jo Leddy, we've got to say, indeed scream, at the darkness, "We beg to differ."[53] We do not just wait for the light; we fight for it. In our love, in our intimacy, in our refusal to submit to the forces of darkness around us, we assault the darkness until it bleeds daylight. Leonard Cohen might sing, "there is a crack in everything / that's how the light gets in,"[54] but Cockburn is saying that if there is to be a crack it will have to be kicked open. We do so in the deep hope and faith that the light shines in the darkness and the darkness cannot overcome it.[55] A thick darkness may well be upon us, but a light will penetrate that darkness, and the dawn will come again.[56]

Here is art that achieves an awakening prophetic power, an art that bears witness to the mystery of lovers open to the thrust of grace, a song that can nurture, nourish, and evoke an alternative consciousness to the dominant ideology. Here is a song that can liberate our imaginations both by naming our time as a time of darkness and by embracing love as a subversion of that darkness, an anticipation of the light. And here is a song that not only calls forth interpretation but also invites appropriation. In the last two lines of the song Cockburn shifts the pronoun. No longer is it, "*you're* lovers in a dangerous time" but "*we're* lovers in a dangerous time." All of us are lovers in a dangerous time. All who practice love in the midst of this culture of death find themselves kicking at the darkness until it bleeds daylight.

It is not surprising to me that this song often is performed at weddings. Couples who are embracing each other in marriage and know this song seem to think that it is appropriate to have it sung in the midst of the ceremony, and I have been honored to preach at such a wedding. One of the ways in which we can engage Cockburn's art is through the creation of our own cultural products. A sermon is such a product and at its best bears some (passing) resemblance to the poetry of psalmists, prophets, and songwriters. This sermon weaves together images from "Lovers" with the language of "abiding in Christ" that we meet in John 15 and the call to "seek the welfare of the city" that Jeremiah writes to the exiles in Babylon in the twenty-ninth chapter of his book of prophecy. A quick reading of these two passages will enhance your understanding of the biblical metaphors and images that are woven with Cockburn's song in this sermon.[57]

## Lovers in a Dangerous Time: A Wedding Sermon

> One day you're waiting for the sky to fall
> the next you're dazzled by the beauty of it all
>
> Apocalyptic dread and creational delight
>     anxiety and joy
>     it's all crashing down or you are overwhelmed
>         by the sheer beauty of it all
>             her beauty
>             his beauty
>             sensual beauty
>             the beauty of gift
>
> That's the way it is for lovers in a dangerous time
>     that's the way it is when you make love in empire
>     that's the way it is when you pledge troth
>     that's the way it is when you get married against the odds
>
> When you're lovers in a dangerous time
> sometimes you're made to feel as if your love's a crime
>     it is criminal to close down your options
>         in a world of infinite choice
>     it is criminal to say enough
>         in a world of insatiability
>     it is criminal to say I do
>         in a world of duplicity
>     it is criminal to tie the knot
>         in a world with no strings attached

*it is criminal to offer yourself in an act of momentous giving*
*in a world where everything has its price*
*sometimes you're made to feel as if your love's a crime*
*criminal activity! . . . at Trinity Anglican Church!*
*. . . on Thanksgiving weekend!*

*When you're lovers in a dangerous time*
*sometimes you're made to feel as if your love's a crime*
*nothing worth having comes without some kind of fight*
*got to kick at the darkness till it bleeds daylight*
*kicking at the darkness*
*getting married in the dark*
*marriage as a shining light in the darkness*
*trothful love as good news in a world of consumer sexuality*

*how?*
*how do we kick at the darkness?*
*how do we live in the midst of empire?*
*how do we live in Babylon?*
*how do we live in exile?*

*Thus says the Lord of hosts, the God of Israel to all the exiles . . .*
*thus says the Lord of hosts, the God of Israel*
*to Andrew and Ericka . . .*
*build houses and live in them*
*plant gardens and eat what they produce*
*take each other as husband and wife*
*have children*
*multiply in all of your ways and do not decrease*

*Build houses in a culture of homelessness?*
*Plant gardens in polluted soil?*
*Get married?*
*Have children . . . in this world?*
*Multiply . . . in a world of debt?*
*That's it?*
*But we want to kick at the darkness!*

*Building houses*
*building a life together of hospitality*
*getting your hands dirty in the soil*
*sharing a life of faithfulness with each other*
*with your community*
*with your neighborhood*
*with the poor*

*raising children of covenant*
*multiplying virtue, justice, kindness, compassion, forgiveness*
    *. . . all of this is kicking at the darkness till it bleeds daylight.*

*Kick at the darkness*
    *seek the welfare of the city*
*kick at the darkness*
    *seek shalom*
*kick at the darkness*
    *spirits open to the thrust of grace*
*kick at the darkness*
    *not out of bravado*
    *not out of triumphalism*
    *not out of bitterness*
*kick at the darkness*
    *rooted in grace*
*kick at the darkness*
    *living in the light*

*Kick at the darkness*
    *with eyes wide open*
*kick at the darkness*
    *because the exile will be long*
*kick at the darkness*
    *because the darkness will not have the final word*
*kick at the darkness*
    *because the darkness is ubiquitous,*
        *but it is not sovereign*

*I have plans for you,*
    *says the homemaking God*
*I have plans for your shalom*
*I have plans for your homecoming*
*Call . . . and I will hear*
*Seek . . . and I will be found*
*Come . . . and I will gather you*
*Come . . . and I will come to you*

*These fragile bodies of touch and taste*
*this vibrant skin . . . this hair like lace*
*spirits open to the thrust of grace*
*never a breath you can afford to waste*
*when you're lovers in a dangerous time*

*Lovers in a dangerous time*
    *need to live somewhere*
*lovers in a dangerous time*
    *need to bear fruit in the wilderness*

*Abide in me as I abide in you*
    *abide in me and bear much fruit*
*Abide in me*
    *be at home in me*
    *be homemakers under the shelter of my love*
*Abide in my love*
    *live in my love*
*Abide in me*
    *my words will abide in you*
    *my word will dwell with you*
    *as you dwell with each other*
    *a word-shaped dwelling*
    *a Christ-shaped dwelling*

*Abiding in Jesus*
    *living in empire*
*Abiding in Jesus*
    *lovers in a dangerous time*
*Abiding in Jesus*
    *open to the thrust of grace*
*Abiding in Jesus*
    *bearing rich fruit*
*Abiding in Jesus*
    *abiding in joy*

*Seek the welfare of the city*
    *seek shalom*
*Seek the welfare of the city*
    *love one another*

*What a friend we have in Jesus*
    *he laid down his life for us*
*What a friend she has in Andrew*
    *he'll lay down his life for her*
*What a friend he has in Ericka*
    *she'll lay down her life for him*

*Seek the welfare of the city*

*Go and bear fruit*
  *fruit that will last*
*Go and bear fruit*
  *fruit of the gospel*
*Go and bear fruit*
  *fruit of the light*
*Go and bear fruit*
  *fruit that will kick at the darkness*
*Go and bear fruit*
  *fruitfulness of committed love*
*Go and bear fruit*
  *fruitful work that seeks shalom*
*Go and bear fruit*
  *fruit that will satisfy and sustain the weary*

*Go forth, my sister, my brother*
  *go forth from this day*
  *and bear fruit*
*Go forth and multiply*
  *go forth as lovers in a dangerous time.*

*And as you go*
  *abide in Jesus*
*as you go*
  *abide in his word*

*And as you go*
  *you do not go alone*
  *we go with you*
  *you see . . . we're lovers in a dangerous time too.*

# Cockburn's Windows

## Getting a Big Picture

Recognizing that while each human necessarily sees the world "from one point of view with a perspective and a selectiveness peculiar" to oneself, C. S. Lewis has noted that it is also characteristically human to want to see "with other eyes, to imagine with other imaginations, to feel with other hearts, as well as with our own." And that is why "we demand windows." Literature, poetry, and art offer us "a series of windows, even doors."[1] In this chapter we want to get a window on the expansive work of Bruce Cockburn. Let's call it a picture window, a big-picture window. And let's take a look through that big-picture window precisely by attending to windows as they appear in Cockburn's work.

"Look out the window, what do I see?"[2] This is the first line that we meet on Bruce Cockburn's self-titled debut album. "Look out the window, what do I see?" Well, nothing too clear—"cows hangin' out under spreading trees / Zoom! They're gone behind the sign." This is the fleeting vision from a car window as we are "going to the country." A window it is, but not a window that affords one the luxury of attending to the view with any depth, with any time.

Windows are constant icons in Cockburn's writing. Indeed, we could sketch the overall shape of Cockburn's career by attending to his windows. While the car window of Cockburn's first recorded track is perhaps less than satisfactory for shaping a vision of the world, it is the destination of that car ride that provides a clue to dominant themes in Cockburn's earliest albums. You see, we are "going to the country." We are going someplace where you can sit by the window and watch, where you can sit by the window and dream.

## Looking for a Window

"I'm looking to be by a window," Cockburn sings on another track on this first album.[3] And this is a window that "looks out on the sea." This is a window that provides a vista of primordial beauty and, if tradition be true, primordial threat. This is, after all, the sea—symbol of chaos, habitat of monsters and serpents. But not necessarily for Cockburn. Later in the song he sings, "you know, these city towers / jewels on the Serpent's crown / twist the space between them / till every eye is blinded." It is the city, not the sea, that is the habitat of the serpent. It is the city, not the sea, that represents the sovereignty of the serpent. Indeed, while the artist longs to be by a window that will shed light and open his eyes—a window by the sea—it is the space between these city towers, these jewels on the serpent's crown, that renders us blind.

Nonetheless, the artist has a vision through this window—"surf of golden sunlight / breaking over me." The problem is that he doesn't know where to find this window. He is *looking* for such a window—"anybody here know / where such a place is?" Why can't this "man of a thousand faces" find this window? Perhaps because he is indeed a man of a thousand faces, and you can look out a window only with one face. He wears a multiplicity of faces, of masks, and clarity of vision requires clarity of identity.

How was such clarity forfeited? To come to grips with the nature of the crisis, the song plays with various images that are mostly biblical in nature. The artist is looking for a window, but the path of his journey began in a garden: "in the Garden paths take form." Which garden? A garden guarded by a hailstorm, a garden of things forbidden, a garden of things unknown. Could this be Eden of the opening chapters of Genesis? Is that where this journey began? And might it be that our journey from this garden must be solitary, that we "must travel on alone" because of the lost innocence, the blinding error in that garden?

Not surprisingly, the artist next alludes to death.

> in memoriam friends come round
> but the hard ground holds its own
> time for pulling, time to ride
> it's my turn but where's the guide?

The garden is now a cemetery. Wasn't that what the discussion with the serpent was all about? Death? So the garden of life becomes a garden of death. And this hard ground holds its own. The artist must now ride—whether away from or toward this place of death we do not know. Whichever direction his path takes him, it appears that he is not content to travel alone. He longs for a guide. This is a journey that requires vision, but he hasn't even found the window that he longs to be looking through.

The imagery returns to the sea:

> *on the jetty shadows lie*
> *and the gulls cry once or twice*
> *swelling thunder, truth is hid*
> *behind the glass eye of the idol . . .*
> *anybody here know*
> *where such a place is?*

The idol hides the truth. The serpent blinds every eye. Another dead end.

Blinded, alone, guideless, longing for the vision that is denied to those who only wear masks and have no sense of authentic identity, the man of a thousand faces asks, "Lord will you trade your sunlit ocean / with its writhing filigree / for any one of my thousand faces?" Having looked for a window that would afford him a redemptive and clarifying vision of the sea—and failed—the artist offers God a deal. How about if I offer you one of my thousand faces, and you give me that vision, you give me that sunlit ocean? If I offer up one of my faces as the authentic face, can I then get the vision that I long for?

It will be a few years before that deal is finalized and Cockburn can sing,

> *All the diamonds in this world*
> *that mean anything to me*
> *are conjured up by wind and sunlight*
> *sparkling on the sea.*[4]

And it will take some time before the artist can see beyond those "jewels on the serpent's crown" to something much more valuable:

> *like a pearl in a sea of liquid jade*
> *His ship comes shining*
> *like a crystal swan in a sky of suns*
> *His ship comes shining.*[5]

But we have a ways to go before we get there.

Windows appear again on Cockburn's second album, the 1971 release, *High Winds White Sky*. And from these windows the artist has a vision of "Life's Mistress."[6] The imagery shifts here from sea to earth, and life's mistress is encountered as something of a sacramental earth mother. Here is a world of vision, but not of sound.

> *Silence*
> *carries*
> *no apprehension here*
> *in the warm sun*

*by the window sill*
*i can just sit still*
*and watch her go by.*

From this window there is afforded a quiet vision of stillness, peace, and order. This life's mistress is "Queen of field and forest pathway," who "understands the speech of stones." This is a mistress/goddess who "weaves peace upon her loom." A window has been found. But this is a window of passivity. The artist sits and watches. Can this be the resolution for this man of a thousand faces? Is the face gazing out that window a singular face, a face of clarified identity and authenticity? From this window, the artist can observe life's mistress at home in her world. There she is interpreting the speech of stones and weaving a household of peace on her loom. And the artist watches. The question is, how long can he just sit there? It doesn't take too long before he is getting impatient.

## Windows Too Small

While the meditative, soft, and sensitive acoustic sounds of "Man of a Thousand Faces" and "Life's Mistress" suggest a sense of passivity and stasis, as soon as the slide guitar and harmonica introduce "Up on the Hillside" on the 1972 album, *Sunwheel Dance*, it is clear that this is a song about movement. Indeed, at the end of the song, Cockburn writes, "The road is waiting and I'm running out of rhyme."[7] What occasions this move from the settledness of the view from the windowsill back to the unsettledness of the road? Well, "up on the hillside you can see the cross shine / out in the alley hear the hungry dog whine." Perhaps this is still a vision from a window, but not of life's mistress weaving peace on her loom. Rather, this is an urban scene of alleys together with an illuminated cross erected on a hillside—perhaps like the cross that shines out over Montreal from the top of Mont-Royal. And you can see this cross shine as you hear the hungry dog whine. The vision is shaped now by the cross, and the silence that carried no apprehension is now disturbed by the sound of a stray dog in the alley. So what do we do when we are sitting by this kind of window? "You and I, friend, sit waiting for a sign / See how the sunset makes the lake look like wine." They are waiting for a sign, perhaps a sacramental sign. A sign of the cross, a sign of creation transformed into sacramental symbol.

A new vision, a new vista, occasions a new sound, a new call. "Over the mountain I can hear myself called." Somehow beyond the cross, on the other side of that mountain, past the cross, there is a call. Who is calling? And what is the call? Could this be the call of the one who hung on that cross? Could this be the call of the one who rose from the dead and bade his disciples to come to a mountain and meet him again?[8] We don't know. But we do know that this call comes from that mountain. This call has something to do with the artist's vocation and that cross that shines.

How will the artist respond? "I want to come running but my window's too small." The window is too small! He is called to get up and follow that call, but the window he has been sitting by—the window of the man of a thousand faces, and the window from which he could sit and watch life's mistress go by—is too constricting. It provides a vision of an outside world but does not allow one the freedom to actually engage that world, to actually come through that window and follow a call that just might provide a redemptive vision for a world that is "in convulsions." Like most windows constructed for safety and security, this window is too small to provide a vista wide enough for real engagement with the world. No wonder the artist sings, "The cliffs are so high and I might fall." Real engagement is so much more frightening and dangerous than enjoying the view from this window. Maybe it's best to ignore the whole business of this cross, the reality of city alleys and being called. "What were you saying?—oh, it's nothing at all." Simply forget the whole thing.

The problem is that such a call cannot be easily forgotten. Such a call has a way of haunting you. It is not surprising that Cockburn's third album, the 1973 release, *Night Vision*, has that sense of being haunted. From the raucous blues tunes "The Blues Got the World" and "Mama Just Wants to Barrelhouse All Night Long" to the quiet laments of "You Don't Have to Play the Horses," "Clocks Don't Bring Tomorrow—Knives Don't Bring Good News," *Night Vision* is permeated with a tone of lament. And in the devastatingly sad concluding track, "God Bless the Children,"[9] Cockburn returns again to images of the sea, death, and idolatry:

> sea swells
> illusion is queen
> in the shallow graves of experience time-centred
> grave silence reigns over the stars
> graven image hanging in time
> while the earth unwinds.

No longer a site of revelation, the sea is now symbolic of illusion and deathly silence. And if you open your eyes, you can now see even more clearly that ever-present graven image, that false idol that guides us all "while the earth unwinds." With that kind of painful clarity of vision imposed upon him, the artist sings, "with pain the world paves us over / Lord let us not betray / God bless the children with visions of the Day." The pain of the world is still an urban, modern, and industrial pain—a pain that "paves us over"—but this ought not lead us to betrayal and a passive compliance in this pain because there are children who see something else. Maybe they are looking out a different window, maybe they have left windows behind, but in the midst of the "night vision" that permeates this album, they have a vision of the Day.

When we get to *Salt, Sun and Time*, it is clear that Cockburn has also caught a glimpse of that Day. Like the children, he has come to see that "two thousand years and half a world away / dying trees still grow greener when you pray."[10] Cockburn is still at a window, but this is a window of stained glass, a sacred window that permits a still-limited vision, but a window and a vision large enough to allow the possibility of following that call that came from the mountain:[11]

> small windows
> looking outward
> show me a sequined sky
> rubies shine in my glass of wine.

A sequined sky and rubies in my glass of wine. A jeweled world indeed, but not the serpent's jewels. A world mediated through glass—stained glass—in which the artist can sing, "like today i'm far away / i see your face behind each time-blurred pane." Whose face? Life's mistress's face? The face of the one who hung from that cross on the hillside? Perhaps both.

What happens if you look at the world through stained glass? Does such a vision leave one with a romanticized, churchly view of the world? Does it in fact result in an inner piety and peace while there is confusion and enmity in the outer world? How does a stained-glass view of the world shape the imagination? Can it comprehend devastating visions of a world that is paved over with pain? Or does it avert its gaze? In "Gavin's Woodpile," on the 1976 release, *In the Falling Dark*, Cockburn returns to themes of *Night Vision* from the perspective of that stained-glass window—a window, perhaps, with a cross.[12]

## Lamp-Warm Windows

"Gavin's Woodpile" begins with apocalyptic images of meteor showers and the groaning of creation.[13] Visions crowd the artist's eyes, and his mind fills with figures of divination or spiritual/cultural discernment not unlike Lappish runes of power:[14]

> working out on Gavin's woodpile
> safe within the harmony of kin
> visions begin to crowd my eyes
> like a meteor shower in the autumn skies
> and the soil beneath me seems to moan
> with a sound like the wind through a hollow bone
> and my mind fills with figures like Lappish runes of power . . .
>> and log slams on rough-hewn log
>> and a voice from somewhere scolds a barking dog.

Such visions bring back memories that perhaps the artist would prefer to suppress. These are memories of a prisoner serving a life sentence for alcohol-induced violence, dismissed as the trash of our society. And as the artist entertains these memories, he sings, "and i toss another log on Gavin's woodpile / and wonder at the lamp-warm window's welcome smile." As he splits wood outside, with a vision of devastating clarity of the terrible brokenness of the world, he glances over at the house—the house where he is safe within the harmony of kin—and wonders "at the lamp-warm window's welcome smile." How can there be such a window? How can there be such warmth, such welcome in a world where some can only look through the windows of their cells?

The visions only get darker as the song continues. The man who is stacking firewood now remembers a fire:

> i remember crackling embers
> coloured windows shining through the rain
> like the coloured slicks on the English River
> death in the marrow and death in the liver
> and some government gambler with his mouth full of steak
> saying "if you can't eat the fish, fish in some other lake.
> To watch a people die—it is no new thing."
>     and the stack of wood grows higher and higher
>     and a helpless rage seems to set my brain on fire.

Even the warmth and serenity of crackling embers recall other windows. These colored windows shining through the rain conjure up images of the mercury poisoning of the Grassy Narrows Reserve and the callousness of government and corporate response to this crisis.[15] So a "helpless rage seems to set my mind on fire," and the artist is "paralyzed in the face of it all / cursed with the curse of these modern times."

The fourth verse of this song seems to be an attempt to find his way through this paralysis by appealing to earlier images and motifs that have failed. First he returns to nature imagery as a source of revelation:

> distant mountains, blue and liquid,
> luminous like a thickening of sky
> flash in my mind like a stairway to life.

But then this revelatory, quasi-mystical vision is interrupted by a technical product of the very modern times by which he feels cursed—"a train whistle cuts through the scene like a knife." So he tries again—"three hawks wheel in a dazzling sky"—but again modernity intrudes—"a slow motion jet makes them look like a lie."

So what then? Cockburn confesses he's "left to conclude there's no human answer near." And yet . . . "there's a narrow path to a life to come / that explodes into sight with the power of the sun." What happens if you keep looking through that stained-glass window? What might one see in the dusk "as the sun goes down"? Even in the apocalyptic darkness that has clouded his eyes, raised questions about that "lamp-warm window's welcome smile," and left him with a paralyzed rage, Cockburn still sees something else:

> *a mist rises as the sun goes down*
> *and the light that's left forms a kind of crown*
> *the earth is bread, the sun is wine*
> *it's a sign of a hope that's ours for all time.*

This stained-glass window provides a sacramental view of the world. His eyes open to the groaning of all of creation under the weight of darkness, oppression, violence, and sin, Cockburn sees this groaning as nothing less than the passion of Christ. The earth is bread; the sun is wine: the bread and wine of the Eucharist, the body and blood of Christ. We are back on that hillside with the cross, and now we are invited to view the world through the perspective of that cross.

## Grimy Windows

"Gavin's Woodpile" wonders at the "lamp-warm window's welcome smile." On the next album, *Further Adventures Of*, we meet a similar window. In "Laughter" Cockburn sings, "a laugh for the dirty window pane / hiding the love within,"[16] and that is the last positive image of windows that we will see for some time. Whether the image is that of "pain takes shape of grimy window,"[17] or you are looking out a window down the gray road at an "old walled monastery / now become a barracks for the paramilitary police,"[18] or we are witness to "neon flame on the window of an upstairs room,"[19] it is clear that these are no "lamp-warm windows" "safe within the harmony of kin" "hiding the love within." And while there may be erotic encounters—"half moon shining through the blind / paints a vision of a different kind"[20]—this new urban experience is more likely to result in bullet holes in the kitchen wall—"so how come the window's broken? / what caused the glass to fall?"[21] And rather than finding stained-glass windows that open vistas on the meaning of Christian faith in a world of oppression, Cockburn encounters the gospel of bondage of the religious Right, with their "shutters on storefronts and shutters in the mind."[22] Shuttered windows, broken windows, neon-flamed windows, windows with the blinds down. These are the windows of the eighties for Bruce Cockburn.

And yet Cockburn's faith is never without hope:

> *You rub your palm*
> *on the grimy pane*
> *in the hope that you can see.*[23]

These are dirty windows, covered with the grime of industrial pollution, looking through a glass so dark that one can hardly see.[24] But if we dare to stand with those who are "waiting for a miracle," then we will rub a spot of clarity onto that grimy pane in the hope that we can see, in the hope that with that kind of vision we will be able to "step out from the past and try to hold the line" while "we're waiting for a miracle."

## Prophetic Windows

And then, for a number of years and a number of albums, windows drop out of the Cockburn lexicon of imagery. That is, until "Get Up, Jonah," on the 1996 album, *The Charity of Night*. And in this song it seems as if we are back at that window with the man of a thousand faces:

> *Somebody stands in a window*
> *Watches the river roll*
> *Trains rumble in the foreground*
> *With the weight of approaching dawn.*

This is no elusive window of vision that the artist seeks but can't find. This is no window by a sea of primordial revelation. Nor is this a window from which one can gaze upon life's mistress. No, this is a window with a moving river and rumbling trains. Is this the river of the prophet Amos—"let justice roll down like waters"?[25] Is this a gospel train, or is it like Gavin's woodpile train—whose whistle cuts through the scene like a knife? Whichever train and whichever river this is, the vista before the artist is neither dusk nor the dawn of a new creation. Rather, through this window he encounters "the weight of approaching dawn." Dawn comes as a weight, a burden—another damn day with the same old burdens, the same old paralyzing forces and curses of these modern times.

Somebody stands in a window confronting the weight of an approaching dawn. And what does he see?

> *Flames from the refinery*
> *Rise broken, red and riveting*
> *And the high vault of heaven*
> *Looks far away and cold.*

Neither "the earth is bread, the sun is wine" nor signs of "hope that are ours for all time" are to be seen from this window. No, in this vista the flames of an industrial society render the high vault of heaven "far away and cold." There is no close divinity out of this window, no sacramental imagery, just the utter absence of God and the deep desolation and coldness that such absence always entails.

Now the artist identifies himself with that person standing in the window. He was always in the window; they have all been his windows.

*There's howling in the factory yard*
*There's pounding in my head*
*I'm swollen up with unshed tears*
*Bloated like the dead*

These are troubling visions coupled with oppressive sounds. No wonder the artist experiences a pounding in his head. No wonder he is swollen up with unshed tears. The sociocultural and military-industrial realities of the outer world now have their parallel—indeed, their deafening echo—in the internal life of the artist: "howling in the factory yard . . . pounding in my head." Moreover, the sense of apocalyptic dread that we met in "Gavin's Woodpile" is now heightened, and the artist is pushed to the breaking point.

*Blood and ashes—time burning*
*On the skyline dark against the stars*
*A solitary horseman—waiting.*

A solitary horseman—that is what the artist sees from this window. The reference would appear to be to the four horsemen of the apocalypse from Revelation 6 who bring judgment on the earth. But which horseman does he see? Pestilence, war, famine, or death? Or is it all four of them bound up into one? Whichever it is, this is a vision of a world of blood and ashes, of violence and death, of oppression and tragic endings. This is no "waiting for a miracle." This is a much more ominous waiting, more akin to the expectations that we meet in the vision of the fall of Babylon in Revelation 18.

So what is the artist to do? All of these windows have led to this window, to this apocalyptic vision. The artist was initially looking for a window that looked out on the sea. But now he realizes that such a romanticized sea is an illusion and that such a safe vista is sheer escapism. If it is the sea that he wanted, the only sea he will get is the sea of the prophet Jonah:

*Lashed to the wheel*
*Whipping into the storm*
*Get up, Jonah*
*It's your time to be born.*

Where does this window lead? If one sees deeply through this window, if this is a stained-glass window that views the world through a cruciform lens, if this is a window that will face the weight of an approaching dawn in all of its apocalyptic threat, then this will be a window through which one will enter into the precariousness and pain of our world. Like the prophet Jonah, who found that the sea was no escape but rather the site of a life-and-death struggle with God, this will be a window through which the artist will be called to nothing less than a prophetic ministry. No peaceful vista this—"lashed to the wheel / whipping into the storm." And no passive observation from the safety of life on the inside of that window—"get up, Jonah / it's your time to be born."

The world is always a mediated place, and that is why we need windows that will provide us vision and perspective in the world. Cockburn's lyrics are not dominated by windows, but there are enough of them to provide a window of their own into the dynamic and always-changing shape of Cockburn's artistic vision. If "Get Up, Jonah" is any clue, then this is a prophetic vision that will refuse to avert its gaze from the apocalyptic endings all around us.

Windows have continued to appear in Cockburn's imagery. Sometimes they are windows that need to be opened up "to let the bad air out."[26] You see, if you're hanging out in a whorehouse, or if political and economic life is subject to the brothelization of culture, full of people screwing each other and screwing the poor in a culture of "drugs and oil and money," and politics is "open for business like a cheap bordello,"[27] then perhaps, "at the risk of being subversive," you got "nothing left to do but shout, 'Open up the window, let the bad air out!'"

But perhaps the prophetic ethos is one more suffused with pathos than with this kind of in-your-face shouting. What happens when being prophetic does not mean looking for fresh air from within a closed-window oppression, but rather changing perspective entirely? What if we are outside looking in? What if the window is looking into a thirty-foot tower near Phnom Penh full of thousands of skulls from the killing fields? Skulls that appear to "whisper, as if from a great distance, / of pain, and of pain left far behind"? "Eighteen thousand empty eye-holes peering out at the four directions."[28] What then? What does this Jonah have to say looking into that window?

## Prayer Windows

Or what happens if the poet is back home and gazes out his window on an urban landscape, "all polychrome grey"? What happens if when you pull back its skin the city reveals that "the beautiful creatures are going away"? What happens if the view from our window opens out onto "the callous and vicious things / humans display," and we see that "we create what destroys" and "bind ourselves to betray"?[29] What happens if this is the view from the poet's window? Well, perhaps, he confesses that

> this is too big for anger,
> it's too big for blame.
> We stumble through history so
> humanly lame.
> So I bow down my head,
> Say a prayer for us all.
> That we don't fear the spirit
> when it comes to call.[30]

All of the vistas opened by these windows push the artist to prayer in the end. Recognizing that neither prophetic denunciation nor artistic imagination is really up to the task, we are called again to wait for a miracle. We are called again to recognize that our stumbling path through human history requires a guide. And so the artist prays for a humility and an openness that will not fear the leading and healing presence of the Spirit in our midst. When the Spirit comes to call, the view outside that window will not be immediately changed. But in the Spirit, recognizing that we are stumblers through history, caught in our own self-destructive webs of despair and betrayal, we will have the prophetic courage to stare at the devastation with open eyes. Indeed, in the Spirit we can also have the faith and courage to rub our hands "on a grimy pane" in the hope that we can see.

There is a sense in which the "Man of a Thousand Faces" was waiting at that window. Perhaps we could say that once he found his own face, once he heard the call from the cross and was set free to follow his vocation, then he kept on waiting by that window. But this is not a passive waiting. Rather, this is a "working and waiting for a miracle."[31]

# Creation
# Dream

One of the joys of teaching courses that attend to the work of Bruce Cockburn is that I get to hear how my students respond to his music and lyrics. Here is how one especially wonderful review essay of *Dancing in the Dragon's Jaws* begins:

> If you wake up early enough, and happen to have the good fortune to be on a lake, there is a good chance you have witnessed the dance. When the temperature is just right, and the sun is just so, and the water is still enough, you will see it. The sun peeks its head above the horizon and begins to dance on the water, shimmering and shining in magnificent glory. Then, as the breeze gently floats by you can catch a glimpse of the cattails swaying melodically. The dance continues. The early morning mist rolls in across the lake and twirls and pirouettes delicately as the water gently steps in and then slides back from the shoreline. This is the dance of creation. Canadian singer and songwriter Bruce Cockburn is no stranger to this dance.[1]

And it would appear that Esther Bowser, the author of this undergraduate paper, is also no stranger to this dance of creation. She is attuned to Cockburn's rich vision of creational dance because she has seen what he has seen and, perhaps, sees it even more deeply because of the experience of viewing the world through Cockburn's artistically allusive vision. This chapter begins to tease out a Christian imagination by asking the first worldview question in dialogue with Cockburn's vision. Where are we?

## Even More, It Depends on the Way That You See

In *The Magician's Nephew* C. S. Lewis tells the story of the founding of Narnia. Uncle Andrew is a man who fancies himself something of a visionary, but in fact he is mostly blind and, as the story unfolds, deaf as well. All of Narnia was springing into being, and talking beasts were embracing their new life, all in response to the song of the Great Lion, Aslan. Uncle Andrew, meanwhile, quite literally cannot believe either his eyes or his ears. At first he recognized that there was indeed a song calling forth this new creation, but once he saw the source of the song to be a lion, "he tried his hardest to make believe that it wasn't singing and never had been singing—only roaring as any lion might in a zoo in our own world. . . . And the longer and more beautiful the Lion sang, the harder Uncle Andrew tried to make himself believe that he could hear nothing but roaring."[2] Uncle Andrew was blind to the dance of creation and deaf to its song. And Lewis tells us why when he writes, "For what you see and hear depends a good deal on where you are standing: it also depends on what sort of person you are."[3]

What you see depends on where you are standing and on what sort of person you are. We see from a particular place. All vision is from a point of orientation, a certain kind of perspective. If Esther Bowser's lake is viewed narrowly from the perspective of its place in a larger watershed that is going to be dammed for the production of hydroelectricity, then perhaps that early-morning dance of creation won't be noticed. And if the person viewing this lake, even if standing at the same place on the shoreline and at the same time as Esther, is an especially self-interested, greedy, apathetic, and uncaring sort of person, then this dance of creation will undoubtedly be lost on him or her. Character shapes vision. What kind of person you are determines what you see.

Bruce Cockburn understands this well.

> *Little round planet*
> *in a big universe*
> *Sometimes it looks blessed*
> *Sometimes it looks cursed*
> *Depends on what you look at obviously*
> *But even more it depends on the way that you see.*[4]

This world can look blessed or cursed. And both are true. Which you see depends both upon what you are looking at and on the way that you see. That is to say, it depends on where you are standing and what sort of person you are. Norman Wirzba notes that perception is more basic than thinking: "How we see and feel the world is more fundamental [than thinking] because it is in terms of our perception that thought and action take shape."[5]

Throughout his body of work, it is clear that Bruce Cockburn sees the dance of creation. He sees both blessing and curse, but blessing is always primordial.

Indeed, without embracing a world that is blessed, it is very difficult to actually discern the world cursed. Without a primordial affirmation of the goodness of this world, perceptions of evil are blurred.

Through Cockburn's eyes we perceive a world of wonders that is suffused with mystery. In Lewis's terms, that's the "sort of person" Cockburn is. But he hasn't always stood in the same place when viewing this world. Quite literally, the world looks different depending on where you stand—whether it be in the midst of poverty-stricken Central Americans, by a Japanese pool, in a remote hot spring, or in the inner city of Toronto. What you see depends on where you are standing. And Cockburn has stood in various places. But standpoint isn't simply a matter of geographical location. Perspective can change over time, and the same view can be seen in different ways.

## From Spring to Christmas

On Cockburn's debut album we meet "Spring Song."[6] There is, in this song, a sense of eternal return. In the turning of the seasons, in the cyclic return of spring we experience a renewal that is at the very heart of things. "When we come / when we come again / to celebrate renewal / at the heart / at the heart of us / our eyes will touch Life." This renewal of the earth is at the heart of our humanity, and in such renewal "our eyes touch Life." In this mixed metaphor, vision and touch are united. Eyes do not just see, they also, in some profound sense, must *touch* Life. And note that this is Life, not life. There is something about this Life that transcends life itself. But this renewal, this touching of Life in its most ultimate and sacred sense isn't simply a natural and necessary phenomenon. While the first chorus has us come again to *celebrate* a renewal that is *at* the heart of us, the second chorus has us come again "to *search* beside the Fool . . . / *for* the heart of us." This renewal might be at the heart of things, but it has been somehow lost, and we must seek it out; we must search for the heart of things. And then the third chorus abandons the future tense of "when we come again" and places us in an eternal present of "till we come / till we come again / to *recognize* renewal / *at* the heart . . . of us."[7] Celebrating, searching, and recognizing. The annual renewal of creation is something to be celebrated, sought out, and finally recognized.

Yet we also know that there is something wrong. While there seems to be an inevitability to this renewal, this coming of spring, it isn't something that can simply be taken for granted. There is a sense of lost identity and disorientation ("though we may be hard to find / where we stand in time"), and there is also some sort of unattributed blame that "we love so well to focus on." Further, this dance through the cycles of creation seems "frenzied" and perhaps impeded "by ornaments entranced." And so we must not just celebrate renewal but also quest for such renewal and "search beside the Fool." There is that unnamed joker again, the one we have met "dancing in the dragon's jaws." We may not know who he is, but it is clear that you need to have the upside-down wisdom of a fool if you are going to plumb the depths of things, if you are going to go for the heart of things, and if your eyes are ever going to touch Life.[8]

In "Spring Song" we see that creational and spiritual renewal is to be celebrated as a gift, and yet it is also something we need to seek out. Moreover, that seeking, that quest for ultimate renewal will continue until we come to the place where we recognize such renewal to be at the very heart of all things. Then perhaps we can sing, "seasons turning yet again / the Mother's breast is full again / as in heaven, so with men / is now and ever shall be." When Mother's breast is full again, when Mother Nature is renewed, or perhaps when the divine Mother brings creational renewal, then there will be a harmony between heaven and human life, and that is the way things are supposed to be.

It is clear that "Spring Song" takes us on a path of spiritual renewal. We are talking here about Life, Mother, the Fool. We are talking about that which is "at the heart of us." And both the lyrics of seasonal renewal and the soft repetitiveness of the music convey a sense of cyclic return.

So where are we? What kind of a world are we invited to inhabit when received through the sounds, words, and vision of this song? There is something sacred about this world. We meet here a world of temporality, cyclical movement, and renewal. This is a world in which our spiritual path is intimately connected to the movement of the seasons. If there is to be rebirth, then it will be experienced through a sense of oneness with natural cycles. And it is clear that in this kind of time-centered world, there can be no standing still. We must embrace the movement of time and find ourselves in union with that movement.[9]

These themes of cyclical temporality are echoed in a number of other songs from the first four albums. Because the world is in temporal movement we must always keep life open[10] and be willing to "turn with the times / change your mind."[11] But if we are to replace the frenzied, life-closing dance identified in "Spring Song" with a dance more conducive to our embrace of temporal circularity, then we need to realize that "we can't dance without seasons upon which to stand / Eden is a state of rhythm like the sea / is a timeless change."[12] We may all be dancers in this life, but that dance must be one with the seasons, one with the creational rhythms of Eden, an embracing of timeless change, of eternal cyclical movement. Only in such oneness with the cyclical rhythms of nature will life be opened to wonder.

> if we can sing with the wind song
> chant with the thunder
> play upon the lightning
> melodies of wonder
> into wonder life will open[13]

Precisely because "the song of the seasons brings life to the land,"[14] we are called to join that song. When we add our song to that of creation, singing in harmony with these "melodies of wonder," then our lives will be taken up into that wonder.

Sounds wonderful. But remember that what you see depends on where you are standing. The way that you see depends on what sort of person you are. While there is something deeply attractive about the world that we meet in these early Cockburn songs, and while themes of wonder, temporality, and the sacred character of life remain constant throughout his body of work, there is something about the romantic naïveté of these early songs of a cyclical return and nature mysticism that could not be sustained.

The turning point seems to come with *Night Vision*. In this 1973 album we "hear the city singing like a siren choir,"[15] find ourselves anxious and alone "when the sun goes nova / and the world turns over,"[16] and end up waiting "beside the desert / nothing left to give away / naked as the Hanged Man's secrets / praying for the break of day."[17] When "the blues got the world by the balls," there is something about cyclical harmony that just doesn't quite match reality.[18] This is a temporal vision of the world, but it is less concerned with seasonal cycles and more attentive to the dynamics of day and night. This album offers us a night vision in which temporality per se is much more ambiguous and ceases to have any salvific significance. What you see may depend on where you stand and what sort of person you are, but if you are in perpetual night, if it is constantly dark, then vision becomes deeply problematic.

The shift can be powerfully discerned in the closing track on *Night Vision*, "God Bless the Children." In this song temporality is not a matter of renewal, but of death. This is a world "devoured by time." In this world of night, we find ourselves drawn not to the heart of reality but to the conclusion that

> illusion is queen
> in the shallow graves of experience time-centred
> grave silence reigns over the stars
> graven image hanging in time
> while the earth unwinds.[19]

The earth doesn't renew itself but unwinds. Experience may well be temporal, but this is the temporality of shallow graves. Cockburn's earlier mysticism may have had the ears to hear the "Spring Song," together with the "ragged branches [that] vibrate / strummed by winds from o'er the hill / singing tales of ancient days,"[20] and "Life's Mistress"[21] may well have understood the speech of stones, but by the time we get to "God Bless the Children," all that we can hear is a "grave silence" in this night vision. This is a sight that neither touches nor hears. There is here a "grave silence" somehow connected to a "graven image," some sort of idolatry that is "hanging in time." Just kind of hanging there. Ominously.

And while this "graven image" is "hanging in time," the Christ doesn't seem to be doing much either. When the night is finished and "day comes," what do we see but that "the hawk of gold / springs forth in flame from a highway paved with diamonds / lion rampant on a green field / ramparts cracked into the sky / while the Christ stands by." These lines can bear multiple interpretations. Perhaps that hawk of gold is the rising sun that "springs forth in flame." Perhaps that "lion rampant on a green field" is an appearance of Aslan's banner. Whatever is going on in these lines, the appearance of a heraldic symbol ("lion rampant"), defensive structures ("ramparts cracked into the sky"), and the imperial overtones of a "hawk of gold" (think of either the Roman or the American eagle) would seem to reveal that this "day" is a day of violence, a day of war. And on this day, the Christ is present, but he merely "stands by."

If what you see depends upon where you stand, and where you stand is intimately connected to what sort of person you are, then as early as *Night Vision* we begin to find a standpoint, an orientation that cannot avert its gaze from the destructive dynamics of time and the painful nature of experience. If sometimes the world looks blessed, and sometimes it looks cursed, then that blessedness will be hopeless escapism if it refuses to face the cursed character of things. Perhaps that is why Cockburn employs the decidedly urban metaphor of pavement at the close of "God Bless the Children": "with pain the world paves us over / Lord let us not betray / God bless the children with visions of the Day." Let us not buy into this cosmic betrayal, this pain that crushes us down like steaming, fresh-poured pavement. And God bless the children who have a different vision. God bless the children who, in their pain, in their disappointment that this "day" finds the Christ merely standing by, still have a vision, but it is a vision of the Day. Not this day of betrayal, but a Day of promise, a Day of trust fulfilled.

Notice that this is a prayer. Moving beyond the assurance offered in "Spring Song" that "our eyes will touch Life," the prayer of "God Bless the Children" is for those who see something more than the Mother's breast full again, more than a salvific turning of the seasons. God bless the children with visions of the Day. When will such a "Day" come? And what does one see when the world is viewed from the vantage point of that Day?

Later in this book we will explore images of Christ throughout Cockburn's songs. It is enough to say here that by the time we are listening to his 1974 album, *Salt, Sun and Time*, a conversion or an evolution to Christian faith has happened. The Christ who is "standing by" at the end of *Night Vision* has entered into Cockburn's world in a profound way in *Salt, Sun and Time*. And the result is that the artist now sees differently, both because he stands in a different place and because something has happened that has made him into a different sort of person. A shift in standpoint and character results in a shift of vision.

This shift is profoundly illustrated in "Christmas Song," the final track on *Sun, Salt and Time*. Here we witness a Christian transformation of the mystical and cyclical vision of life that characterizes much of Cockburn's earlier work. As Martin Wroe has written, "The blurred vision of the creator that nature's thick lenses offered now gave way to the crystal-clear vision of God in Jesus."[22] Reminiscent of "Spring Song," "Christmas Song" perceives salvific implications in the cyclic process of the seasons. Indeed, here at the beginning of winter, a deeply buried spring, asleep in the frozen earth, is nothing less than a "prayer," "pregnant with force." In the cycle of the seasons, in this transition from winter to spring, "we melt away and return again." And in this cyclic return, this natural process of life, death, and rebirth, we find that we are "stronger for the tempering flame." We are stronger for enduring this process year after year. But in the added fifth line of the third verse, Cockburn identifies more explicitly the source of that strength—"stronger for the Saviour's name."

It is important to consider where this song stands in relation to what we have seen to be the cyclical earth mysticism of "Spring Song." "Christmas Song" is not just a baptism of an earlier belief, a remythologization of a previously held nature mythology. Rather, in the interface between this earlier worldview and this newly expressed Christian faith, a radical transformation has taken place. Neither the artist nor we as listeners are standing in the same place, and therefore we both see differently, have a different way of seeing, and perhaps end up being different sorts of people. This is, after all, "Christmas Song." In the midst of the ever-recurring cycle of the seasons, in the midst of this clearly cyclical world, a contingent, unrepeatable, historical event has occurred. A baby was born in a manger. A star appeared in the heavens. Angels made visitations. Yes, the cycles of nature continue, and yes, there are important images of salvation in the cyclic return of the spring and the thaw of winter, but those images are deepened and given a profoundly Christian interpretation by seeing that this hope of renewal is rooted distinctively in the events of Christmas.

The cosmic harmony of "Spring Song"—"as in heaven, so with men / is now and ever shall be"—is now a harmony realized and achieved not in the universal cycles of nature but in the particular events of the incarnation. It is through this vision that "our eyes will touch Life," and it is beside this "Fool," this "glittering joker," that we will come again "to recognize renewal." If you put "Christmas Song" beside "Spring Song," you find that you can "celebrate renewal" because such renewal happens through the history-transforming events of Christmas. "At the heart of us," we are "stronger for the Saviour's name." At the heart of things, the thaw of winter and the arrival of spring is a function of the arrival of the Son. We can see here the influence of C. S. Lewis on Cockburn's emerging Christian imagination. In *The Lion, the Witch and the Wardrobe* the thaw of the interminably long winter occurs only when Aslan returns.[23] So also is it the arrival of the Incarnate One that heralds the arrival of spring in "Christmas Song." The Christ who "stands by" at the end of *Night Vision* is the force of cosmic renewal at the end of *Salt, Sun and Time*.

## Cockburn's Creational Triptych

If a Christian faith is to be vibrant and prophetically engaged in the world in all of its brokenness, then it must be rooted in a Christ who does much more than just "stand by." If we are to find ways to bring justice and healing to a world that sometimes looks deeply cursed, then we will need to have a vantage point, a vision of life, that can see both the deep blessed character of the world and how the Christ who enters into the dragon's jaws of this cursed world has been intimately involved with this creation from the beginning. On the albums *Joy Will Find a Way*, *In the Falling Dark*, and *Dancing in the Dragon's Jaws*, we find three songs that deeply explore the riches of biblical images of creation. Respectively, "Starwheel," "Lord of the Starfields," and "Creation Dream" form something of a triptych, a three-paneled altarpiece that the artist presents as hymns of praise to his redeeming Creator.

Cowritten with Kitty Cockburn, "Starwheel" embraces life in all of its ambiguity. We hear a resonance with the Old Testament book of Ecclesiastes in this song. The biblical sage writes, "Vanity of vanities! All is vanity."[24] The contemporary sage writes, "you're bound to move on and so am I / on this world we've had time to burn / how come nobody ever seems to learn?"[25] And in the second verse we learn again that "constant change is the space we're in." There is here, and repeated throughout Cockburn's body of work, a sense of the inevitability of change, and a sense that in this changing, moving world, we've all "had time to burn."[26] Whether this metaphor of burning refers to the idea that we've all had time to be burned, to be hurt or victimized (as in "Burn" on the same album), or alludes to living with passion and intensity (as in "O love that fires the sun / keep me burning" from "Lord of the Starfields"),[27] or expresses that we all have had too much time on our hands, the artist's observation is that this time to burn is wasted time. So he asks, "how come nobody ever seems to learn?"

What is it that we never seem to learn? The parallel lines in the third verse give us an answer: "we're given love and love must be returned / that's all the bearings that you need to learn." Both the artist and the ancient sage recognize that there is a certain meaninglessness to a movement of life in which the most fundamental lessons remain unlearned. The ancient sage answers his own existential predicament with this summary statement: "Fear God, and keep his commandments; for that is the whole duty of everyone."[28] Cockburn's answer isn't all that different, but it has the sharp focus of the New Testament's vision of human duty being fundamentally rooted in love. Jesus teaches that the commandment that fulfills all other obligations is the love command—love God and love your neighbor. This, says Jesus, is what it means to be truly human.[29] Cockburn is saying that if we want bearings in this ever-changing, ceaselessly shifting world, then there is only one bearing that is available and only one that we need. Set your sight by the bearing of love, and it will transform your futility into meaning.

Why do we find it so difficult to get that bearing? What hampers our learning of this lesson? What clouds our vision so that we cannot find that bearing of love in our lives? In the second and third verses of this song, Cockburn suggests two impediments. The first is the attempt, by means of scientific control and political power, to deny change in the world—"you may use a slide rule or a golden crown

/ but nothing's worth it that you can pin down." Love is a bearing that one sets for a journey. In this song, love is a navigational image. Love is a bearing for people on the move, who are growing and changing, and who are in tune with the changing, dynamic character of reality. As such, it is a bearing that is of no use to anyone who wants to deny change, pin life down, and remain stuck in a statically and oppressively controlled present.

This leads to the second impediment. This autonomous grasp for control is in fact nothing less than playing "shell games with God"—"don't go playing no shell game with God / only Satan's going to give you odds." A shell game could be a reference to the game where a pea is hidden under one of three shells. The shells are shuffled and the player has to guess where the pea lies. Typically, there is a wager at stake, and the one who initiates the game and manipulates the shells is a con artist. In this case, these lines could mean, "Don't try to outsmart God; don't try to get this complex world figured out and pinned down on your own and without the bearings of love." Or perhaps a shell game carries overtones of "going into a shell," in the sense of hiding away in an enclosed, controlled environment, somehow sealed off from the outside world and from God. Either way, such isolation is yet another dead end; perhaps the cul-de-sac par excellence! Love is the opposite. Love opens us up: to God, to one another, and to life itself.

But how does this all relate to the starwheel, to the galaxies in interstellar space, and to Orion, "high in the southwest sky"? Here we find a profound theological depth in this song. Cockburn ends each verse with the call for us to "see how the starwheel turns." Look at Orion! Observe the stars! Listen to what they will say! This would appear to be an allusion to Psalm 19:

> The heavens are telling the glory of God;
>     and the firmament proclaims his handiwork.
> Day to day pours forth speech,
>     and night to night declares knowledge.
> There is no speech, nor are there words;
>     their voice is not heard;
> yet their voice goes out through all the earth,
>     and their words to the end of the world.[30]

As a contemporary psalmist, Cockburn inhabits the same world of creational eloquence as the ancient psalmist. This is a world that speaks, if we have the ears to hear. The heavens declare the glory of God. The stars speak. Though they make no sound, their voice goes out to all the earth. Orion is high in the southwest sky and has something to say: "We're given love and love must be returned— / that's all the bearings that you need to learn." The stars, the constellations of the night sky that serve as a source for navigational bearings, point beyond themselves to the ultimate bearing of all of creation: Love. Love is a reciprocal relationship. And the stars themselves bear witness to this love and this reciprocity, because the very turning of the starwheel is a response of love to Love.

This is nowhere more clear than in what could well be seen as a companion piece to "Starwheel" on Cockburn's next album, *In the Falling Dark*, namely, "Lord of the Starfields." How does the starwheel turn? Cockburn answers this question in the chorus: "O love that fires the sun / keep me burning."[31] In these lines Cockburn gives voice to a worldview that is in stark contrast with the autonomous projections of modernity. If the spirit of modernity can be captured in René Descartes's individualistic dictum *cogito ergo sum* ("I think, therefore I am"), then a vision of life rooted in biblical spirituality will confess, *Sumus amamur, ergo sumus* ("We are loved, therefore we are"). In harmony with the ancient psalmist who offered the breathtaking observation that "the earth is full of the steadfast love of the LORD,"[32] the contemporary psalmist recognizes that it is precisely such love that fires the sun. The creating, sustaining, ever-involved Creator, who is Love, *fires* the sun, and this song, which is by its own admission a song of praise (a psalm, if you will), prays for that same love to keep the artist burning. If it is love that fires the sun, then it is no surprise that paying attention to how the starwheel turns will teach the lesson that "we're given love and love must be returned— / that's all the bearings that you need to learn."

The magnificence of the God to whom this psalm is sung is unmistakable. This is the "Lord of the Starfields." The vast and incomprehensible realm of space is the realm of this God's lordship. This eternal and Creator God ("Ancient of Days / Universe Maker") is the "beginning and end," the alpha and omega.[33] Such a God is the "sower of life," and, therefore, wherever there is life there is witness to this God.[34] Indeed, the very light of the starfields themselves testifies that "heaven and earth are / full of your light."

I find the most striking images in this song, however, in the contrasting two lines that begin the fourth verse: "Voice of the nova / smile of the dew." Voice of the nova! This is the voice of a supernova, an atomic explosion of a star that could be as much as a hundred million times the power of our sun. Yet that deafeningly explosive and cosmically generative "big bang" has the gentle "smile of the dew." And while Cockburn's response in the second verse to the "wings of the storm cloud" is to confess, "you make my heart leap / like a banner in the wind," here his response to a Creator whose voice is as powerful as a supernova, and whose smile is as gentle and as inviting as the morning dew, is to simply confess, "all of our yearning / only comes home to you." Echoing St. Augustine's prayer that "our hearts are restless, O Lord, until they find their rest in Thee," this song openly confesses that the Creator God is the fulfillment of our deepest needs, loves, and desires. Our yearning can find its appropriate home in only one place, with the Lord of the starfields.

If "Starwheel" and "Lord of the Starfields" belong together as a pair, then "Creation Dream," from *Dancing in the Dragon's Jaws*, completes our triptych. This song is a celebratory vision of the Christ singing and dancing the creation into being. The opening lines clearly refer to the primeval waters at the dawn of creation, depicted in the first chapter of the book of Genesis: "centred on silence / counting on nothing / I saw you standing on the sea."[35] Before the Word that calls creation into being, before the divine "let there be," and dependent on nothing that preexists creation, "I saw you standing on the sea." This is a *creatio ex nihilo*, a creation out of nothing. And because this is before the Creator sings the first words, "Let there be light," it all begins in the dark: "everything was / dark except for / sparks the wind struck from your hair / sparks that turned to / wings around you." Reminiscent of the "wings of the storm cloud" in "Lord of the Starfields," this ecstatic vision is accompanied by something like "angel voices mixed with seabird cries." Or maybe this is akin to the "voice of the nova." But whatever it sounds like, it is a voice or a song of power. It is like "fields of motion / surging outward / questions that contain their own replies." This is a questioning, calling, beckoning, inviting voice. These questions elicit their own answer. This is deeply suggestive of the creational "let there bes" that contain their own reply—"and it was so."

This *creatio per verbum*, a creation in response to a calling, enacting, and powerful word of the Creator, is deeply biblical and wonderfully rich. Creation has a responsiveness built into its very fabric because creation is itself, in its very being, a response to the creational word of God. But Cockburn pushes the metaphor further. This isn't just a word but a song—"lines of power / bursting outward / along the channels of your song." And we find ourselves back with C. S. Lewis in *The Magician's Nephew*, with Aslan singing Narnia into being.

> In the darkness something was happening at last. A voice had begun to sing. It was very far away and Digory found it hard to decide from what direction it was coming. Sometimes it seemed to come from all directions at once. Sometimes he almost thought it was coming out of the earth beneath them. Its lower notes were deep enough to be the voice of the earth herself. There were no words. There was hardly even a tune. But it was, beyond comparison, the most beautiful noise he had ever heard. It was so beautiful he could hardly bear it. . . .
> Then two wonders happened at the same moment. One was that the voice was suddenly joined by the other voices; more voices than you could possibly count. They were in harmony with it, but far higher up the scale: cold, tingling, silvery voices. The second wonder was that the blackness overhead, all at once, was blazing with stars.[36]

Here is a vision of creation that begins with sound before it can move to sight. Not just a *creatio per verbum* but a *creatio per cantum*, creation through the most beautiful song ever sung! Narnia is sung into being before there is light enough for sight. Indeed, the celestial lights arise in response to the song!

Cockburn pushes the aural metaphor of voice and song even further, however, to the metaphor of dance. And why not? Shouldn't a good song, indeed, the song that calls creation into being, inspire dancing? So Cockburn portrays the Creator as not only singing but dancing creation into being:

> *you were dancing*
> *I saw you dancing*
> *throwing your arms toward the sky*
> *fingers opening*
> *like flares*
> *stars were shooting everywhere.*

From *creatio per verbum* to *creation per cantum* and now *creatio per salatum*, creation through dance! The Lord of the starfields, who makes the starwheel turn with a love that fires the sun, here creates those very stars in the midst of a wild, ecstatic, sensuous dance. This dance is so wild, indeed so electric, that the stars come shooting out of the fingers of his joyously outstretched hands. This dancer is full of cosmic power, and will appear again in the very next song on this album "dancing in the dragon's jaws."[37] As we will see later in this book, the dance of creation must be performed anew in the face of all that threatens creation if the dance is to go on. The one who ecstatically danced creation into being will dance in the dragon's jaws for the renewal and restoration of that very creation.

## A World of Wonders

While not everyone would readily read these three early Cockburn songs as a religious "triptych" or so explicitly in terms of biblical themes, there can be little argument that these songs are deeply spiritual interpretations of creation and that they are profoundly expressive of a Christian faith. While "Lord of the Starfields" identifies itself as a hymn of praise, and "Starwheel" makes explicit reference to God and the revelatory power of the stars, "Creation Dream" cannot be interpreted as anything less than a prayer. And there should be nothing surprising about any of this. It has often enough been noted, including by the artist himself, that during this period in the mid-to-late seventies Cockburn freely explored his emerging Christian faith in his songwriting.

But it is also clear that this creational vision is alive throughout the Cockburn corpus. Consider a song like "The Gift," from the 1988 album, *Big Circumstance*. Those earliest themes of a radically temporal world suffused with grace return in lines like "everything is motion / to the motion be true" and the chorus:

> *The gift*
> *keeps moving—*
> *never know*
> *where it's going to land*
> *you must stand*

*back and let it*
*keep on changing hands.*

The gift of creation, and all the gifts that can be received as the good fruit of creation, must be received and not controlled. As in "Starwheel," there is wise counsel here against any autonomous attempt to grasp this world. If life comes to us from the generous hands of grace, then it must be received and passed on with just such grace. No wonder Cockburn will later sing, "I believe it's a sin to try and make things last forever / Everything that exists in time runs out of time some day / got to let go of the things that keep you tethered / Take your place with grace and then be on your way."[38] Temporality, movement, and change are all good dimensions of this gift-laden creation. And since grace is at the foundation of such a time-shaped world, we need to take our place with grace and then keep moving.

A world rooted in grace is fundamentally sacred in character. And so, in the second verse of "The Gift," Cockburn sings,

*In this cold commodity culture*
*where you lay your money down*
*it's hard to even notice*
*that all this earth is hallowed ground*
*harder still to feel it*
*basic as a breath*
*love is stronger than darkness*
*love is stronger than death*

If it is love that fires the sun and calls forth the light in the face of primordial darkness, then of course "love is stronger than darkness"! If "we're given love and love must be returned," then it is precisely love that will give us our bearings in the midst of darkness.

A cold commodity culture in which everything is reduced to its market value will blasphemously obscure our vision that "all this earth is hallowed ground." This kind of narrow materialism will cloud our vision and render us numb to what we know most deeply to be true. "You stare at too much concrete—you forget the earth's alive."[39] But this artist will continue to write songs that will help us both to see and to feel. Just as Cockburn employed metaphors of speaking, singing, and dancing in his creation songs of the seventies, so here in "The Gift" does he highlight that the issue isn't just that we don't "notice" that "this earth is hallowed ground" but that this cold commodity culture makes it "harder still to feel it / basic as a breath." If we are to engage this world with grace and receive our lives as generous gift, then the sacredness of all things, the hallowedness of this earth, must be something that we feel so deeply and so integrally that it is as basic as the very air we breathe. This is a sacramental view of the world that insists that reality "bears witness to its own gratuitous givenness" before it becomes an object of human control and manipulation.[40]

Perhaps it's a matter of both seeing "just beyond the range of normal sight" and hearing just beyond the range of normal hearing. Have you ever seen the floods clap their hands or heard the hills sing for joy?[41] Have you ever noticed sun and moon, mountains and hills, fruit trees and cedars, wild animals and cattle, creeping things and flying birds all singing praise to their Creator?[42] Have you ever heard trees sing for joy or the stones on the side of the road sing, "Hosanna"?[43] If you enter the world through the music and lyrics of Bruce Cockburn, you just might see and hear such things. You see,

> light pours from a million radiant lives
> off of kids and dogs and the hard-shelled husbands and wives
> all that glory shining around and we're all caught taking a dive
> and all the beasts of the hills around shout,
>     "such a waste!
> don't you know that from the first to the last
>     we're all one in the gift of Grace!"[44]

The beasts of the hills understand that we're all one in the gift of grace. The very hills themselves, the rocks, the vegetation, the birds, all know that this is hallowed ground. Not only is their very creatureliness a response to grace, but they also make their response with considerable eloquence. All of creation speaks, if we but have the ears to hear. Both biblical faith and Cockburn's lyrics call us beyond a narrow anthropocentrism that renders everything else in the world an object for our analysis, manipulation, and exploitation. In contrast to this myopic and egocentric worldview, we are called to a sense of cosubjectivity, as cosubjects with all other creatures in a creation-wide communion. What you see depends on where you stand and on what sort of person you are. The same is true for what you hear. Whether you hear the beasts of the field cry out "such a waste"—indeed, whether you hear all of creation groaning in travail in the face of ecological destruction—depends on whether you live in a world that is taken to be eloquent and not dumb.[45]

In a spirituality infused with biblical insight, all of creation is revelatory. All of creation sings of its Creator and is the very locus of wisdom and truth. So in a much more recent song, Cockburn sings,

> In grains of sand and Galaxies
> In plasma flow and rain in trees
> In the sepia swell of silted-up surf
> in the ebb and the flow of dying and birth
> In wounded streets and whispered prayer
> The dance is the truth and it's everywhere.[46]

If dance is at the heart of things, if creation is itself a dance in response to a dancing Creator, then it is no surprise that the dance is the truth and is everywhere. From the grains of sand on the seashore to the vast expanse of the universe, in the ebb and flow of life and death, from the public pain of our city streets to the private prayers whispered in a longing hope, in and through the dance of all things, there is truth, there is revelation. And when that dance is inhibited or denied, there are only lies, deception, and blasphemy.

In the presence of such truth, however, the only appropriate response is humility and wonder. And so Cockburn sings in "Understanding Nothing,"[47]

> *weavers' fingers flying on the loom*
> *patterns shift too fast to be discerned*
> *all these years of thinking*
> *ended up like this*
> *in front of all this beauty*
> *understanding nothing.*

There is an inscrutability to this world. The arrogance of a modernist worldview that seeks to capture and control the world here meets the humility of a vision that knows that discernment of the intricate patterns and movements of this world is ultimately beyond us. The question is whether the world is conceived as the autonomous construction of modernist hubris or as a beautifully complex tapestry woven by a divine weaver. Cockburn's vision is clear. We stand in front of all this beauty, if we still have the eyes to perceive beauty, and confess that when it comes right down to it, we understand nothing.

This is a world of wonders, alive with possibility. Before such a world the artist sings, "I stand here dazzled with my heart in flames (at this) / world of wonders."[48] And while we will see that there is much to trouble our hearts in this world, much blasphemy going around, there are moments when we can sing with Cockburn:

> *moment of peace like brief arctic bloom*
> *red/gold ripple of the sun going down*
> *line of black hills makes my bed*
> *sky full of love pulled over my head*
> *world of wonders*
> *world of wonders.*

In this world of wonders there are moments of peace, moments of harmony, moments of things being as they always were intended to be. And in those moments the prayer of "Lord of the Starfields"—"all of our yearning / only comes home to you"—is fulfilled in a decidedly this-worldly way. To come home to God is not to escape the good world that God has created. To come home to the "Lord of the Starfields" is to experience this world of wonders, in all of its grace and in all of its beauty, as a blessed and secure place under the canopy of love. "Line of black hills makes my bed / sky full of love pulled over my head," Cockburn sings. If in "Joy Will Find a Way" he sang, "make me a bed of fond memories / make me to lie down with a smile,"[49] then in "World of Wonders" we realize that the very creation itself is that bed. We are offered in these lyrics an image of being "tucked in" to sleep in a creation founded in nothing less than the creative love of God.

This, I suggest, is the foundation of Cockburn's creative vision. In this affirmation of the creaturely character of the world, the goodness and beauty of creation, the eloquence of all things, the blessed temporality of the world, creation's responsive and revelatory character, and the love that permeates and engenders all things, Cockburn evocatively offers us a vision of life in this world of wonders. Again, in "World of Wonders" Cockburn sings, "there's a rainbow shining in a bead of spittle / falling diamonds in rattling rain." But you have to have the eyes to see those diamonds, and you need to have a spiritually attuned imagination to discern a rainbow in a bead of spittle. A rainbow! Nothing less than that most ancient biblical symbol of God's faithfulness to all of creation.[50] If you can't discern God's covenantal love for creation in a bead of spittle, you won't likely see it anywhere else either. Commenting on these lines, Cockburn once said, "Grace lives in the dirt, you know? . . . If you've got to wait until you're sitting out on a mountaintop somewhere to experience grace, you're probably going to miss it. It's not really grace then. You've constructed an atmosphere for yourself to get in touch with an aspect of yourself. But it's that gleam in a 'bead of spittle.' That's where the grace is. It's all over the place."[51] Grace lives in the dirt because dirt is graced.

This is a world received as a gift of grace, suffused with mystery. That's why Cockburn sings, "You can't tell me there is no mystery / It's everywhere I turn."[52] Whether it is in the "Moon over junkyard where the snow lies bright," the "star-strewn space," or this intoxicating "feast of beauty," one thing is clear to Cockburn—this is a world of mystery born of love.

> So all you stumblers who believe love rules
> Believe love rules
> Believe love rules
> Come all you stumblers who believe love rules
> Stand up and let it shine
> Stand up and let it shine.

# At Home in the Darkness, but Hungry for Dawn

At the beginning of his short novel *Remembering*, Wendell Berry offers a poem/prayer to the "Heavenly Muse, Spirit who brooded on / The world and raised it shapely out of nothing." His prayer is, "Touch my lips with fire and burn away / All dross of speech, so that I keep in mind / The truth and end to which my words now move / In hope." A prayer to the very source of all creativity, the brooding Spirit who birthed creation, that the creativity of the author be true and that his words be moved in the direction of hope. "Keep my mind within that Mind / Of which it is a part, whose wholeness is / The hope of sense in what I tell." If there is to be truth, then the author's mind must find its place somehow within that Mind that conceived this creation; and if there is to be hope, there must be wholeness in the face of fragmentation. This is the sense that he attempts to evoke through his words. "And though / I go among the scatterings of that sense, / the members of its worldly body broken, / Rule my sight by vision of the parts / Rejoined." Because wholeness is shattered, hope is scattered and the "worldly body broken," the poet prays this brooding Spirit would rule his sight by a vision of the parts rejoined. If what God has joined no one should tear asunder, then hope must be found in a vision of wholeness restored. This path of restoration is a path from exile to home. "And in my exile's journey far / From home, be with me, so I may return."[1]

## One Day I Shall Be Home[2]

This vision of parts rejoined is something "just beyond the range of normal sight." We need artists and poets, storytellers and songwriters, to help us catch a glimpse of such restoration. And along this path of restoration, this path of homecoming, we need stories and songs that are "at home in the darkness, but hungry for dawn."[3] We need a vision that faces the darkness, the brokenness of the world, and our profound homelessness with both candor and grace. Indeed, we can only honestly face the darkness of our spiritual, ecological, and cultural displacement if we understand deeply that "grace lives in the dirt." We can grasp the tragedy of a broken world in all of its horror only if we can first see a rainbow in a bead of spittle[4] and understand that from "the first to the last we're all one in the gift of Grace."[5] And it is only out of a deeply spiritual sense of the joy of home that we can begin to face what Edward Said has described as "the essential sadness" of exile, this "unhealable rift . . . between the self and its true home."[6]

Home, however, is an elusive thing. It is both our deepest longing and the site of our most devastating disappointments. Perhaps this is why themes of exile and return are so prevalent in all great literature. We find exile and homelessness so devastating precisely because we have a primordial sense somehow that "home" is our original state and it is to home that we must go if there is to be any healing in our lives, any rejoining of that which has been torn asunder.[7] And the richer the imagination of the home that has been lost, the more eloquent and passionate will be the imagination of homecoming, of return from exile.

Cockburn's "creation dream" is nothing less than a vision, an evocative memory, of homemaking. As we saw in the last chapter, this is a world of wonders suffused with grace. This is our creational home. When that dream devolves into the nightmare of homelessness—whether that be the homelessness of a personal nomadism and broken relationships, the forced homelessness of socioeconomic oppression, or the wanton destruction of habitats—then we need hopeful and empowering images of homecoming, a vision of parts rejoined, a narrative of return from exile.

Such themes have been constant throughout Cockburn's work. Perhaps his very early song "One Day I Walk," sets the stage for what will come:

> One day i walk in flowers
> one day i walk on stones
> today i walk in hours
> one day i shall be home.[8]

This panhandling, busking artist on the street corner knows he is not at home. And while he may be a beggar today ("and shall be one again") and may well be a nomad throughout most of his life, he offers this simple little song in the clear conviction that "one day i shall be home."[9] Before he identifies that homecoming with the "Lord of the Starfields" ("all of our yearning / only comes home to you"[10]), he is already yearning for home.

There is also a sense in this song that if there is to be homecoming, it will not be for those who arrogantly grasp for and construct home but for those who receive home as a gift. It is as a beggar that the artist is confident that this journey will arrive home someday. Home is received as a gift into an open hand. Cockburn will later sing in "Shipwrecked at the Stable Door":

> Big Circumstance has brought me here—
> wish it would send me home.
> Never was clear where home is
> but it's nothing you can own.
> It can't be bought with cigarettes
> or nylons or perfume
> and all the highest bidder gets
> is a voucher for a tomb.[11]

The artist is still on the path and is not yet home. In fact, it is "Big Circumstance" that has brought him to this homeless place. "Big Circumstance" appears to be a suggestive way to refer to divine providence. It isn't just "circumstance" that shapes our lives, a sort of arbitrary happenstance. Rather, this is Big Circumstance; this is a direction of life that is somehow caught up with bigger things, bigger purposes. And the artist gives voice again to a longing for home—"Big Circumstance has brought me here / wish it would send me home." But where and what is home? The artist confesses that he doesn't know where home is, but he knows that it is "nothing you can own." Kimberly Dovey has written, "Home is a relationship that is created and evolved over time; it is not consumed like the products of economic process."[12] Home in the midst of exile or occupation is not something that you can barter for with other commodities. Home is not a commodity at all. In fact, if that is the way you approach homemaking, says Cockburn, then "all the highest bidder gets / is a voucher for a tomb." That kind of economic reduction of home results in little more than the ultimate homelessness of a well-proportioned place of death.

Herein is the paradox of home. If you seek to autonomously construct home, you will lose it. If you understand that home is a gift from the very gift-giver who created our creational home, then home can be yours. The ecstatic, world-birthing "creation dream" is personally appropriated in "A Dream like Mine":

> Beautiful rocks—beautiful grass
> Beautiful soil where they both combine
> Beautiful river—covering sky
> Never thought of possession, but all this was mine.[13]

Never thought of possession, never thought of control, of claiming this as something over which I had proprietary rights, and yet, by receiving this world as the beautiful gift that it is, "all this was mine."

Bring this back to "Shipwrecked at the Stable Door," and we hear, "Blessed are the poor in spirit / Blessed are the meek / for theirs shall be the kingdom / that the power mongers seek." Echoing the Beatitudes of Jesus,[14] Cockburn sings that the poor in spirit and the meek are blessed with the kingdom because they receive the kingdom as gift. Because the meek are "those who love the gift of earth" and have made no proprietary claim on it, the earth will be theirs. With such a gift there can be no sense of entitlement or accomplishment. The "power mongers," however, are those who abuse the gift, who claim ownership and the right to exploit the earth. Their home-wrecking economies and lifestyles only perpetuate exile and close the door to homecoming.

## Oh Sweet Fantasia of the Safe Home

Between "Creation Dream" and "A Dream like Mine," however, there is another dream. In his 1980 song "How I Spent My Fall Vacation," Cockburn asks,

> i wonder if i'll end up like Bernie in his dream
> a displaced person in some foreign border town
> waiting for a train part hope part myth while the
> station changes hands.[15]

Consider the depths of Bernie's homelessness here. He is a displaced person, a person in the wrong place, and perhaps with no place at all. And he finds himself in a foreign border town. Not only is his displacement demonstrated by the foreignness of his location, this very location is in a liminal space on the border, neither here nor there. And there is nothing that this character can do about his displacement. There is no proactive response available to him, no way to simply get on the move back to home. All he can do is wait for a homeward-bound train. But even this waiting is full of ambivalence. This train is "part hope part myth." He is hanging his hope of homecoming, his hope of moving beyond displacement, on this train, but he's not so sure that he can believe this hope. And then to top it all off, this very liminal place of a train station in a foreign border town is itself profoundly unstable, as it is "changing hands." Who is in control here? Who can help me find a way home?

The poet who confidently and longingly sang, "one day I shall be home," now isn't so sure. Home may be our most primordial memory and longing. Home may be a site of identity, orientation, rest, dwelling, and inhabitation. But what if home is broken and those memories are shattered? What if instead of singing, "make me a bed of fond memories / make me to lie down with a smile,"[16] you find yourself a hopeless, insomniac loner struggling with "days of striving, nights of novocaine"?[17] Perhaps home becomes little more than a "sweet fantasia" devoid of hope because it is rooted in an unbelievable myth.

> *Oh sweet fantasia of the safe home*
> *Where nobody has to scrape for honey*
>  *at the bottom of the comb*
> *Where every actor understands the scene*
> *And nobody ever means to be mean*
> *Catch it in a dream, catch it in a song*
> *Seek it on the street, you find the candy man's gone*
> *I hate to tell you but the candy man's gone.*[18]

Another dream, but this dream is a romantic lie. This is the nostalgic vision of home that we all know is neither true nor attainable. This vision of everyone knowing their place, everyone finding security and sustenance in the warm embrace of home, might make for a lovely pop song, but if you seek it on the street, or take a mere glance at the homeless shelters, or dare to take a brief glimpse into the heart of family violence, then you will see that home often degenerates into a precarious site of fear, disrespect, confusion, and estrangement.

Or do we really need to look at the street to see that this vision of home is a "sweet fantasia"? Might we simply need to look deep within ourselves and our own proclivity to home breaking? We won't dwell on these themes here except to say that Cockburn understands the devastating reality of home breaking too well to locate the cause of such displacement and dislocation exclusively outside of himself.

The 1980 song "Fascist Architecture" is pivotal in Cockburn's work at this time.[19] Writing in the context of his own broken marriage and struggling with the issue of what home might look like in the face of a broken home, Cockburn sets a path toward homecoming by acknowledging his complicity in the dynamics of home breaking:

> *fascist architecture of my own design*
> *too long been keeping my love confined*
> *you tore me out of myself alive.*

The secure home that has crumbled was a well-constructed edifice of well-confined love. This is a "fascist" architecture both in its grandiosity and in its self-enclosure. And it is a fascist architecture not imposed upon the artist, but of his own design. Such an architecture, such edifices of home, can only crumble. And there is a severe mercy in the crumbling:

> *walls are falling and i'm ok*
> *under the mercy and i'm ok*
> *gonna tell my old lady*

> *gonna tell my little girl*
> *there isn't anything in this world*
> *that can lock up my love again.*

If the fascist walls are falling, this creates an openness to the world outside of home, an expansiveness in the very understanding of home. Love can no longer be locked up but must be open to the embrace of hospitality. This, I suggest, is an impetus for the radical politicization of Cockburn's lyrics in the 1980s. On this reading, abrasive political songs such as "Rocket Launcher,"[20] "Call It Democracy,"[21] "People See through You,"[22] "Stolen Land,"[23] and "Where the Death Squads Live"[24] are impassioned protests against the political and economic forces that have rendered late modernity a culture of displacement and homelessness.

## From a "Shell-Pink" to a "Santiago" Dawn

In Cockburn's "Creation Dream," this creational home is born out of the ecstatic dance of the Creator and the generative power of the divine song. And it all happens "in the shell-pink dawn." Home is born on that first morning. And if home is to be reborn in the face of the darkness of exile, then it will require a new morning, a new dawn. This new morning is nowhere more powerfully or beautifully portrayed than in Cockburn's song "Santiago Dawn," on the 1985 *World of Wonders* album. Recounting revolutionary opposition to the regime of Augusto Pinochet in Chile, some ten years after the CIA-supported coup that overthrew the elected government of Salvador Allende on September 11, 1973, Cockburn takes us to the heart of a shantytown on the outskirts of Santiago. Here, in this regime-imposed poverty and homelessness, something awakens.

It is Sunday and the tension builds as the sound of military thugs moving through the community is mirrored in the music. South American panpipes and *charango* play a typically Latin American tune, only to be punctuated by the aggressive bang of a military drum.

The forces of oppression are "hunting for anyone who still has a voice." These are forces of silence and repression that engage in violent intimidation tactics to keep opposition to the regime cowering in fear. But they got more than they bargained for.

> *they come in strong but it's not that long*
> *before they know its not so easy to leave*
> *to keep a million homeless down takes more*
> *than a strong arm up your sleeve*

The captors have become the captives. The forces of homelessness find that the longing for homecoming in the face of exile and oppression cannot be eradicated, and it will take much more than brute force and military might to keep the homeless down.

So while the regime's thugs launch their attack—"at the crack of dawn the first door goes down / snapped off a makeshift frame"—they find themselves facing a full-blown rebellion. And it is in the midst of this struggle for home in the face of homelessness that a new dawn rises in Santiago.

> first mass rings through smoke and gas
> day flowers out of the night
> creatures of the dark in disarray
> fall before the morning light

Then the music swells, the drums move from oppression to the rhythm of hope, and a horn section announces a new day, perhaps even a day of Jubilee, a day of restoration and redemption.[25]

> bells of rage—bells of hope
> as the ten-year night wears down
> sisters and brothers are coming home
> to see the Santiago dawn
>
> Santiago sunrise
> see them marching home
> see them rising like grass through cement
> in the Santiago dawn.

With strong echoes of Isaiah's vision of the exiles coming home from Babylon, Cockburn sings of a dawn of new beginnings in which darkness can be "dead and gone."[26] Homecoming is an ineluctable force in the human spirit, and that is why he can see the displaced "rising like grass through cement / in the Santiago dawn." But notice which bells are ringing, calling the people home in the face of the forces of homelessness—"first mass rings through the smoke and gas / day flowers out of the night." These "bells of rage—bells of hope," bells of homecoming, are church bells. They are the bells calling the faithful to the first mass on this Sunday morning. These are bells calling the people to a meal of bread and wine, a passover from slavery to freedom. This is a meal of liberation rooted in the story of the one who first said, "Let there be light," and who overcame darkness not through violent opposition but through a sacrifice that stripped the forces of homelessness of their oppressive and violent power.

Perhaps it is dark; perhaps it is difficult to have any hope of homecoming beyond this oppression, but there is in the very ringing of these bells a call to a subversive story of liberation, a eucharistic narrative of day flowing out of the night. The mass proclaims, "Christ has died, Christ has risen, Christ will come again." In this song, Cockburn sees Jesus crucified again in the bodies of the poor, but he also sees resurrection ("rising like grass through cement") and the coming of Christ in the struggle for justice in Chile and around the world. The hope for homecoming cannot be snuffed out—not by right-wing dictators or even by a fascist architecture of our own design. The hope for homecoming is constitutive of the human condition. Like grass rising through cement, it will irrepressibly emerge and animate human action against all odds.

## At Home in the Southlands of the Heart

Authentic homecoming requires both a profound grasp of one's own homelessness and deep solidarity with the most desperate of the homeless. And since Cockburn's work displays both of these stances, it is not surprising that we encounter a delightful sense of settled homecoming in the albums of the early 1990s. While the rootsy *Nothing but a Burning Light* (1991) and the romantically beautiful *Dart to the Heart* (1993) albums perhaps lack some of the lyrical vitality and passion of earlier offerings and at times border on a smug self-satisfaction ("I ride and I shoot and I play guitar / And I like my life just fine"[27]), there is still much to be learned about homecoming here.

For example, while the revolutionary homecoming of "Santiago Dawn" is rooted in a eucharistic vision that provides the homeless with a memory that subverts the forces of the regime, this does not mean that the painful memories of homelessness are erased. Homecoming is rooted in liberating memories but happens, if at all, in honest confrontation with broken memories. This fine tension between broken memory, liberating memory, and homecoming is profoundly explored in the song that could be seen to capture the thematic heart of these two albums, "Southland of the Heart," found on *Dart to the Heart*.

While the song's refrain, "Lie down / Take your rest with me," is a clear allusion to Jesus proclaiming, "Come unto me, all you that are weary and are carrying heavy burdens, and I will give you rest,"[28] this invitation to come home is offered in the face of painful memories. When does one most profoundly need to hear such an invitation to rest?

> When the wild-eyed dogs of day to day
> Come snapping at your heels
> And there's so much coming at you
> That you don't know how to feel.

And when is a memory of Jesus offering rest to the heavy laden most powerfully evoked? "When thoughts you've tried to leave behind / Keep sniping from the dark" and "When your heart's beset by memories / you wish you'd never made."

You see, the "rest" of homecoming and the good night's sleep that such rest affords are most authentically received

*When the nightmare's creeping closer*
*And your wheels are in the mud*
*When everything's ambiguous*
*Except the taste of blood.*

The dream of homecoming must always confront the nightmare of broken memories. Home as a place of safety, clarity, and connectedness is always received in the face of life's most fearful ambiguities.

## Dark Dreams

We could summarize our discussion thus far by saying that homelessness is both internally generated through "fascist architecture" of "our own design" and externally imposed by home-destroying regimes of oppression. And if we consider Cockburn's body of work as a whole, it is clear that he never loses sight of this dialectic between the internal and the external. He never gets so taken up in introspection that he misses the big picture of historical forces of geopolitical and economic oppression. Nor does he externalize the forces of homelessness at the expense of understanding the personal complicity that we all share in the dynamics of home breaking. To speak in theological terms, Cockburn understands that sin is both personal and structural.

Consider Cockburn's beautiful hymn of confession "Dweller by a Dark Stream":

*It could have been me put the*
*thorns in your crown,*
*rooted as I am in a violent ground.*
*How many times have I turned*
*your promise down,*
*still you pour out your love,*
*pour out your love.*[29]

Addressing Jesus, the hymn begins with human violence as intensely personal. We are all rooted in a violent ground, and that ground proves to be unsustainable for homemaking. A violent ground is not a habitat that can generate the shalom of homemaking. If home is rooted in gift and promise, then this is a gift that is constantly rejected through our incessant breaking of trust.

*I was a dweller by a dark stream*
*a crying heart hooked on a dark dream,*
*in my convict soul I saw your love gleam,*
*and you showed me what you've done.*
*Jesus, thank you, joyous Son*

We remain deeply homeless because we have taken up residence elsewhere. We are "dwellers" by a dark stream. Here we find neither the homemaking vision of "Creation Dream" nor the homecoming dream of "darkness dead and gone" of "Santiago Dawn," but an addiction to a dark dream, a dream in which home is not possible. And yet, in the midst of such darkness, "I saw your love gleam." In the face of an imprisoned spirituality, a path home is an offer yet again.

The darkness that renders us homeless may be deeply personal, but it is never just personal. In the third verse of "Dweller by a Dark Stream," Cockburn sings, "So I'm walking this prison camp world." It may be "my convict soul" that is a "dweller by a dark stream," but there is something about a society constructed out of our collective convict souls that deforms this world of wonders into a prison camp world. And the structures of that world invariably result in homelessness.

In "All Our Dark Tomorrows" Cockburn offers a critique of the regime of George W. Bush and the political, military, and economic machinations of that period in US presidential history. Under such conditions, sings Cockburn, "All sane people, die now / Be lifted up and carried away / You've got no home in this world of sorrows."[30] In a world of "excess and the gaping need," and of "shrunken men stuffed up with greed," in a world in which greed supplants generosity, and hospitality gives way to xenophobic fear, "you've got no home." There is simply no space for homemaking here. There is no energy left for the joy of home in the face of such sorrow.

## Where Is My Pastureland?

Getting hooked on dark dreams—both personally and societally—means that the fears and nightmares of homelessness are never far away. Homecoming, at least in this life, can never be final. If there is one thing clear about Cockburn's 1996 album, *The Charity of Night*, it is that any self-satisfied homecoming will always be short-lived.[31] Indeed, if "home" is often construed as a place of escape, then this album claims that there is no escape possible. Representative of this sentiment is "The Whole Night Sky."[32]

> *Derailed and desperate*
> *How did I get here?*
> *Hanging from this high wire*
> *By the tatters of my faith*
> *Sometimes a wind comes out of nowhere and*
> *Knocks you off your feet and look—see my tears—*
> *They fill the whole night sky*
> *The whole night sky.*

While homecoming happens at dawn, when "the creatures of the dark" are in "disarray," this album is primarily concerned with night—and night is often connected with memory.

These two themes come together in "Birmingham Shadows."[33]

> *Head full of horrors*
> *Heart full of night*
> *At home in the darkness but hungry for dawn*
> *I can only remember scenes, never the stories I live.*

When our lives have been irrevocably formed by dark memories, then we had better get used to being at home in the darkness. But this is not a defeated acquiescence for Cockburn. This is not an abandonment of the pilgrimage home, because he is still "hungry for dawn." It is just that some of his memories are so horrific that they are untellable as story and become reduced to disjointed, fragmented scenes.

Without a story, however, homecoming is impossible. And while Cockburn's dark memories seem to resist narrative, he still tries to tell their story on this album.[34] In the last track, "Strange Waters," we meet fragments of a personal narrative set in the context of a postmodern meditation on the Twenty-Third Psalm.[35]

Cockburn, I have suggested, is a troubadour on the way home. In "Strange Waters" he pauses to reflect on the journey. In the opening verses we meet a series of snapshots, or moments, from the artist's life. Things he's seen, places he's stood in or walked. From "a high cairn kissed by holy wind" in the Himalayas and a "mirrored pool cut by golden fin" in a Japanese garden; to the alleys and the dark side of cities where you might meet a mad person "whose blessing you must accept without pity"; to airports, those portals of late-twentieth-century transience; to the sites of modern warfare and carnage; to an Arkansas forest fire or to the deep and painful fires that have burned in the artist's own heart—through all of this, Cockburn confesses, "you've been leading me." Through all the paths he has walked and love he has burned, his pilgrimage has been led by a divine hand. Along this path of contrasts and so many unexpected turns, Cockburn discerns the hand of the shepherd God leading him. "The LORD is my shepherd, I shall not want . . . he leads me beside still waters . . . he leads me in paths of righteousness."[36]

In "Pacing the Cage," earlier on this album, Cockburn sings, "sometimes the road leads through dark places / sometimes the darkness is your friend."[37] And now, at the end of the album, he can say more. In that darkness he has never been alone. Along this sometimes-tortured homeward path, he has a profound sense of being led. But different from Psalm 23, this path has not been to a safe home; it has led not to "still waters" but to "strange waters." Not passive, comforting, secure waters, but menacing, disconcerting, threatening, "strange waters."

Unlike the exodus journey of the Israelites, this path is not through a natural wilderness but a cultural wilderness. This is a path "across the concrete fields of man," across the uninhabitable cityscapes of alienated civilization. And Cockburn senses a profound vulnerability in those concrete fields. In this panoptic society— "Sun ray like a camera pans"—you feel as though you are being watched. In such a context there seem to be only two options available: "some will run and some will stand." Some will seek escape (perhaps by "going to the country"?[38]), while others will militantly oppose this culturally oppressive wilderness (perhaps evidenced in songs such as "People See through You"?[39]). But neither stance will do. Neither romantic escape nor violent revolt will make for home. Neither flight nor fight will heal the violence at the heart of all home breaking.

You see, "everything is bullshit but the open hand." Running or standing, both are bullshit compared to the open hand. In the Torah we read that we should not be "hard-hearted or tight-fisted" toward our needy neighbor. Rather, we are instructed, "Open your hand to the poor and the needy neighbor in your land."[40] Don't be tightfisted (the posture of both running away and militant opposition); be openhanded. With love, compassion, justice, and hospitality, find those who are languishing in those concrete fields of men and open your hand to them in radical fellowship.

"Oh, you've been leading me / beside strange waters," but there has been guidance along the way. I know that this is a pilgrimage of openhandedness. And while the waters have been strange, there are also "Streams of beautiful / Lights in the night." There are pointers along the way, perhaps even revelatory words to help us navigate in the night.

Maybe I can handle strange waters even though I would prefer still ones. And maybe I can trust that in the valley of the shadow of death, in these concrete fields of man, you are with me. But where is the pasture in which I can finally lie down in security? Where is the table set in the presence of my enemies? Where is the cup overflowing? Where is the homecoming in the house of the LORD?[41] The poet is still not home, so he transposes the thankful confidence of Psalm 23 into a lament:

> But where is my pastureland
> In these dark valleys?
> If I loose my grip
> Will I take flight?

In this last question, of this song and of this album, we have another allusion to the question of opening our hands. But now the echo is not so much to the biblical injunction to be openhanded and not tightfisted as to an image Cockburn employed earlier on the album. Recall these lines from "The Whole Night Sky":

> Derailed and desperate
> How did I get here?
> Hanging from this high wire
> By the tatters of my faith.

It is hard to experience the world as a pastureland, as a home, when you're hanging from a high wire by the tatters of your faith. This pilgrimage across these concrete fields, the destruction of ecological habitats, the tearing apart of home by violence, these encounters with the insane, and even the diverse spiritual paths of homecoming that are on offer, all have taken their toll. And we are left hanging by the tatters of our faith, on the very precipice of ultimate homelessness.

Cockburn doesn't ask what happens if he should happen to "lose" his grip. No, the issue here is much more intentional. Not "lose" but "loose." "If I loose my grip / Will I take flight?" If the artist follows his own claim that "everything is bullshit but the open hand" and actually opens his hand, lets go of control, then will he fall to his death, or will his tattered faith take flight?[42] You can't open your hands to either God or your neighbor if you are hanging on for dear life to that high wire. And without open hands, there is no pathway home.

For Cockburn, home is neither an accomplishment nor a possession, but a gift to be received with an open hand. As a gift, home cannot be secured with a tight, self-protective grasp. We must loose our grip and open our hands to an embracing hospitality. Only with such a stance can we sing with confidence, "one day i shall be home."

# Creation Dreams and Ecological Nightmares

In chapter 2, I suggested that a *theological* engagement with the work of any artist, and certainly an artist like Bruce Cockburn, needs to be faithful to the work itself and allow Scripture to be a dynamic dialogue partner with the art if it is to bear the fruit of cultural discernment and serve the awakening of the imagination. Having reflected in the last two chapters on themes of creation and home, perhaps it is appropriate to now bring certain biblical texts into conversation with the creational vision that we have met in Cockburn's music. What happens when the rich images of these lyrics meet similarly rich metaphors in the Bible? What cultural discernment might be achieved, and how might this interaction serve to shape our imaginations?[1]

Specifically, I want to bring these songs and texts to bear on the ecological crisis. It seems to me that the environmental crisis is, at heart, a failure and a perversion of the human imagination. Our imaginations have been taken captive by an ecocidal ideology of economic growth that invariably will render us homeless in a world unfit for habitation. If imagination is the issue, then a redirection of our lives toward creation care will not emerge out of statistics of ecological despoliation, as important as those statistics might be. What we need is liberated imagination, imagination set free to envision an alternative life, an ecological imagination that engenders a life of restorative homemaking in our creational home. Cockburn's art, especially when interpreted in dialogue with biblical visions, is a rich resource for funding such an imagination.[2]

We have already spent some time in Cockburn's creationally focused songs and traced the theme of home throughout his work. Now I ask you to consider this series of readings from the Hebrew and Christian Scriptures. I begin by placing various texts from the first chapter of Genesis in counterpoint tension with the voices of prophets like Jeremiah, Isaiah, and Hosea. I do this by interspersing the creation account of Genesis 1, which describes God's good creation, with texts of prophetic lament and judgment from the prophets. I will let these texts speak for themselves. Then I will move on to the Christian vision of the first chapter of John's Gospel and a few verses from Paul's Letter to the Colossians.

As you read these texts, pay attention to the themes, tensions, and metaphors that you meet there. Also attend to any resonances that you might hear between these texts and some of Cockburn's lyrics that we have been interpreting. Specifically, you might want to keep in mind songs like "Creation Dream," "Lord of the Starfields," "One Day I Walk," "All the Diamonds in the World," "In the Falling Dark," and even "Night Train" as you read these texts.

## Genesis and the Prophets in Tension

In the beginning when God created the heavens and the earth, the earth was a formless void and darkness covered the face of the deep, while a wind from God swept over the face of the waters. Then God said, "Let there be light"; and there was light. And God saw that the light was good; and God separated the light from the darkness.[3]

I looked on the earth, and lo, it was waste and void;
and to the heavens, and they had no light.[4]

And God said, "Let the waters under the sky be gathered together into one place, and let the dry land appear." And it was so. God called the dry land Earth, and the waters that were gathered together he called Seas. And God saw that it was good. Then God said, "Let the earth put forth vegetation: plants yielding seed, and fruit trees of every kind on earth that bear fruit with the seed in it." And it was so. The earth brought forth vegetation: plants yielding seed of every kind, and trees of every kind bearing fruit with the seed in it. And God saw that it was good.[5]

The earth dries up and withers,
the world languishes and withers;
the heavens languish together with the earth.
The earth lies polluted
under its inhabitants;
for they have transgressed laws,
violated the statutes,
broken the everlasting covenant.
Therefore a curse devours the earth,
and its inhabitants suffer for their guilt.

> . . . all joy has reached its eventide;
> the gladness of the earth is banished.

> The earth is utterly broken,
>   the earth is torn asunder,
>   the earth is violently shaken.[6]

And God said, "Let the waters bring forth swarms of living creatures, and let birds fly above the earth across the dome of the sky." So God created the great sea monsters and every living creature that moves, of every kind, with which the waters swarm, and every winged bird of every kind. And God saw that it was good. God blessed them, saying, "Be fruitful and multiply and fill the waters in the seas, and let birds multiply on the earth."[7]

> Hear the word of the LORD, O people of Israel;
>   for the LORD has an indictment against the inhabitants of the
>   land.
> There is no faithfulness or loyalty,
>   and no knowledge of God in the land.
> Swearing, lying and murder,
>   and stealing and adultery break out;
>   bloodshed follows bloodshed.
> Therefore the land mourns,
>   and all who live in it languish;
> together with the wild animals
>   and the birds of the air,
>   even the fish of the sea are perishing.[8]

And God said, "Let the earth bring forth living creatures of every kind: cattle and creeping things and wild animals of the earth of every kind." And it was so. God made the wild animals of the earth of every kind, and the cattle of every kind, and everything that creeps upon the ground of every kind. And God saw that it was good.[9]

> Take up weeping and wailing for the mountains,
>   and a lamentation for the pastures of the wilderness,
> because they are laid waste so that no one passes through,
>   and the lowing of the cattle is not heard;
> both the birds of the air and the animals
>   have fled and are gone.[10]

Then God said, "Let us make humankind in our image, according to our likeness; and let them have dominion over the fish of the sea, and over the birds of air, and over the cattle, and over all the wild animals of the earth, and over every creeping thing that creeps upon the earth."

> So God created humankind in his image
> in the image of God he created them;
> male and female he created them.

God blessed them, and God said to them, "Be fruitful and multiply, and fill the earth and subdue it; and have dominion over the fish of the sea and over the birds of the air and over every living thing that moves upon the earth."
. . . And it was so. God saw everything that he had made, and indeed, it was very good.[11]

> I looked on the earth, and lo, it was waste and void;
>     and to the heavens, and they had no light.
> I looked on the mountains, and lo, they were quaking,
>     and all the hills moved to and fro.
> I looked, and lo, there was no one at all,
>     and all the birds of the air had fled.
> I looked, and lo, the fruitful land was a desert,
>     and all its cities were laid in ruins
>     before the LORD, before his fierce anger.[12]

## Creation Restored

There is an abrasive honesty to how the prophets understand the tension between creational goodness and ecological devastation. And yet hope for creational restoration is at the very heart of biblical faith. Escapist piety that has humans exploit and dominate this earth only to be whisked off to some otherworldly heaven has no support from an integral reading of the Bible.[13] Humans are earth creatures and this world is indeed our home. It is therefore central to Christian hope that the "gospel" of Jesus is not about the destruction of the world but its redemption. So it is not surprising that John begins his story about Jesus by making direct allusions to the first chapter of Genesis.

> In the beginning was the Word, and the Word was with God, and the Word was God. He was in the beginning with God. All things came into being through him, and without him not one thing came into being. What has come into being in him was life, and the life was the light of all people. The light shines in the darkness, and the darkness did not overcome it.[14]

As far as John is concerned, the story he is going to tell about Jesus is nothing less than a retelling of the creation story. The gospel is about the redemption of all of creation.

Saint Paul's understanding of what the good news of Jesus is all about is equally cosmic in scope. In a text that has had the commentators (and translators!) bending over backward to say that Paul doesn't really mean what he appears to be saying, the apostle writes,

> And you who were once estranged and hostile in mind, doing evil deeds, he has now reconciled in his fleshly body through death, so as to present you holy and blameless and irreproachable before him—provided that you

continue securely established and steadfast in the faith, without shifting from the hope promised by the gospel that you heard, *which has been proclaimed to every creature under heaven.*[15]

Every creature under heaven? Could the apostle really be saying not only that "all creatures" are recipients of the good news found in Christ but also that they somehow have heard this gospel proclaimed to them? From the context in Paul's letter to the Colossians, I conclude that this is precisely what the apostle means and that it is a failure of imagination that creates problems for Paul's modern interpreters.[16] Perhaps if they read this passage with Cockburn's music playing in the background, they would have a less constricted imagination. They might even have a liberated imagination.

So to an act of imagination we now turn. Bringing together these biblical texts with Cockburn's vision of creation and the journey home, I come up with the tension between creation dreams and ecological nightmares. And I have crafted these reflections into a sermon. And like a song, this sermon is less concerned with the imparting of information than with the shaping of the imagination. Rooted in both the biblical texts and in a close interpretation of Cockburn's lyrics, the sermon attempts to put before us the stark realities of the ecological crisis and seeks to engender an alternative imagination and way of life.

## Creation Dreams and Ecological Nightmares

*The contrasts are stark.*

*In the beginning the earth was a formless void;*
*I looked on the earth, and lo, it was waste and void.*

*Let there be light;*
*and they had no light.*

*A lush, well-watered world of rich fecundity;*
*the earth dries up and withers.*

*A world recognized as delightfully good;*
*all joy has reached its eventide,*
*the gladness of the earth is banished,*
*. . . the gladness of the earth is banished.*

*Creation dreams;*
*ecological nightmares.*

*A creation of rich interrelatedness and wholeness;*
*and yet the earth is utterly broken,*

*the earth is torn asunder,*
*the earth is violently shaken.*

*The earth, the earth, the earth.*

*Waters swarming with living creatures;*
*and the fish of the sea are perishing.*

*Winged birds of every kind fly across the dome of the sky;*
*and the birds of the air are perishing.*

*And God blessed them and said . . .*
*but a curse devours the earth.*

*A world of primordial peace;*
*and bloodshed follows bloodshed.*

*The contrasts are stark.*
*Biblical contrasts.*
*Ecological contrasts.*
*Dreams and nightmares.*

*Be fruitful and multiply;*
*the birds of the air and the animals have fled and gone.*

*A flourishing creation;*
*a languishing land.*

*Creatures of every kind;*
*fewer and fewer creatures of any kind.*

*A generative world that brings forth life upon life;*
*the degenerating force of a culture of death.*

*Fertile garden;*
*barren wastelands.*

*A creatio per verbum,*
*a creation by the Word of the Creator God,*
*let there be, let there be*
*let the waters bring forth,*
*let the earth bring forth,*
*in the beginning was the Word,*
*all things came into being through this Word,*
*a covenant word,*
*a life-engendering, calling, loving,*
*inviting, directing, ordering*

*Word of a Creator overflowing in creative love,*
*an extravagant Word,*
*a Word of blessing;*
*and yet,*
*the earth lies polluted under its inhabitants;*
*for they have transgressed laws,*
*violated the statutes,*
*broken the everlasting covenant,*
*a broken Word.*
*The true Word of life*
*meets the deceptive words of death.*
*The contrasts are stark.*

*And God saw,*
*God saw,*
*God saw,*
*God saw,*
*God saw,*
*God saw,*
*it was good,*
*good,*
*good,*
*good,*
*good,*
*very good.*

*And I looked,*
*I looked,*
*I looked,*
*I looked,*
*I looked,*
*it was waste and void,*
*no light,*
*mountains quaking,*
*no one at all,*
*no birds,*
*no fruitfulness,*
*cities in ruins.*

*God saw,*
*it was good.*
*I look,*
*and see desolation.*

*Creational dreams;*
  *ecological nightmares.*

*Loving dominion*
  *degenerates into disdainful domination.*

*Creaturely kinship*
  *overthrown through human centeredness.*

*A rich diversity of many creatures "according to their kinds"*
  *reduced to a world depleted of thousands upon thousands of species.*

*Seed-bearing fruit and plants with their self-generating seed*
  *meet monocrop terminator seeds.*

*Wildly creative diversity*
  *nipped in the bud by industrial agriculture.*

                                                              *Selah*


*A creation dream that begins in silence,*
  *before that first creative word,*
*drowned out by the cacophony*
  *of a world with too much communication*
  *and too little to say.*

*Counting on nothing,*
  *a creatio ex nihilo,*
  *a creation of pure gift*
*meets a culture that counts only commodities,*
  *and entitlement renders gratitude impossible.*

*An ecstatic creation dream,*
  *a dream of energy "sparks the wind from your hair,"*
  *engendering "fields of motion surging outward"*
*meets the ecological nightmare of consumer affluence*
  *fueled by oil fields and tar sands,*
  *firing the engines of progress.*

*Creation dream degenerates into a dark dream.*

*A dream of an eloquent creation,*
  *a responsive world wherein*
  *questions contain their own replies*
*gives way to a world of mute objects,*
  *natural resources,*
  *commodities.*

*You were dancing,*
*I saw you dancing*
*throwing your arms toward the sky.*
*Not just a creatio per verbum,*
*not just a creation by powerful Word,*
*but a creatio per salatum*
*a creation by dance.*

*Fingers opening,*
*like flares*
*stars were shooting everywhere*
*lines of power*
*bursting outward*
*along the channels of your song.*

*Like Aslan singing Narnia into being,*
*here is a dream of creation*
*through a song so beautiful that you could hardly bear it.*

*From creatio per verbum,*
*creation by the word;*
*to creatio per salatum,*
*creation through dance;*
*to creatio per cantum,*
*creation through song.*

*And song calls forth song.*
*Creation sings,*
*trees clap their hands,*
*hills dance for joy,*
*the storm clouds praise,*
*birds and animals sing in the choir,*
*even the rocks on the side of the road will cry out!*

*And the image bearer can't help herself,*
*she too must sing.*
*Lord of the starfields*
*Ancient of Days*
*Universe Maker*
*Here's a song in your praise*

*Wings of the storm cloud*
*beginning and end*
*you make my heart leap*
*like a banner in the wind*

*A liberated imagination begins in praise.*
*Blessed care of our creaturely neighbors*
*begins in gratitude born of love,*
*love at the very heart of creation.*

*O Love that fires the sun*
*keep me burning.*

*May my love,*
*may that which animates my life,*
*may that passion and liberated imagination*
*be rooted in nothing less than the very love*
*that fires the sun,*
*nothing less than the very animating Spirit*
*that is the real driving force of all of life.*

*Lord of the starfields,*
*sower of life*
*heaven and earth are*
*full of your light.*

*May our praise not descend into blasphemy,*
*may we not be sowers of death,*
*may we not block out the light that illuminates heaven and earth,*
*may we live in the light*
*and say to the darkness, "We beg to differ."*

*The light shines in the darkness,*
*and the darkness did not overcome it.*

*Voice of the nova*
*smile of the dew*
*all of our yearning*
*only comes home to you.*

*Deafening voice of a supernova,*
*the powerful, commanding voice of the Creator's*
*creation-calling Word,*
*that is as gentle and as inviting*
*as the smile of the morning dew.*

*In the face of habitat destruction*
*we long for restoration,*
*in the face of species eradication*
*we long for care,*
*in the face of global warming,*
*we long for repentance,*

*in the face of economic captivity,*
    *we long for ecological liberation,*
*in the face of our broken hearts in a broken world*
    *we confess that our hearts are restless*
    *until they find their rest in thee,*
*all of our yearning,*
        *only comes home to you.*

        *One day I walk in flowers,*
        *one day I walk on stones,*
        *today I walk in hours,*
        *one day I shall be home.*

*Coming home,*
    *ecological rape meets stewardly love.*

*Coming home,*
    *that which is despoiled is made whole.*

*Coming home,*
    *defilement meets forgiveness and restoration.*

*Coming home,*
    *every tear is wiped away.*

*Coming home,*
    *ecological vandals become homemakers.*

*Coming home,*
    *home to the Father,*
    *home to the family,*
    *home to the community,*
    *home to the earth.*

*Home was born with shots of silver*
    *in the shell-pink dawn.*
*Home was born in a garden.*

*Home is born anew in another garden,*
    *another dawn,*
    *the resurrection dawn of the new creation.*

*What once was estranged is reconciled,*
    *what once was hostile is befriended,*
    *what once was defiled is holy,*
    *what once was guilty is blameless.*

*This is the gospel,*
    *this is the good news,*
    *this is the faith,*
    *this is the hope.*

*Anything less,*
    *and we remain homeless.*
*Anything less,*
    *the rape continues.*
*Anything less,*
    *our piety is blasphemy.*
*Anything less,*
    *Jesus is still on the cross.*

*Reconciliation of all things,*
    *in heaven and on earth,*
    *visible and invisible,*
    *all things created,*
    *all things redeemed,*
    *all things brought back home.*

    *Two thousand years and half a world away,*
    *dying trees still will grow greener*
    *when you pray.*

*This is the gospel,*
    *not just for humans,*
    *not just for "our sins"*
    *not just for "our souls."*

*This is the gospel,*
    *proclaimed to every creature under heaven.*

*This is the gospel grasped by atoms and amoebas,*
    *good news for habitats and house wrens,*
    *restoration for eagles and ecozones,*
    *salvation for seed-bearing plants and seas swarming with life.*

    *All this glory shining around*
        *and we're all caught taking a dive,*
    *and all the beasts of the hills around shout,*
        *"such a waste!*
        *don't you know that from the first to the last*
        *we're all one in the gift of Grace!"*

*The beasts of the hills know,*
*the winds and rains know,*
*the fish of the sea and birds of the air know,*
*the fruit trees and vegetation know,*
*all of creation knows*
*that the dawn has come.*
*All creation knows*
*that homecoming is at hand.*
*All creation knows*
*that the one who dies for the world*
*has exercised the true dominion.*
*All creation knows*
*that the tomb is empty.*
*All creation knows*
*that the New Adam has risen with healing in his hands.*
*All creation knows*
*that we're one in the gift of grace.*
*All creation proclaims,*
*"Alleluia! Christ is risen!"*

*O love that fires the sun,*
*keep me burning.*
*O love that is the heart of all things,*
*set our imaginations free.*

*Creation dreams or ecological nightmares.*
*Life or death.*
*Blessing or curse.*

*Without vision there are nightmares.*
*Without dreams there is death.*

*So choose life,*
*live out of a creation dream,*
*practice resurrection.*

# Into a World of Dancers

*"You were dancing, I saw you dancing."*
*"This glittering joker was dancing in the dragon's jaws."*
*"The dance is the truth and it's everywhere."*[1]

Dance is a constant metaphor in Cockburn's writing. All of creation is founded in the ecstatic dance of the Creator. *Creatio per salatum*. Creation dances in harmony with the Creator. The stars, the seasons, all of creation are taken up in the "cyclic ballet" of the cosmos.[2] And since Jesus is the creation-calling Word made flesh, the "dust motes dance" around his feet, rejoicing in the appearance of the Lord of the dance, even as he comes to "dance in the dragon's jaws."[3]

## Who Are We?

To help us understand these images, we are drawn back to the first chapter of Genesis. The movement, dynamism, joy, harmony, and symbolic rhythm of the creation story are well appropriated by the metaphor of creational dance. But the dream of creational dancing in respectful harmony has devolved into the disrespectful and destructive nightmare of ecological devastation. And we know that this nightmare has everything to do with one particular dancer in the cosmic ballet. Humans. When creation dreams become ecological nightmares, it is invariably the human creature who is at the heart of it all. So, with Cockburn's help, we need to reflect further on a biblical understanding of what it means to be human. In the last three chapters we have been addressing the worldview question, Where are we? What is the nature of the world in which we find ourselves? We must now move to the second worldview question, "Who are we? What does it mean to be human?" And again, the metaphor of dancing will prove fruitful. If both God and creation are suggestively understood in terms of dance, then wouldn't the same metaphor also disclose certain dimensions of what it means to be that particular creature who is called to be in the "image" of this God?

Notice, first, that to be human is to be a creature. In the unfolding of the biblical creation story, the human is first and foremost a creature. We are not gods. We don't even receive a day of our own in the creation story but share our moment of creation with all the other animals. Creaturely kinship is at the heart of a biblical understanding of what it means to be human. And there can be no human flourishing, no human dancing, that is divorced from our integral and dependent place in creation. Just as "waves can't break without the rocks that dissolve into sand"—as Cockburn sings in his 1972 song "Life Will Open"—so "we can't dance without seasons upon which to stand."[4] Human dancing is not autonomous, somehow standing on its own. There can be no dance, there can be no human activity, apart from the cyclic ballet of the seasons, apart from the dance of all creation. "Eden is a state of rhythm like the sea / is a timeless change." Therefore, the creatures who are called to be the stewards of Eden must dance in rhythmic harmony with their creaturely kin. We are all part of a cosmic dance, all called to our own place within that dance.

The modernist notion of human autonomy whereby "man" is the measure of all things is a deceitful and dangerous pretense.[5] So Cockburn invites the listener, "Turn your eyes to the world where we all sit and dream." Take a look at the way things are in our world. Employing the metaphor of "dreaming" in a negative way, Cockburn notices that we are all "busy dreaming ourselves and each other into being." Rather than receiving life as a gift of the Creator, our lives and the world in which we live are constructed through the autonomous exercise of human reason directed by scientific discovery and technological control, all in service of the dream of an economic utopia. We dream ourselves and the world into being. And we construct and exploit the world in service of this dream.

But "dreaming is a state of death, can't you see? / we must live through who we are," Cockburn wisely counsels. Who we are cannot be divorced from the creation in which we stand. Who we are cannot be divorced from our most elemental character as creatures. Refusing to recognize and receive the givenness of life, the gift character of creatureliness, our deathly dreaming becomes a creation-wide nightmare. So "let's hear a laugh for the man of the world / who thinks he can make things work / tried to build the New Jerusalem / and ended up with New York." And while we are laughing at the pretensions of this worldly autonomy, let's not forget those who have put their faith in human technological power: "A laugh for the sun redballing / through the thermal inversion haze / a laugh for the nuclear good-time boys / numbering all our days / Ha Ha Ha."[6]

So much for human autonomy. The world of wonders is reduced to the banal and profane world of economic growth, greed, consumerism, war, and ecological destruction. But this is not the way things need to be.

> *if we can sing with the wind song*
> *chant with thunder*
> *play upon the lightning*
> *melodies of wonder*
> *into wonder life will open.*[7]

If human singing, chanting, and playing can join the harmonies and rhythms of creation, and if we abandon the pretense of autonomy and subject the human dance to the creational dance, then "into wonder life will open." Those primal creational melodies of wonder will be reawakened, and the enclosed world of modernist control will be transformed.

## Principal Dancers

Is such reawakening possible, however, if we take our cue from the beginning of Genesis? Isn't that ancient text, with its view of humans having "dominion" over creation and "subduing" the earth, diametrically opposed to a vision in which human life is subject to the patterns and processes of creation? Isn't that Judeo-Christian view of humanity precisely our problem? Isn't such an elevated view of humans at the heart of our ecological crisis?[8] This isn't the place to offer a full discussion of the perils and promise of the Jewish and Christian religious traditions in terms of environmental care,[9] but perhaps rereading the first chapter of Genesis through the metaphor of dance might suggest an alternative ecological imagination rooted in a richer understanding of what it means to be human, created in the image of God.

Cockburn's early intuition that the human dance must stand upon and be in harmony with the generative dance of creation makes good biblical sense. The first chapter of Genesis situates human life in the context of a creation that is good, blessed, and gifted. To properly "image" God, and thereby be fully human, is to "rule" and to "have dominion" over the rest of creation.[10] But these terms, which seem so domineering and hierarchical, need to be read in their context.[11]

Humans are created in the image of God. In this telling of primal beginnings, humans are called to rule the creation in the image of the Creator. This is a royal metaphor wherein we are called to be vice-regents of the Creator-King. As image bearers we are called to rule and exercise power as this King rules and exercises power. And in the context of this creation story it is clear that the Creator-King exercises power precisely to evoke, call into being, and bless the creation. Repeatedly Genesis 1 tells us that the Creator recognized the goodness and delight of creation. Repeatedly we read that the Creator "blesses" creation. The Creator's rule is a rule for life, not death. This is a rule that is the direct opposite of a violent, destroying, and exploitive use of power.[12]

We are called, as male and female, equal copartners created in the image of God, to be stewards of creation. We are called to use human culture-forming power to open up creation, not to close it down. Such an opening up of creation evokes new possibilities of creativity, justice, care, generativity, and fulfillment. We are given the high office of being gardeners in God's creation of delight, called to till and to keep our creational home, to open it up and make it fruitful, to protect and love it.[13] If it is true that the Creator calls forth this world of wonders out of the unfathomably deep resources of divine love, then the only appropriate way to "rule" creation will bear the imprint of that love. If it is true that "the earth is full of the steadfast love of the LORD," if it is true that love goes all the way down, if it is true that it is love that fires the sun, then the only way to rule in the image of the Creator is through love.[14] If "we're given love and love must be returned / that's all the bearings that you need to learn," then such love must be at the heart of what it means to be human, created in the image of God.[15]

Love is neither arrogant nor insists on its own way.[16] Love takes on the mantle of a servant committed to the flourishing of all creation. Norman Wirzba notes that this capacity for a servanthood driven by love is unique and "unparalleled in any other species." Indeed, because "we do not live by instinct and because we do not have to fight and claw our way through life (we have no natural predators), we are freed to restrain our wants and drives and make room for the needs of others."[17] As a result, our "dominion" takes on the celebratory character of maximizing creation's health.

Perhaps you have noticed that the only way that I can talk about what it means to be created in the "image" of God is by employing various other images. We are stewards, gardeners, rulers, servants. These various images come together and acquire new meaning through the metaphor of dance. We could say that this wonderfully complex, dynamic, interrelated, pulsating, moving, breathing, living, responding creation is a fantastic cosmic dance before the face of the Lord. Indeed, God is not just the audience of this dance but also a participant—"You were dancing / I saw you dancing."

To be created in the image of such a God, then, is to join that dance in a God-like way. Humans are called to take their place in this cyclic ballet of creation as the prima ballerina, the principal or leading dancer in God's creation-wide dance troupe. But this principal dancer is not in the dance troupe to arrogantly strut his or her stuff so much as to serve a leading, loving, nurturing, and healing role in the creation. Dancing in the image of God, the human creature is called to enhance, not hinder or inhibit, the dance of creation.

## Lord of the Dance

Dancing requires choreographic skill. That is why great dancers spend many hours in front of a mirror—not out of narcissistic self-indulgence but to work hard at getting the dance right. But what image do we see in that mirror? Nothing less than the image of God! And from a Christian perspective that image is most richly manifest in the Christ—this glittering joker, dancing in the dragon's jaws. Saint Paul says that Jesus is the "image of the invisible God."[18] He is the New Adam. In Jesus we see both who God is and what it means to be truly human. He is the Lord of the dance, and in him we learn how to be image-bearing dancers in God's creational dance troupe. From a Christian perspective we can't answer the question, who are we? without asking the question, who is Jesus? Jesus is the image of God par excellence, the principal dancer of all principal dancers. We must take our cue from him.

And what cue does Jesus give us for our culture-forming, creation-blessing dance? Perhaps the most profound interpretation of Genesis 1:26–28 is found in St. Paul's Letter to the Philippians. Genesis tells us that humans are created in the image of God to have dominion over creation. Paul says that though Jesus was the very form and image of God, he "did not regard equality with God as something to be exploited, but emptied himself, taking the form of a slave, and being born in human likeness." In human likeness and in the image of God, Jesus does not grasp for power, does not exploit his status, but manifests what it means to truly bear the image of God through taking up the role of a slave, a servant with no power. Paul continues, "And being found in human form, he humbled himself and became obedient to the point of death—even death on a cross."[19] So what does it mean to "have dominion" over creation as God's image bearers? How do we exercise the appropriate rule and authority of a principal dancer? By dancing in step with the principal dancer par excellence as servant of all. By following the Lord of the dance to a cross. In this interpretation, the call to dominion is the call to lay down one's life in service of those over whom we have dominion. Paradoxically, the call to rule is the call to sacrifice one's own power and one's own gain for the sake of others. In the Christian understanding of things, Jesus is enthroned as premier dancer, as the "Lord" of all. But he is enthroned on a cross. There he offers up his ultimate performance, the "dance" that turns out to be the renewal of the world. This is the most profound meaning of having "dominion" in creation.

## Into a World of Dancers

Some of these images come together in Cockburn's 1977 song "Feast of Fools." Inspired by theologian Harvey Cox's book by the same title, this song stands out on the *Further Adventures Of* album.[20] The Feast of Fools was an annual event in medieval society in which all the rules of feudal society were suspended. And in this song the image of such a feast creatively evokes the radical reversals that characterize both the prophetic literature and the teachings of Jesus. At the Feast of Fools the first will be last, and the last will be first.[21] This "Fool" may well remind us of a certain glittering and dancing joker in whose wake "tears can sing and joy shed tears."[22]

At the Feast of Fools there is humor, but unlike the distanced, gentle irony of a song like "Laughter," this humor "can sometimes be cruel." Perhaps it seems cruel because more is at stake. Indeed, the whole song conveys, both lyrically and musically, a profound intensity and pathos, especially in the passionate electric guitar solo before the last verse.

Such a feast is liberating because "everybody has a voice." The voices of those who have been oppressively silenced in a tightly controlled hierarchical society are released. At the Feast of Fools "it's time for the silent criers to be held in love." These voiceless criers must be silent no longer. Being held in love, they must be given back their voices, the voices of their pain. And as we have seen in our previous discussion of this song in chapter 2, such a prophetic reversal will necessarily entail judgment on their oppressors. If "it's time for the silent criers to be held in love," then it is also "time for the horizons of the universe to be glimpsed even by the faceless kings of corporations / it's time for chaos to win and walk off with the prize which turns out to be nothing." Silent criers and faceless kings. What does it mean for faceless kings to glimpse the "horizons of the universe"? Perhaps it is time for such people to hear the "voice of the nova" and "see how the starwheel turns." Maybe it is time for them to understand where they stand in the big picture of things. In the face of all attempts at autonomous control, it is time for chaos to win, for primordial chaos to overthrow oppressive order.

All of this may seem harsh, and this humor can indeed be cruel, but ultimately the Feast of Fools is a time of redemption. At the Feast of Fools "outlaws can all come home." Those who have been ruled out, rendered homeless, ostracized, or rejected are welcomed home. And at this feast, all things are laid bare. You can try to disguise yourself, hide who you really are, "but you'll be naked past the bone." There can be no pretense here.

"At the feast of fools / people's hands weave light / there is a diamond wind / flowering in the darkest night." Anticipating the images of light and homecoming in "Santiago Dawn," at the Feast of Fools light flowers out of the dark. "People's hands weave light." Weaving—that archetypal human culture-forming activity— produces light. The darkness of oppressive control is dispelled together with its worthless products and replaced by something akin to a "diamond wind."

In the last verse, Cockburn continues to name names, but he gets personal. "It's time for the singers of songs without hope to take a hard look and start from scratch again." In this broadside at the whole "pop music" scene, Cockburn is saying that if your music doesn't "weave light," if you don't offer your listeners a vision of hope beyond the present darkness, then you are no better than those faceless kings of corporations who are your overlords, and you will likely suffer their same fate.

But it is also time to forget "these headlights racing against inescapable dark."[23] Yes, we need light. Yes, people's hands must weave such light. But there is a certain kind of light that will not help. Perhaps "these headlights racing against inescapable dark" is a reference to the whole progress ideal of Western culture. We need to abandon and forget that "Enlightenment" vision wherein light is autonomously produced out of human reason, economic expansion, and technology. (These *are* headlights, after all!)

What does all of this have to do with dancing? Consider the last lines of this song:

> It's time for Harlequin to leap out of the future into
>     the midst of a world of dancers
> It's time for us to stand hushed in the cathedral
>     of silence waiting at the river's end.

What time is it? It is time for Harlequin, the Fool who will hold the silent criers in love, to leap out of the future into the midst of a world of dancers. If this is the Feast of Fools, if it is a time of redemptive reversals, then it is time for that glittering, dancing joker to make that decisive choreographed leap that will transform and liberate this dance of all creation. It is time for the Christ to return and to lead us—dancers all—as the principal dancer of all principal dancers.[24]

But to be sure that we do not fall back into our own autonomous, self-serving, and oppressive dance again, Cockburn wonderfully mixes his metaphors. On the one hand, we are dancers, full participants in the shaping of this world. It is into the world of such dancers that Harlequin must leap. On the other hand, "it's time for us all to stand hushed in the cathedral / of silence waiting at the river's end." We are dancers, and yet we are called to stand still and be silent. This coming, this ultimate resolution of our often painful dance, is not something that we can produce. We must stand hushed before the one who comes, before this Harlequin. We must receive our dance direction in the quiet that is appropriate to such sacred moments. After all, we are in a cathedral of silence. This sacred world, this creational cathedral, remains silent before the one who comes to bring its redemption.

At the end of the book of Revelation, the river of life flows from the very throne of God, and all of creation becomes a temple, a cathedral.[25] And at this river's end, in the presence of God, our dance takes on a stance of expectant waiting. No longer is this a salvation to be produced from our own "frenzied dance," entranced by the ornaments of our own making.[26] The redemptive resolution of the dance to which we were called must be received as a radical gift, equal to the gift of that original dance that birthed creation. Creation and creation restored. Both dances of grace.

Humans are dancers because they image a dancing God in the midst of a creation deeply characterized as dance. Sometimes our dance can "get a rhythm that can shake creation."[27] Other times this is an ironic "dancing in paradise."[28]

Sometimes the dance doesn't ring true—"table-dancing in black tights."[29] And then there are those nights when it's "a dancer oscillating on weightless feet," but it doesn't really matter.[30] At its best our life is revealed as "dancing scenes,"[31] moments of deep meeting in which "I'm heading for you / And you're headed for me / and we dance and we dance / and we dance."[32]

Of course, our culture-shaping dance isn't always at its best. There are power games being played. Good-looking, well-manicured folks are strutting their stuff while stomping all over the other dancers.

> Down there in the realm of power
> Somebody's manicured hands
> Play the Ace of Influence
> Against the Jack of Demands
> I reach for the deck—
> Draw the seven of hearts—
> Doesn't mean the world
> But it's a better place to start
>     and we dance and we dance
>     and we dance.[33]

If you are going to dance in this world of broken dancers, then you are going to have to take risks. The stakes are high as influence is played off against demand in the competition of prima ballerinas. What is the artist to do? The question isn't whether to play or not to play, to dance or not to dance, but rather, How will we dance? In whose image will we dance? So the artist reaches for the deck and draws the seven of hearts, and while this low card "doesn't mean the world" and will not likely win in this game, "it's a better place to start."[34] Rejecting both influence and demand, the artist embraces the heart and dances accordingly.

## And the Dance Flows On

What kind of a dance proceeds on the foundation of the seven of hearts? What kind of a dance is appropriate if it is directed by love, indeed, by love made flesh? Perhaps it is a dance that leaves no footprints. Cockburn concludes his seminal album *Dancing in the Dragon's Jaws* by returning to the theme of dance. The album began where it all begins, with the "creation dance." Then it moves to that glittering joker dancing in the dragon's jaws. In the next track, "Badlands Flashback," we meet someone "dancing like a flame," challenging us to remember the dance of creation. And then in the final song on the album, the nature of the dance is revealed, and we are given direction for how to join in.

Forming a wonderful *inclusio* with "Creation Dream," "No Footprints" brings us back again to creational glory while also picking up themes from

"Wondering Where the Lions Are" that get us thinking about eternity. The song begins:

> *mist hangs above hills*
> *above mist hangs stone face of mountain*
> *above mountain hangs a net of sky—*
> *crack! there are wings and they rip the net.*[35]

Here is a creational vision suffused with a transcendence that points beyond this world in a way that deepens our understanding and love for this world. Above hills, mist; above mist, mountain; above mountain, sky. Above, above, above. And the sky is cut by the wings of a free-flying bird, perhaps opening our vision to what lies above the sky.[36]

And this revelatory moment, this seeing of creation that orients us to the Creator, also discloses what we have known about creation since the beginning of this album. It is a dance.

> *and the dance flows on*
> *everything flows toward the rim of that*
> *shining cup.*

And not only is creation a dance, it is a sacramental dance. Perhaps this is a wedding dance, bride and groom dancing toward that cup of union. Or perhaps this is a dance that understands "the earth is bread, the sun is wine / it's a sign of a hope that's ours for all time."[37] Perhaps this vision of creation has placed us again, standing hushed, in the cathedral of silence. The dance flows on. Everything, every creature, every moment, every time, all of creation "flows toward the rim of that shining cup." This is a cup of salvation and a dance of renewed covenant.[38]

The song continues:

> *through these channels/words*
> *I want to touch you*
> *touch you deep down*
> *where you live*
> *not for power but*
> *because I love you*
> *so love the Lord*
> *and in Him love me too*
> *and in Him go your way*
> *and I'll be right there with you*
> *leaving*
> *no footprints when we go*
> *no footprints when we go*
> *only where we've been a faint and fading glow.*

This is not a dance of mastery. This is not a dance of manipulation, seduction, or power. This is a dance of communion. "I want to touch you / touch you deep down / where you live." This is a dance of love. "Not for power but / because I love you." And this is a dance with the Lord of the dance. "So / love the Lord / and in Him love me too." Dance . . . in God, subject to the Creator's redemptive leading.

Such a dance will require us to be light on our feet. If this is a redemptive dance in harmony with one another and all of creation, then it is a dance that will not leave deep footprints on the earth. While this song was written before the phrase "ecological footprint" was coined, there is a sense here of a dance with creation that leaves a light footprint. This is a dance that is carefully attuned and responsive to all of our dance partners. So let's not leave our mark on creation by a heavy footprint. Rather, let the memory of our dance here be something like a faint and fading glow. Let our dance enhance creation.

Humans are dancers. At our best we leave few footprints in our wake. At our worst, we leave boot marks on each other's bodies and on the body of creation. Usually, we are at our worst. Cockburn reflects on humans at their best and worst in the album that followed *Dancing in the Dragon's Jaws*, the 1980 offering appropriately titled *Humans*. The next chapter will enter into this ambiguous world of what humans can be.

# Humans

Bruce Cockburn's 1979 release, *Dancing in the Dragon's Jaws*, begins with the very dawn of creation and ends with a vision of all things as a sacramental dance. This is a dance of communion in which we are encouraged to leave no footprints when we go. The 1980 release, *Humans*, also opens with a dawn, but, in contrast to the ecstatically joyful dawn of "Creation Dream," on this album we are greeted by "grim travellers in dawn skies." It may be dawn, but there is no joy in the meeting of this new day. Rather, this dawn brings with it renewed anger, confusion, and pain. And by the end of the album, it is clear that this particular traveler is bearing the imprint of many a footprint on his body and his soul.

In "Hills of Morning," on *Dancing*, the artist is watching a group of people who are ill at ease, a "fraying rope getting closer to breaking." As we begin to listen to *Humans*, however, it is clear that the artist is no longer merely watching others who are ill at ease. Songs like "More Not More," "You Get Bigger as You Go," and "What about the Bond?" are reports on the state of his own dis-ease. This "fraying rope" has finally broken. And while experiences of this world get Cockburn thinking about eternity and occasion some kind of ecstasy in "Wondering Where the Lions Are," on *Humans* the artist sees the beauty of this world and it makes him "cry inside": it "makes me angry but I don't know why."[1] Where *Dancing* exudes a sense of creational generativity, newness, and joy, *Humans* has a devastating sense of futility—"all been done before / planet breathes exhaustion."[2]

For Cockburn, as for many other artists, life on the road occasions many songs. The road songs on *Dancing* convey a sense of transcendence. There may be a lonesome violin playing in "Incandescent Blue," but "the notes float up into the overcast / and change to white birds as they sail on through / and soar away free into incandescent blue." And in "Northern Lights" we meet a "sky full of rippling cliffs and chasms / that shine like signs on the road to heaven." The road songs on *Humans*, however, paint a very different picture. Such transcendence is brought to earth by the stark realism of songs like "Tokyo," "Grim Travellers," "Guerilla Betrayed," and "How I Spent My Fall Vacation." What the artist bears witness to both from the road and from the journey of his life is betrayal, displacement, disillusionment, disintegration, loss, and death.

As we saw at the end of the last chapter, Cockburn concludes *Dancing* by singing,

> through these channels/words
> I want to touch you
> touch you deep down
> where you live
> not for power but
> because I love you.[3]

When we turn to *Humans*, however, something has changed. Words can be hateful and used to hurt and to alienate. Relationships are always about an exercise of power that more often than not is about control and devolves into violence. The vision of love and touch in "No Footprints" is beautiful but does not reflect the artist's experience on *Humans*. It is in the painful absence of such love and deep touch that Cockburn sings,

> there must be more . . . more
> more songs more warmth
> more love more life
> . . .
> more current more spark
> more touch deep in the heart.[4]

"Not for power but / because I love you" meets there must be "more love, more life." "I want to touch you . . . deep down where you live" is countered by the cry that there must be "more touch deep in the heart."

But what about the touch of God? What has happened to God between these two albums? Again the contrast is stark. On *Dancing* Cockburn sings, "I've been cut by the beauty of jagged mountains / and cut by the love that flows like a fountain / from God."[5] By the time we get to the end of *Humans*, however, the metaphor of cutting has taken on a more tragic meaning. Cockburn sings, "all you can do is praise the razor / for the fineness of the slash."[6] The cut of love meets the slash of irreparably broken relationships.

One of the ground rules that I established in the second chapter of this book was that I would not be overly concerned with biographical details about Bruce Cockburn. If there was one album that would tempt me to break that rule, it would be *Humans*. It is clear that this album stands as a sad and pained witness to the dissolution of Bruce's marriage with Kitty Cockburn. In fact, the four songs that speak most painfully out of that experience ("More Not More," "You Get Bigger as You Go," "What about the Bond?" and "Fascist Architecture") were written one after another from February 14 to May 5, 1980. The four road songs ("Tokyo," "How I Spent My Fall Vacation," "Grim Travellers," and "Guerilla Betrayed") were all written during the fall tour of 1979. "Rumours of Glory" stands between these two groups of songs, written on New Year's Eve, 1979. One could interpret this as a song that brings together the painful extremes of what Cockburn has witnessed on the road with the painful extremes he is experiencing at home. This leaves one more song. While "The Rose above the Sky" closes the album, it was in fact the first song written (in August 1979). I find this interesting, because if there is any song that could offer hope in the midst of such pain, this is it. But this song was written first. It is almost as if Cockburn could see where things were going and could anticipate the pain that the next ten months would bring to him and so wrote "The Rose above the Sky" as a statement of anguished hope. This is my only biographical speculation. Whether this is true, I do not know. And in a sense it doesn't matter. In my interpretation of *Humans* I will make very few assumptions about the possible relationship between the songs and the personal details of the artist's life. This album is called *Humans*. It is a testimony to the human condition in its brokenness and in hope of its present and future healing. It is an album about us, the listeners, as much as it is about Bruce Cockburn, the artist.

## On the Road, East of Eden

If dance proves to be a suggestive metaphor for understanding what it means to be human, called to be the steward and loving servant of all creation, then the songs on *Humans* bring us to the shape of the human dance east of Eden. We are no longer in the garden. We are no longer at home in a place of identity, security, and communal love. We are grim travelers, on the road, displaced, frightened, and broken. We have found out "what the luxury of hate is,"[7] and in the words of a much later song, we are "dancing arm in arm towards the looming end of days."[8] That covenantal bond, "sealed in the loving presence of the Father," has been broken, and our calling to healing love in creation has devolved into "I'd like to put a bullet through the world."[9]

The opening track on *Humans* sets the stage. Who are we? What does it mean to be human? We are grim travelers in dawn skies. We are subjects of a capitalist system in which the powerful elite move capital around the world so it can reproduce itself while also moving human beings "as if we were so many cattle." In such a world we face the violence of both totalitarian coups ("12 mercenaries got weapons primed / gonna take that African nation / in record time") and anarchist revolutions ("bitter little girls and boys from the / Red Army Underground / they'd blow away Karl Marx if he had the nerve / to come around"). In the face of such violence and in the shadow of rampant industrialism, all previous allusions to hopeful transcendence lose their appeal:

> down on the plain of 10,000 smokestacks
> trucks butt each other to establish dominance
> the newspaper next to me leans over
> and says matter-of-factly
> "sacred mountain towers above meadows"
> uh huh and above us
> . . . grim travellers in dawn skies.

The power-struggling reality of life "down on the plain" cannot be mitigated by quick and easy reference to transcendence. A newspaper leaning over and saying, "sacred mountain towers above meadows" sounds surreal. And the artist's response to this platitude, "uh huh," has the ring of "yeah, right." That's a lovely sentiment, but we are not in some alpine meadow. We are down on the plain, and above us there is no "sacred mountain" but only these grim travelers.

People may well see the beauty of this world, but it "makes them cry inside / makes them angry and they don't know why." As the song progresses, the artist shifts the pronoun in the chorus from the second person (you), to third person (them), and then to the first person (me). This is no longer someone else's problem. Seeing this beauty against the backdrop of such violence fills the artist with both tears and anger, even if he doesn't quite understand why.

This is a road trip of disorientation and displacement. In "How I Spent My Fall Vacation" the artist wonders if he will "end up like Bernie in his dream / a displaced person in some foreign border town." Will he be stuck out here on the road, homeless, out of place? Is that the human condition east of Eden? Or will he end up "just sitting at home growing tenser with the times"? Both home and road are sites of tension and displacement. Or is his and our fate to be "like that guy in 'The Seventh Seal' / watching the newly dead dance across the hills"?[10] Dancers still, but this is the dance of the "newly dead," not the death-defying and life-affirming dance in the dragon's jaws.[11] Or maybe he'll end up "wearing this leather jacket shivering with a friend / while the eye of God blazes at us like the sun."

Or, or, or. Which way will it be? There is no resolution in this song. But whatever the human condition, however we resolve the meaning of human life, the images are all alienated, all cold. The dancer created in the image of God is still under the gaze of this God, but this no longer feels like the warm gaze of love. The "eye of God" forms an *inclusio* for this song. While the opening lines tell us that the "sun went down looking like the eye of God / behind icy mist and stark bare trees," the song closes with the artist and a friend shivering "while the eye of God blazes at us like the sun." It may well be that love fires the sun, but we can still be left shivering, far from that love, subject to a divine gaze that does not comfort. We are in the midst of a spiritual, cultural, and emotional winter.

At the Feast of Fools things were turned upside down. This glittering joker dancing in the dragon's jaws was dancing a dance of redemptive revolution. This, I have suggested, is the human calling. This is what it means to be created in the image of God. But how do we engage in redemptive change when the forces of the status quo are so powerful? Perhaps the revolution takes on a violence of its own. When we meet up with the revolutionaries who would "blow away Karl Marx if he had the nerve to come around," we find that this too is a world of betrayal. In "Guerilla Betrayed" the hope that "we could change something" devolves into violent anger. The song begins with a revolutionary resolve.

> ships moving into this cave of cloud
> out of the white light up river
> at a certain point you can only die.

But the revolutionary conviction that "we could change something" even if it will require our death falls apart into disintegrating fragments in the concluding two lines:

> up river at a certain point you can . . .
> ships . . . white light . . . only

Trust is at the heart of any authentic human life. Identity, vision, hope, and life are possible only in the context of trust. When trust is betrayed, everything is up for grabs.

Death is a constant companion on this road trip. Tragic death. Deep loss. Death on the road.

In "Tokyo" we enter into what seems like a dark movie.

> They're getting prepared to haul a car out of
> the river
> Noise and smoke and concrete seem to be
> going on forever
> Grinding gears and drivers getting high
> on exhaust
> I'm thinking about the water down below
> and what got lost

There is a cinematic sense to this song as images and sounds cut across our perceptual horizons. Noise, smoke, grinding gears, pachinko's jingle (a Japanese pinball/slot machine), violence, and businessmen pissing against the wall assault us, and then "cut to crumbling guardrail, slow motion car falls." This car falling over the bridge, a slow-motion plunge of death, symbolizes all that Cockburn has seen. Indeed, the artist finds himself in that car:

> Tonight I'm flying headlong
> to meet the dark red edge of dawn
> I know somebody will be crying
> and somebody will be gone.

With such images "ringing like a fire alarm" in his mind, it is no wonder that the artist sings, "Oh Tokyo—I never can sleep in your arms." Pushed to the edge—"Didn't I get enough shaking up?"—the artist feels like we are all "dice bouncing around in the cup." We are all stuck in this crap shoot, this wild gamble that constitutes human life. And again, the dawn brings with it only grief, not new life.

## Lament and Disorientation

Why is all of this violence, betrayal, and displacement so disorienting? Why can't the artist just shrug it off and accept what is? Why does he find it necessary to sing such passionate songs describing these experiences? Because he wants to live in a world of harmony and peace, of trust and fidelity, of home and knowing one's place "safe within the harmony of kin."[12] We find ourselves disoriented when reality isn't what it's supposed to be. Disorientation occurs when our most fundamental orientation in life is thrown into doubt by what we actually confront in our lives.

We can, however, keep disorientation at bay if we can find a way to dismiss the broken realities that we confront as things that are external to us. We could say to ourselves: "That may be the way things happen 'out there' in the world, but my own world is secure and serves to consistently confirm my worldview, my orientating vision of life. I know who I am, where I am, and where I'm going." But what happens when the disorientation of the "outer world" is mirrored in a disorientation of the "inner world"? What happens when the death, betrayal, and exhaustion that seem to be the norm for sociocultural life find their way into the very depths of our own lives, our own homes? It is this tragic parallel that makes *Humans* such a remarkable album. Precisely by giving voice to his own pain and loss, the poet gains deeper insight into the tragedy of the human condition. There is an anguished synchronicity between the world on the road and the world at home.

If Bono is right and Cockburn is a psalmist, then *Humans* is a collection of psalms of lament. And while "Grim Travellers," "How I Spent My Fall Vacation," "Guerilla Betrayed," and "Tokyo" could be heard as laments about the state of the world, "More Not More," "You Get Bigger as You Go," and "What about the Bond?" are laments of deep personal brokenness. Like the psalmist who composed Psalm 88, these are songs of a soul "full of troubles," composed from "the depths of the Pit, in the regions dark and deep." The poet is overwhelmed with grief. These songs come from one who is "shut in so that I cannot escape; my eye grows dim through sorrow." These troubles come "from all sides," "they close in on me."[13]

Psalms of lament are pained and abrasive cries of the heart. They name and embrace negativity, loss, and betrayal. Refusing to cover up pain through a conservative repetition of the prior orientation, these psalms allow the disorientation of broken life to come to full expression. And such psalms are intensely erotic. *Eros* is the passionate longing for that which we lack. While we often take this term to refer to a sexual longing, its meaning runs even deeper. Eros cries out in a longing ache for redemption, for healing, for wholeness. The psalms of lament and the songs on *Humans* are deafening with such cries. But note that eros is always directed to the fulfillment of our deepest desires.[14] Lament is always voiced in the hope that redemption is possible. Psalms and songs of disorientation are always rooted in a failed orientation and long for the time when we will be able to sing new songs of reorientation. Lament keeps us alive with hope when the temptation is to surrender to a defeated numbness.[15]

## What about the Bond?

If ever there was a song that depicted the pain of life east of Eden with an utter rawness, it is "More Not More." With a vocal performance that reaches a raw intensity not previously seen in the Cockburn corpus, "More Not More" literally screams for something deeper, more true, and more authentic in human experience. After a road tour that could render one exhausted and cynical, the artist cries out for "more." But this is not the "more" of an insatiable consumerism, feverishly seeking out new experiences to consume. No, this young and emerging artist sings, "not more fame / not more money not more games." None of this will satisfy. None of this will fulfill the deepest yearnings in the human heart, because fame, money, and the games that we are all required to play cannot address the thoughtless cruelty and loneliness that keep us in chains. Having composed a number of songs that chronicled the advent of a cultural winter of loss, pain, and death, the artist sings that there must be more than this:

> more songs more warmth
> more love more life.

Rooted in a deep conviction that the dancing Creator is the source of "lines of power / bursting outward,"[16] and that it is "love that fires the sun,"[17] the artist insists that "there must be more . . . more / more current more spark."

The worn-out, depleted experiences of life can't be the last word. The cynical dismissal of hope must not rob us of our passion and render us silent. Those who think that the artist is "a fool for thinking / things could be better than they / were today" cannot strip him of his tormented hope. Maybe he is a fool, but we have seen that this is precisely what we are called to be. In the face of personal and cultural stagnation and deception, there simply must be "more growth more truth." If authentic human life is found in free communion with one another, God, and all of creation, then we need "more chains" to be "more loose." The shackles that restrain us from love must be undone. The chains of injustice must be broken.[18] Created in love and for love, and declared to be delightfully good by the Creator, we cry out in the face of all that would rob us of our true humanness,

> not more pain not more walls
> not more living human voodoo dolls.

This is quite a song to be composed on Valentine's Day, 1980. This is a song of deep lament that stubbornly insists that things don't have to be this way, a song that refuses to accept our human brokenness as normal while desperately hanging on to hope.

"Sorrow is a creative act," wrote Nick Cave.[19] The love song, Cave insisted, "is the sound of sorrow itself." It is "clothed in loss and longing." We can hear that sound of sorrow in all of its bitterness and disappointment in "You Get Bigger as You Go." This is as painful an account of a marriage breakdown as you will ever hear. The development of images in this song mixes together the exhaustion and brokenness of a failed relationship with the exhaustion and brokenness of the world itself.

> you walk away to see a film see some
> people see a man
> stab in throat twist in gut all too clear
> not too new—all been done before
> planet breathes exhaustion
> staggers on
> enemy anger impotent gun grease
> too many thoughts
> too dogshit tired
> one small step for freedom
> from foregone conclusion

Notice that the artist is removed from the events. He is telling us about someone else who has walked away from him to watch a film in which other people watch a man who has been violently assaulted. The artist narrates from a distance a tale of watching someone watching others watching someone else's pain, captured through the watching eye of the camera. This literary distancing symbolizes the distance and alienation that he is artistically depicting. The staccato adding up of images also gives a sense of no center, no integration—and, in this song, no hope. If Cockburn is going to long for freedom in "More Not More" ("more chains more loose"), then this song insists that not all freedom is liberating. This is "one small step for freedom / from foregone conclusion." This step, this walking away, enacts the painful conclusion. We are free of each other. The relationship is over.

And yet, as the lover departs, "you get bigger as you go." Maybe it is those "bales of memory like boats in tow" that make her seem bigger in her absence. She looms large because the memories—joyful and painful—are so deep. She may be gone, but the story of their marriage, and the story of all that brought them together in the first place, remains. Or maybe she gets bigger as she goes because the artist is haunted by the pained silence—"spent all day afraid to talk"—or the angry break in communication between them—"telephone snarls 'don't touch me.'"

Like the psalms, this is a cry in the night. In a later song, Cockburn will sing, "Look, see my tears / they fill the whole night sky."[20] And the psalmist sings,

> I am weary with my moaning;
>  every night I flood my bed with tears;
>  I drench my couch with my weeping.
> My eyes waste away because of grief;
>  they grow weak because of all my foes.[21]

Make no mistake, the lover is now a foe. The artist feels as if he is a target of derision, and the lover is nothing less than a "vector of this weird dis-ease." And now, after a night of grief, a night of growing hurt, a night in which the lover seems to get bigger and bigger as she goes, a night of "news reruns" in which "it's all been done before"—the same old shit out there in this exhausted planet as there is in this night of anger and loss—after this long night, "dawn comes rainbow." Perhaps a hint of hope? Perhaps a faint echo of a covenant renewed? Perhaps a memory of God's covenant with Noah and all the earth, sealed by the rainbow?[22] Might there be hope for marriage, hope for the communion of one with another even in the shadow of such betrayal, such violence? Is it possible that as "pain takes shape of grimy window" on this morning of tears, the covenantal bond "sealed in the loving presence of the Father" might be restored? Not so quick.

In the next song on the album, "What about the Bond?" we are confronted with the unsurpassable distance between orientation and disorientation. Often psalms of lament will name the prior orientation, the prior settled faith, that has been brought into crisis by the recent turn of events. Indeed, it is the strength of that faith, the clarity of that earlier orientation, that makes the disorientation so deeply unsettling. It is because the psalmist can recall earlier times of joyful worship in the house of God in communion with others that he can sing with such passion:

> Why are you cast down, O my soul,
> and why are you disquieted within me?
>
> Why must I walk about mournfully
> because the enemy oppresses me?
> As with a deadly wound in my body,
> my adversaries taunt me.[23]

"What about the Bond?" stands in this tradition of psalms of disorientation. It is the composition of one deeply disquieted and wounded. It is written from the perspective of someone who experiences his present crisis in terms of oppression.

In the face of disharmony, mute helplessness, dysfunction, and confusion, the artist cries out for a renewal of covenant, a renewal of the bond between lovers:

> what about the bond
> what about the mystical unity
> what about the bond
> sealed in the loving presence of the Father.

Citing Genesis 2:24 almost verbatim, "man and woman / made to be one flesh," the artist appeals to an understanding of marriage rooted in nothing less than the order of creation. This is a covenantal bond, a mystical unity that goes beyond social conventions. This is a bond sealed in the loving presence of the Father that cannot be abandoned glibly in the name of "moving on." Life is indeed a journey, one involving near-constant change, but this is not change for its own sake. Change, if it is to be healing, must be rooted in and directed by a "love that will abide." The bond must be maintained or all is lost, all is wasted, the artist cries.

"What about the Bond?" is more than a chronicle of the end of a marriage. It is also a song that bears witness to a profound worldview crisis and one possible reaction to such a crisis. In this song we meet someone who is desperately hanging on to a worldview, a fundamental life orientation, when all the evidence suggests its failure. In the face of a worldview crisis, it seems to me that there are four options available: denial, abandonment, entrenchment, or reinterpretation. When life experiences bring into question the truth of our worldview, when our deepest orientation faces realities that are disorienting, we can simply hide our heads in the sand and *deny* what is going on within and around us. Or we can face the crisis in such a way that requires us to *abandon* that worldview (and likely adopt a new worldview through some sort of conversion). The old worldview is not able to withstand the pressures of life experience, so it must be left behind. Or we can hang on for dear life in a heroic act of *entrenchment* that battles the disorienting reality by stubbornly insisting that the only way to address the problem is by more militantly applying the prior orientation to it. Or the time of disorientation could give rise to a reorientation, a *reinterpretation* of that orientation for a new situation. Occasioned by deep crisis, a new path forward is found that can lead us through the pain and confusion to a deeper worldview rooted in the prior orientation but transformed through the fires of disorientation, doubt, lament, and pain. In the book of the Psalms we meet such reorientation in psalms that call us to "sing a new song."[24] The philosopher Paul Ricoeur considered this move from orientation to disorientation to reorientation the establishment of a "second naïveté."[25] This is a *second* naïveté because the prior orientation has gone through the refining fire of life in disarray. But it is a naïveté nonetheless, because the orienting faith has not been abandoned but maintained.

In my opinion, "What about the Bond?" is a song that gives voice to a desperate strategy of *entrenchment*. While I appreciate and understand the emotional dynamics of the song, and even agree with the theological orientation to which the artist appeals, the song doesn't seem to go beyond restating with increasing intensity an orientation that cannot deal with the painful realities it faces. The frustrated "c'mon" shouted at the end of the song is the cry of a person at his wit's end. While hanging on for dear life is perfectly understandable in the face of a worldview crisis, such entrenchment will invariably fail. In the face of disorientation, shouting the prior orientation more loudly will not help. Any creative path forward will require the kind of reinterpretation that can lead to a more profound reorientation.

Such a step toward reorientation is found in "Fascist Architecture." We have already looked at this song in chapter 5, so here my comments can be brief. If there is to be movement beyond the anger of "More Not More," "You Get Bigger as You Go," and "What about the Bond?" then the artist is going to have to get beyond his own pain and the scapegoating of his estranged lover. This construct of marriage, this orientation that is now in crisis, is not some eternal given handed down from on high. No, this is an architecture of our own design. And it is a self-enclosed, highly protective, and imposing "fascist architecture." Love cannot flourish and grow under such restrictive conditions.

Notice that this is not a matter of abandoning a worldview that understands love to be the very foundation of all creation. We are not giving up our commitment to the "mystical unity," "sealed in the loving presence of the Father." Rather, the artist leads us into a deeper understanding of the human condition, a tempered and more mature perception of the love that fires the sun. In the face of "blood like sweat," "while the magnificent facades crumble and burn" the artist catches a glimpse of "the billion facets of brilliant love / the billion facets of freedom turning in the light." The facades of our constructions of human life crumble—as they should, being only facades. And in that crumbling, in the falling of these Jericho-type walls, new things are revealed. In the light cast from the flames of such judgment, love and freedom are revealed to be more wonderful, mysterious, and incomprehensible than they have ever been. Love and freedom have been in crisis, and yet it is love and freedom that we glimpse in the midst of this collapse. And, with the artist, here we stand, "bloody nose and burning eyes / raised in laughter to the skies." The laughter of gratitude. The laughter of one who knows that he's "under the mercy and i'm ok." And in this moment of second naïveté, the artist recognizes anew the nature of unlocked love. Things will never be the same again.

The fascist architecture of confined and self-enclosed love must crumble if love will ever be unlocked. This is a severe mercy that requires a radical relinquishment of the structures that we have erected for our own protection. Militant self-defense can never creatively lead us through our disorientation. If lament is to be transformed into praise, then a certain kind of surrender is necessary. While *Humans* never brings us to praise, never quite gets us to a resolution of the crisis of the inner and outer worlds, it nonetheless closes with a profound song that takes an important step in the direction of reorientation. As the ending song on this album, "The Rose above the Sky" appropriately looks back and forward. This song pauses to reflect on what has happened and places the past in the context of a vision of the future, an eschatological vision. What you see depends on which direction you are looking. Ultimately, the meaning of life is determined from the perspective of the end. This is a world-weary, battered, and bruised ending song that looks forward to an eschatological resolution of all things in God.

"Something jewelled slips away," the song begins. Something of great value and beauty has been lost. And with a note of quiet resignation, rather than vindictive anger, the artist acknowledges that what is gone is gone. His hands are still held out, but there is "only air within their grasp." So "all you can do is praise the razor / for the fineness of the slash." It could have been uglier, he says. I may have the "bloody nose and burning eyes" of "Fascist Architecture," but the cut is a clean one. The memory of the wound will always be there, and the scar will never disappear, but this kind of a slash can be healed. Such healing, however, will have to wait "till the Rose above the sky / opens / and the light behind the sun / takes all."

The artist acknowledges that all attempts at resolution were sabotaged by "gutless arrogance and rage." The two tend to go together. But the truth of the matter is that this kind of brokenness is deeper than the anger and jealousy of the present. "You carry the weight of inherited sorrow / from your first day till you die." This sadness and brokenness invariably seems to lead us to "burn apart the best of tries." Such sorrow has become a deeply ingrained dimension of human life. And this sorrow is bigger than any of us. It is a collective sorrow, a sorrow that has permeated human life to its core. We carry this inherited sorrow from the first day until we die. But we carry it in a certain direction: "toward that hilltop where the road / forever becomes one with the sky." Whether this is a reference to that hill where we first caught a glimpse of the glittering joker dancing in the dragon's jaws in "Hills of Morning," or a reference to Calvary, the hill on which this joker was crucified, or an allusive movement in the direction of transcendence (the direction is clearly "up"), we will be traveling towards that hilltop "till the Rose above the sky / opens / and the light behind the sun / takes all."

We carry the weight of inherited sorrow, yet our lives are filled with mercies. In a moment of deep grace and gratitude, the artist remembers "the mercies of the currents that brought / me to you and you to me." Reorientation cannot simply reject a broken past. Mercy must be discerned there as well. Memories of mercy must not be blotted out by the painful memories of discord. While we may scream, "what about the bond?" in our longing for reconciliation, in the end we must still be grateful for the mercies that allowed that bond to be established in the first place. We cannot understand all of this. There is no revelatory word that will make it all clear. But that is, perhaps, for the best. You see,

> in the silence at the heart of things
> where all true meetings come to be
> 'Til the Rose above the sky
> opens
> and the light behind the sun
> takes all

Words are exhausted. There is nothing left to say, only a vision to be seen. At the heart of things, where true communion happens, there is silence. The "mute help-lessness" of "What about the Bond?" finds its resolution in silence. Communion is a mystery that runs deeper than words. If we are to grasp it, if we are to have any path beyond our anguished disharmony toward restored wholeness, then it will be found in a vision of the eschatological reconciliation of all things.

Notice that when Cockburn sings the chorus after the first and second verses, the words are "*till* the Rose above the sky." None of this will be resolved until the divine future opens up to us. But after the final verse, as Cockburn sings the concluding lines on this album, he testifies, "i *see* the Rose above the sky." There is silence at the heart of things; there is nothing left to say, but the artist tells us what he sees. He can see the future. Once again, his faith gives him a vision "just beyond the range of normal sight," but now instead of a glittering joker he sees "the Rose above the sky." In Latin Christian iconography the rose functions as a symbol of salvation in the next world. Sometimes identified with Mary, the Queen of Heaven (our Lady of Roses), in Gothic cathedrals the rose window invariably has Christ at the center. Similarly, the labyrinth at Chartres has a white rose at the center as a symbol of the love of God, a love made flesh in Christ. And Dante's final vision of spiritual resolution in *The Divine Comedy* is a mystic rose, which is itself alluded to in T. S. Eliot's *Four Quartets*. In the vision of the Rose above the sky, there is hope for an ultimate resolution in which our inherited sorrow is turned to joy.[26]

The artist sees and invites us to see the opening of this Rose above the sky. In this album he has taken us into the depths of the human condition in all of its betrayal, displacement, disillusionment, disintegration, loss, and death. And now he opens to us a vista of salvation beyond the brokenness. The human condition may be bleak, but that is not where we have come from or where we are going. There is an opening of new possibilities, a divine consummation of all things. We may well feel like "dice bouncing around in the cup" in "Tokyo"; our dance in this creation may well be a gamble with high stakes, but in the end "the light behind the sun / takes all."[27] In the end, the light that enlightens the sun, the love that fires the sun, the one who in the beginning said, "Let there be light" and who is himself the "light of the world" takes all.[28] He fills all things. All things find their end and meaning in him. All things are reconciled in him. All things consist in him. All things are welcomed into his glory.[29]

## Rumors of Glory

Maybe "glory" is a clue to what it means to be human. In Psalm 8 the psalmist confesses that human beings seem insignificant when compared to the glory of God above the heavens, rather inconsequential in contrast to that "light behind the sun." "What are human beings that you are mindful of them, mortals that you care for them?" the psalmist asks. And then he provides his own answer.

> Yet you have made them a little lower than God,
>     and crowned them with glory and honor.
> You have given them dominion over the works of your hands;
>     you have put all things under their feet,
> all sheep and oxen,
>     and also the beasts of the field,
> the birds of the air, and the fish of the sea,
>     whatever passes along the paths of the seas.[30]

Humans are made for glory. Not the self-glorification of human exploitation of the world, but the glory of being created in the image of God, called to loving stewardship, protection, and care of all creation. We have seen in chapter 4 that this is not a dominion of domination but of sacrificial service. In fact, it is precisely when loving dominion devolves into anthropocentric domination, when stewardly care is defiled by violent abuse, that our glory is turned to shame. Yet, somewhere in that tension, somewhere in that chasm between loving care and exploitive violence, we can still hear a "rumour of glory."

"Rumours of Glory" is another moment on the path to reorientation on *Humans*. Written as a New Year's Eve reflection on the nature of human life, the song stands temporally between the road trip of the autumn and the painful personal songs of that winter and spring. Somehow in the midst of the crises that the artist has met on the road and at home, openly facing "the extremes / of what humans can be," the confusing ambiguity of "smiles mixed with curses," and the danger of plunging "your hand in" and drawing "it back scorched" in all human relationships, the artist nonetheless perceives that "something is shining / like gold but better / rumours of glory." There is a glory to be seen, a rumor to be heard, but it lies "behind the pain/fear / etched on the faces." Behind it all, behind fascist architectural facades, behind the tears and anger of those grim travelers in dawn skies, behind the noise and smoke and concrete of our failed attempts at constructing life, behind the snarled "don't touch me," behind the gutless arrogance and rage, if you have the eyes to see, "something is shining / like gold, but better / rumours of glory."[31] This is like gold after the dross has been burned off, but it is better. Human life has been subjected to the fires of doubt and pain, betrayal and hate, and through it all glory shines.[32] In the midst of the disorientation, we catch a glimpse of what is to come and what once was. We are creatures crowned with glory. We are created in the image of God. And while we can tarnish that image and defile it through idolatry, the rumor of this glory cannot be eradicated. Indeed, this rumor is our only hope.

# 9

# Broken
# Wheel

We all know that something is wrong. We all know that things are not what they ought to be and that there is a brokenness that runs deep through our own lives. We may name this brokenness in different ways, but we all know it is there.

We have met that brokenness in the lives of humans as portrayed by Bruce Cockburn. Ours is a life of broken bonds, betrayal, hatred, disappointment, grief, and displacement. And we name such experiences as broken because we all live out of moral frameworks that say things ought not be this way. There is something deep in the human psyche that refuses to simply acquiesce to brokenness. Precisely because all of life is "drenched in, patterned by, glued together with moral premises, convictions and obligations," do we find ourselves passing judgment on certain acts, attitudes, and ideologies. "There is nowhere a human can go to escape moral order. There is no way to be human except through moral order."[1] And we need a moral order, a normative vision of life, because we constantly confront moral *dis*order within ourselves and the world within which we live. To even ask the question, what's wrong? requires some sort of moral order, vision, or framework.

Moreover, we can answer this third worldview question only on the basis of answers to the first two questions. For example, if *where we are* is in a world of raw resources waiting for our extraction and exploitation, and if we understand *who we are* to be fundamentally acquisitive economic creatures out to serve our own self-interest, then we would likely answer the question, *what's wrong?* in terms of anything that might happen to be in the way of this kind of economic expansion. What's wrong? Primitive aboriginal peoples standing in the way of civilizational progress is what's wrong. So we have to eradicate them. Limitation in our knowledge that hinders our exploitation of the earth is what's wrong. So we need more intense scientific research and more aggressive technological applications of that science. Economic growth has been slowing down. So we need to encourage consumption and reduce taxes for the rich so they will then stimulate the economy through their investments.

You see the point. How we answer the first two worldview questions about the nature of the world and humankind will set the contours for how the third question (and the fourth) will be answered. For example, because Cockburn's vision of life is rooted in a creation born of love wherein humans are called to direct their lives by that love, the breaking of the bond of marriage is experienced as something fundamentally wrong in the world. Employing more theological language, we could say that if creation is rooted in covenant and humans are called to be covenant keepers, then the dissolution of a marriage goes against the very grain of the universe.

So it is that we live in the falling dark. And so it is that we are counseled to kick at the darkness until it bleeds daylight. But where did the darkness come from? Is it enough to understand the darkness of our world in terms of forces external to us? Doesn't "kicking" at the darkness end up objectifying the dark as something "out there," something that oppresses us from the outside? Is it enough to kick at the darkness? And how do you kick at the darkness once you realize your total complicity in darkness? Recalling our discussion of home and homelessness in chapter 5, what do you do when you come to realize that it isn't just that external forces have rendered you homeless but that you have engendered your own homelessness through a "fascist architecture" of your own design? Which darkness do you kick at once you realize that there are no innocent bystanders and that you and I, "we are the break in the broken wheel"? This brings us to one of Cockburn's most profound songs, "Broken Wheel" from the 1981 album *Inner City Front*.

## Broken Wheel

In his earlier song "Starwheel," Cockburn confesses that love is the very life force of the universe. It is love that turns the starwheel and moves the galaxies. But now it is apparent that this starwheel suffers from a deadly flaw.

> *Way out on the rim of the galaxy*
> *The gifts of the Lord lie torn*
> *Into whose charge the gifts were given*
> *Have made it a curse for so many to be born*
> *This is my trouble—*
> *These were my fathers*
> *So how am I supposed to feel?*
> *Way out on the rim of the broken wheel.*

"See how the starwheel turns"—it bumps along on a broken rim! And precisely because Cockburn understands creation as fundamentally gifted, a gift of the Creator, the tearing or rending of those gifts creates deep disorientation.[2]

Since the gifts of creation have been entrusted to the stewardly care of human beings, created in the image of God, the tearing of those gifts is fundamentally a human responsibility: those "into whose charge the gifts were given / have made it a curse for so many to be born." But notice that this is not a predicament located outside of the artist, nor is this a situation in which the artist allows the listener to take comfort in the stance of a victim: "this is my trouble / these were my fathers / so how am I supposed to feel? / way out on the rim of a broken wheel?" And that means that "no adult of sound mind / can be an innocent bystander." "You and me—*we* are the break in the broken wheel." It is human brokenness, the distortion of human stewardship, that occasions cosmic brokenness. This brokenness is not merely a theological assertion about human fallibility and culpability. No, this is a deeply personal confession. "So how am I supposed to feel?" Indeed, how *are* we supposed to feel when we realize not only our complicity in brokenness but also our willful participation in and propagation of evil? How are we supposed to feel when we realize that our mismanagement of the gifts of creation, our failed stewardship, has made it no less than "a curse for so many to be born"?

"Broken Wheel" explicitly rejects any spirituality of escape. There can be no bystanders, there is none who is without sin, and there can be no averting our gaze from the curse that our sin has caused. In this song we are called to engage the world in all of its pain precisely because it is only by embracing the brokenness of creation that we can begin to affirm the possibility of change. As Walter Brueggemann has put it, "Only grief permits newness."[3] Those who do not want the new are afraid of grief; they deny it to themselves and repress it (or ignore it) in others. But grief permits newness because grief, mourning, and tears are not expressions of powerlessness. Rather, grief functions as a radical critique of the distortedness of our own lives by bringing what is wrong to conscious awareness. "Broken Wheel" refuses to cover up and insists that we confront the brokenness, oppression, failed expectations, and empty promises of our lives.

If grief permits the newness of hope, then this song gives voice to a profound hope:

> *Water of life is going to flow again*
> *Changed from the blood of heroes and knaves*
> *The word mercy's going to have a new meaning*
> *When we are judged by the children of our slaves.*

The embrace of pain is the door of hope. In a world characterized by "pain and fire and steel," Cockburn is bold enough to proclaim that the "water of life is going to flow again." "Water of life" alludes to a prominent biblical metaphor for God's presence. Significantly, this metaphor is often employed in the Bible during times of deep spiritual thirst and desolation. It is used by Isaiah during the Babylonian exile.[4] Jesus refers to himself as living water, and the book of Revelation concludes with a river of life flowing in the new Jerusalem and the announcement that the waters of life are on offer to all who are thirsty.[5]

This water, however, is acquired at a cost. The water of life is going to flow again, but it will be changed from the blood of heroes and knaves. But who are they? Perhaps we need to look again at the book of Revelation. Before we ever get to those waters of life in the last chapter of Revelation, there's a lot of blood—the blood of the martyrs and the blood of the Lamb, the sacrificial blood of Jesus.[6] Might these be Cockburn's heroes and knaves? Perhaps. After all, what is a knave but another name for a fool, a joker, a trickster? Cockburn has consistently used such metaphors for Christ. The waters of life flow from the pierced side of the Christ. If there is hope for this broken-wheeled world, then it is a hope that walks the path of the cross.

So there will be waters of life; there will be mercy, but this mercy will have a new meaning. The kind of radical reversals that we see throughout the teachings of Jesus now appear in this song. We are going to be "judged by the children of our slaves." The very children for whom our brokenness has made it a curse to be born now return, scathed by that curse but alive nonetheless, to judge us. And so "the last will be first, and the first will be last."[7] It is only in the context of such prophetic reversals that there can be any hope for this broken-wheeled world. Anything less would be cheap and escapist.

The coda of the song brings us to new depths of spiritual insight. "You and me—we are the break in the broken wheel / bleeding wound that will not heal." Echoing the prophet Jeremiah, the contemporary prophet knows that our wound is incurable, our injury beyond healing.[8] And so he reaches beyond Jeremiah to Jesus the great healer as he prays, "Lord, spit on our eyes so we can see / how to wake up from this tragedy." Alluding to the healing story from the Gospels in which Jesus made a paste of mud with his own spittle and applied it to the eyes of a blind man, the song confesses that we are blind and asks for Jesus to come with healing in his spittle.[9]

But notice how Cockburn mixes the metaphors of blindness and sleep in these lines: "spit on our eyes so we can see / how to wake up from this tragedy." Our problem isn't just that we are the break in the broken wheel. Nor is the problem that we are blind to this devastating truth. No, all of this is compounded by the fact that we are asleep to this tragedy. We have numbed ourselves until we are asleep. Our bleeding wound will not heal because we are desensitized to it in our anesthetized slumber. Spit on our eyes so we can see. Spit on our eyes so we can be awake.

This is an amazing prayer to be uttered by an insomniac. Many of Cockburn's songs are set at night.[10] It is hard to sleep when you are deeply troubled. But the artist doesn't ask for the peace of a good night's sleep. Cockburn doesn't ask for a healing that will alleviate the pain. Rather, he asks for a healing that is deeper, a healing that will be awake to the pain and conscious of the brokenness. In this world, sleep is inappropriate. At a time of such crisis, we need to keep awake. If healing must walk the path of the cross, then we must try to do better than the sleepy disciples on the eve of Good Friday. We must be alert in prayer both to the pain of the world and to the painful path of redemption.[11]

The song concludes by structurally manifesting brokenness. With the exception of the penultimate line ("in a world of pain and fire and steel"), the third verse consists of disjointed quotations from the previous two verses and the coda. This is, indeed, a broken verse for a broken-wheeled world.

## Souls Turned Back on Love

What's wrong? The gifts of the Lord lie torn. The very gifted fabric of the universe has been ripped apart by humanity not fulfilling its creational calling to tend the garden. Cockburn's worldview is formed by what philosopher Paul Ricoeur has called the "Adamic myth."[12] This is an anthropological understanding of evil. Rather than locate evil in the nature of the material world or in some sort of cosmic battle among the gods, the Adamic myth identifies evil as an alien intruder into the good creation. And it is human misdirection that gives entrance to such an intruder. What's wrong with the world? We are. The world that was born of the love of the Creator is to be cared for, tended, and opened up by the creature made in the image of that Creator. We are called to image that love, to embody that love in our relationship with God, one another, and the rest of creation. But we have turned our back on love.

> *Terrible deeds done in the name*
> *of tunnel vision and fear of change*
> *surely are an expression of*
> *a soul that's turned its back on love.*[13]

To turn our back on love is to turn our back on the very life force of the universe, the very love that fires the sun! And the consequences are devastating.

With backs turned on love we become dwellers "by a dark stream."[14] Once sin dwells in us, St. Paul writes, then we are at home in evil, at home in sin, far from the house of love, far from the house of God.[15] We dwell in darkness. We find ourselves with "crying hearts, hooked on a dark dream," as we walk "this prison camp world." There is something imprisoning and addictive about evil. While we will perversely claim that our actions are expressions of freedom, we are in fact held captive, held in slavery by our sin.[16] "Hooked on avarice," sings Cockburn, "how do we get off it?"[17] We have all the freedom of a junkie looking for the next fix. The prophet Hosea observes that "their deeds do not permit them to return to their God."[18] Having so valued our own freedom, we find ourselves caught in a way of life that has no exit, entrapped by our own deeds. We want to believe that we are all autonomous islands unto ourselves. And yet Cockburn tells us that if we are to consider ourselves islands, then we are the islands of "Alcatraz, St. Helena, Patmos and the Château D'If."[19] Islands of exile. Islands of imprisonment.

## In the Falling Dark

If it was the voice of love that first said, "Let there be light," then it is no surprise that biblical writers identify evil with the absence of light. Turning our backs on love is to turn our backs on light and to embrace darkness. Cockburn weaves such images of light and darkness throughout his lyrics. Consider again "In the Falling Dark":

> light pours from a million radiant lives
> off of kids and dogs and the hard-shelled husbands
>     and wives
> all that glory shining around and we're all
>     caught taking a dive
> and all the beasts of the hills around shout,
>     "such a waste!
> don't you know that from the first to the
>     last we're all one in the gift of Grace!"[20]

The light is everywhere, even radiating from the hard-shelled lives of people like us. But we miss it; we're caught taking a dive. The beasts of the hills get it. They see the light. They understand that grace is at the heart of all things. They can bask in the glory of God shining through all of creation. But we miss it. We find ourselves living in the falling dark.

The darkness is thick. You think that maybe you have begun to grasp the depths of this darkness, that maybe you have begun to understand just how pervasive and devastating this darkness is, and Cockburn comes along and tells you that "you've never seen everything."[21] There are depths of darkness not yet seen.

Themes of vision preoccupy the 2003 album, *You've Never Seen Everything*, both lyrically and in the album art. From the cover, where we see Cockburn looking intently to the viewer's right with light emanating from his eyes, to the face of the CD, to underneath the CD in the album case, to almost every page of the album booklet, we are confronted with an open eye.[22] In "All Our Dark Tomorrows" Cockburn sings, "I can see in the dark, it's where I used to live,"[23] and the album invites the listener to join the artist in that darkness, with eyes wide open. On the third and fourth pages of the album booklet, we meet Cockburn's eyes staring directly at the reader of the lyrics of "Tried and Tested" and "Open." Just as we cannot avoid the gaze of the artist himself on these pages, so we cannot avert our eyes from what he sees in the dark.

Eyes are notably absent, however, at the very center of the album booklet. Here, in the middle of the album art, we are confronted with a large image of an anatomical heart. Here is the "heart" of the album. Across this image we see just one lyric, "You've Never Seen Everything." If we are to see in the dark, then we will need to look deep into the heart of things, into our own hearts, because that is where the darkness dwells. "The heart is devious above all else; it is perverse—who can understand it?" writes the prophet Jeremiah.[24] And in Genesis we meet perhaps the most devastating verses in the whole Bible:

> The LORD saw that the wickedness of humankind was great in the earth, and that every inclination of the thoughts of their hearts was only evil continually. And the LORD was sorry that he had made humankind on the earth, and it grieved him to his heart.[25]

God can also see in the dark, and what he sees is the human heart held captive by the imagination of evil. This terribly distorted heart ends up breaking the heart of the Creator to such a degree that God is sorry he created us in the first place. I cannot imagine a more devastating verse in the Bible. God is sorry that he made us. And if we listen closely to Cockburn's song "You've Never Seen Everything," we can see why.

"Nobody's making me say this / I'm talking to you," it begins. This song is intensely personal and could have been avoided. The artist doesn't have to take us on this journey into darkness, but he wants to look us in the eye, tell us the truth about the human condition, and unveil for us what lies in our hearts.

While the immediate context of the song would appear to be a very long air flight, it is clear that there is a deeper meaning when he says, "Like exiled angels we swing out of the clouds / Above night city— / Fields of light broken by the curve of dark waterways." Like exiled angels no longer at home in the heavenly realm, so are we exiled from the creational home that love built. As we look out on this broken home, there are still fields of light to be seen, but they are broken by the curve of dark waterways. Again, the immediate reference is likely an aerial view of an illuminated city at night in which there are curves of dark waterways, or rivers, where there is no light. But the rest of the song suggests that more is going on here. Light is always broken by darkness, and this song is a devastating chronicle of precisely that brokenness. The artist is haunted by insomniac visions of bizarre and gruesome violence. From teenage suicide, to police brutality, to a murder/suicide, to mass murder of one's neighbors, the narrative sinks deeper and deeper into a painfully graphic portrayal of human depravity. And we are repeatedly reminded that "you've never seen everything." There is always more; there is always something worse than the last thing. Not the kind of song destined to hit any Top 40 list or get any radio airplay!

This depravity is not limited to interpersonal violence, however.

> *I see:*
> *A leader of the people with a ring in his nose*
> *And the leaders of business tell him which way to go*
> *With tugs on the golden chain which once led the golden calf*
> *And we're supposed to be impressed with their success*

*But my mind goes blank before the unbelievable indifference*
*shown life*
*spirit*
*the future*
*anything green*
*anything just*

The political and economic structures of the world participate in this depravity. When you turn your back on love and dwell in the darkness, you treat life, the spirit, the future, the environment, and the rights of others with indifference. Why? Because "greed twists eternal in the human breast." Turning our backs on love means that we turn our backs on the exorbitant generosity of the Creator. Forgetting that we are all one in the gift of grace, we turn in on ourselves and are captivated by a self-serving imagination of greed. When grace is replaced by greed, and generosity is displaced by avarice, there is no limit to the depths of evil that can result.

"You've Never Seen Everything" is a haunting song. The artist speaks the words of all the verses over a darkly ambient music laced with dissonant and mournful harmonica, vibraphone, and guitar riffs. Only the chorus is sung. In a duet with Emmylou Harris, Cockburn sings,

*Bad pressure coming down*
*Tears—what we really traffic in*
*ride the ribbon of shadow*
*Never feel the light falling all around.*

Having taken the pulse of the human condition, the artist comments on the climate of human culture. There is a bad pressure coming down. It weighs heavily upon us and leaves us in tears. When you ride the ribbon of shadow, and when the darkness of that shadow is this deep, wide, and long, then it is no surprise that you never feel the light falling all around. What's wrong? We live in the falling dark. What's wrong? We've got a "head full of horrors / heart full of night." What's wrong is that we are "at home in the darkness." The good news is that we are also "hungry for dawn."[26]

## Cold Absence

Dawn, however, can be a long time coming. When it is "the coldest night of the year" and you are living in the shadow of a broken relationship, you find yourself staying up all night "trying to keep the latent depression from crystallizing."[27] When your "eyes fill with memories poisoned by intimate knowledge of failure to love," then "sometimes, sometimes, doesn't the light seem to move so far away?"[28]

Perhaps the first casualty in this broken-wheeled world is our relationship with one another. The story tells us that upon eating the forbidden fruit, the eyes of Adam and Eve were opened and that, noticing their nakedness for the first time, they covered themselves in shame.[29] Joyful intimacy devolves into fearful and self-protective distance. Just as this broken-wheeled world is described as "this bluegreen ball in black space / filled with beauty even now / battered and abused and lovely,"[30] so in the brokenness of our relationships we are "the numb and confused / the battered and bruised / the counters of cost / and the star crossed." You see, in the minefield of love, "you pay your money and you take your chance / when you're dealing with love and romance."[31] Life was made for intimate communion, but once covenant has been broken, we find ourselves "confused and solo in the spawning ground," watching "the confusion of friends all numb with love."[32] And it all leads us to the cynical conclusion that "when two lovers really love there's nothing there / but this suddenly compact universe / skin and breath and hair." No wonder we are "alone and sleepless" on the coldest night of the year.[33]

What's wrong? Our sexuality is deeply broken. While a popular Freudianism has simplistically said that sex was the original sin, there is no basis for such a view in the biblical text. Sex is not the original sin, but our sexuality is one of the first casualties of sin. Cockburn addresses this brokenness with an explicit candor.

> *Woman-in-kitchen, man-in-palace*
> *Worshipping the performance of the phallus*
> *Gaming for power till their hearts grow callous*
> *As if a human's just an animal with malice*
> *Limp lance, phallocrat, finger on the trigger*
> *Go ahead and stay small while everything gets bigger*
> *It's a bully's game and I don't want to play*
> *Why don't you think about the better way.*[34]

While Cockburn also writes songs of explicit erotic joy,[35] these lines lament a sexuality that destroys intimacy precisely by making an idol out of sexual performance. In fact, the artist will suggest that a sexual practice that worships the performance of the phallus in a callous game of sexual power in the end leaves us with a "limp lance" that will "stay small while everything gets bigger." Sexual idolatry results in impotence.

These are all erotic songs. They are filled with an eros, a longing for that which is lost. An eros for intimacy, for restored fidelity, for trust. In his 1999 "Love Song Lecture," Nick Cave suggested that while love songs come in many guises, "they all address God, for it is the haunted premise of longing that the true love song inhabits." He continues:

> [The love song] is a howl in the void, for Love and for comfort and it lives on the lips of the child crying for his mother. It is the song of the lover in need of her loved one, the raving of the lunatic supplicant petitioning his God. It

is the cry of one chained to the earth, to the ordinary and to the mundane, craving flight; a flight into inspiration and imagination and divinity. The love song is the sound of our endeavour to become God-like, to rise up and above the earthbound and the mediocre.[36]

A love song, says Cave, "is never truly happy" because it must always be "clothed in loss and longing." And that longing, while perhaps directed to a particular person, is always, at its deepest level, a longing for God.

Consider Cockburn's 1984 song "Lily of the Midnight Sky."[37] While many of his songs of the seventies were suffused with a sense of the divine presence, there is in this song a "cold absence." The "glittering joker," "Lord of the starfields," and "joyous son" has become "Lily of the Midnight Sky."[38] With images of arid loneliness and barren isolation, the artist weaves for us a love song that breathes the kind of loss and longing that Cave is talking about. This artist may be hungry for the dawn, but this day dawns with an intensity of absence:

> in the rising day
> you keep fading away
> don't I know that you're always around
> I can reach you if I try
> Lily of the midnight sky.

This Lily of the midnight sky is a "shimmering crescent moon" that "recedes into working dawn." This is a dawn that hides the moon, so the artist speaks, "I raise a fist to the marauding sun that has hidden you away." And in the anguish of losing this object of his love, he exclaims, "i'm the rag in a bottle of gasoline. / longing to ignite / *ich will alles* / all of you." The artist is driven by a burning passion, a longing for full communion, a longing to have it all. While such passion may well be directed to a lover, I think that we do well to take Nick Cave's advice and recognize in a song like this nothing less than a howl in the void, a cry to an absent God.

> nobody else could be you
> if only I could see you
> I should be able to touch you somehow
> I can reach you if I try
> Lily of the midnight sky

Again, Cockburn is a psalmist. The psalmist laments that his soul thirsts after God and that his tears have been his only food, day and night. The divine absence occasions a taunt from others that painfully resonates in his own heart: "Where is your God?" Where indeed? With the same tone of abrasive spiritual honesty, Cockburn complains, "you keep fading away." While the psalmist asks, "When shall I come and behold the face of God?" Cockburn cries out, "if only I could see you." And yet, while the psalmist is downcast and deeply disquieted within himself, he nevertheless reassures himself, "put your hope in God, I'll be praising him again someday."[39] So also does Cockburn insist in the midst of his lament, though God has been hidden away, and though he can neither see nor touch this God, "I can reach you if I try / Lily of the Midnight Sky." The song concludes with these evocative images:

> while you look from on high
> spare a smile as i
> put on my dog mask and howl for you
> I can reach you if I try
> Lily of the midnight sky.

While I am howling my lament, howling into the void, howling in longing for restored communion, can you, like that crescent moon, spare a smile for me? Might there be a moment, might there be a brief glimpse of blessing in the midst of this cursed world, of presence in the face of such devastating absence?

What's wrong? In this falling dark we live in the ruins of broken relationships. In our relations with one another and with God, a cold absence has a grip on our lives.

## Dialogue with the Devil

The darkness is of our own making, and neither Scripture nor Cockburn will allow us to escape our culpability by appeals to how "the devil made me do it." God created us in his own image as "choosers not clones," and we can never escape our responsibility for the choices that we make by appealing to an external force of evil that somehow controls our lives.[40] Nonetheless, images of Satan, or the devil, do appear in Cockburn's early work.

Biblical faith doesn't make anywhere near as much of the character of Satan as does a lot of fundamentalist religion. Nonetheless, Scripture does have a place for a personalization of evil in a figure such as Satan, or the devil. While it may be the case that evil is rooted in the human heart, there also seems to be a dynamism in evil, a certain force or power of evil, that somehow goes beyond the sum total of all human evil combined. Once set loose in the world, evil seems to take on a certain demonic life of its own. I think that it is this quasi-autonomous force of evil, undoubtedly rooted in human sinfulness, that the Bible refers to when it speaks of Satan. The Evil One, however, is not so much a force that creates evil as it is a symbol of that which tempts us to evil. From the fall narrative in the third chapter of Genesis to the story of Jesus's temptation in the wilderness, the Evil One appears as the tempter, the one who seduces us to evil and lures us into the imprisonment of sin.[41]

We meet such a tempter in "Dialogue with the Devil."[42] The song begins on an island of sorts—"standing on a rock in a river." And from this vantage point there is a veneer of arrival, a possibility of victory. "You could drown yourself in jewels / like a thousand other fools / while you stand there looking down at what you've won." From this standpoint, from this place in the story of your life, you could join all the others, drowning yourself in the jewels, in the wealth that you have achieved. That is one possibility, one path.

But what happens if instead of "*standing* on a rock in a river," we move to the next verse and are "*sitting* on a mountain of ashes / face to face with past regrets"?[43] What happens if those jewels are gone and all that you have left is the painful memories of broken relationships and past sins? What happens if the veneer of arrival and success has been torn off, and you have nothing but the ashes of the life you have burned? Well, maybe then "you could roll down to the canyon / piss away this incarnation." Maybe the only option is to say "piss it all" and surrender yourself to self-annihilation. That's another option, "but remember that you pay for what you get." There are consequences to all actions, even suicide.

In this moment of indecision we hear the voice of the tempter:

> and he says, "but don't you know
> how hard it is
> to hit the ground and mean it,
> and mean it?"

Do you really think that you could pull this off? Do you really think that you would have the courage and the resolve to jump off that mountain of ashes? Interestingly, there is no diabolical tone to this question. The lines are delivered in gentleness, perhaps even with a feigned kindness of concern.

The quest resumes. From *standing* on a rock in a river to *sitting* on a mountain of ashes, we now find ourselves walking—"*walk* the jangling streets of the city / trying to find the buried sun." While we stared "at the splintered sun" refracted off the water in the first verse, now we are looking to find that sun buried somewhere under the city streets. Perhaps this buried sun, the source of light and life, will help us deal with those past regrets from that mountain of ashes. But again, maybe this is an illusion. Again, "you could drown yourself in jewels / like a thousand other fools / while you wander waiting for it to be done." Whether this is a reference to the end of life or to the revelation of the sun that will bring resolution to the quest, it is clear that we are still left wandering, still left without an answer.

So the devil makes a second appearance, but this time with more intensity:

> and he cries, "why don't we celebrate?
> why don't we celebrate?
> love can make you sad
> come on, let's drive ourselves mad."

Forget this quest. Forget looking for a buried sun. Forget those past regrets. All of that is rooted in a love that can make you sad. Forget it and embrace a Dionysian celebration. Come on, let's party! Let's drive ourselves into a madness that can leave all of this dreary reality behind!

And then the artist quietly and wisely comments on the devil's invitation.

> *and he's aware*
> *how hard it is*
> *to kiss the sun and mean it*
> *and mean it.*

The devil may have told us how hard it is to hit the ground and mean it, but it is the artist who uncovers the devil's knowledge that is being used against us here. The devil knows how hard it is to kiss the sun and mean it. To kiss the sun would seem to be an allusion to the act of homage afforded to kings in ancient times (and to the pope today through the kissing of his papal ring). We meet such an image in Psalm 2:

> *Now therefore, O kings, be wise;*
> > *be warned, O rulers of the earth.*
> *Serve the Lord with fear,*
> > *with trembling, kiss his feet.*[44]

But it's not so easy to kiss the sun (or the "Son") and mean it. It is not easy to give up one's autonomy by subjecting oneself to the sovereignty of another. Perhaps Judas learned this as he offered Jesus that kiss of betrayal.[45] And in that moment of indecision, the devil reaches for the jugular.

> *and he screams "why don't we celebrate?*
> *why don't we celebrate?*
> *life can make you sad*
> *come on, let's drive ourselves mad."*

The intensity of this scream is matched by the frenzied guitar solo that follows. Don't kiss the sun! Don't seek a resolution of this story or an absolution of those past regrets! Embrace the satanic celebration, a fist in the air against the marauding sun, a finger in the air to anything that would restrain our self-indulgent celebration! Three moments of dialogue with the devil. Three moments of temptation that culminate in a screaming invocation.

We need some time to consider this offer. So the artist gives us that time with a passionate guitar solo that brings us back to the beginning. The solo moves from the scream of the third temptation to a resolution that returns us to the original tune and the opening images.[46] In the last verse we are again "standing on a rock in a river." But now we are "staring at the rain made one." There is here a revelation of unity. Instead of "staring at the splintered sun" of the first verse, and instead of drowning ourselves in jewels, on the surface of this river we now see "flashing diamonds / rolling down the twilight canyon." No longer will we be tempted to roll down to the canyon in an act of suicidal desperation. This is a canyon of salvation; this is a river of flashing diamonds. So what should we do? "We shall kiss the sun in spite of him." We know how hard it is to kiss the sun and mean it. About this the devil was right. But the difficulty of offering such homage, the difficulty of such a spirituality of trust, is not enough to keep us from embracing the sun/Son. And in such an embrace, in such a resolution, there can indeed be a celebration. The artist now takes the devil's words as his own, and with an inviting sweetness of unspeakable beauty he concludes the song by singing repeatedly and in descending notes, "why don't we celebrate?" Here is an invitation to celebrate the forgiveness of those past regrets, the resolution of the quest for meaning, the unity of all things, and the resistance of the devil's temptation.

Such a resistance to Satan's temptation is also found in "Lament for the Last Days," on the 1975 album *Joy Will Find a Way*. In a song where we meet a dancer whose "flying footsteps in the snow / rhyme the rhythm of ruin" while a "night-bound choir inside chants on— / a hymn to brick and pistols," it is clear that we are living in the last days. Things are about to fall apart. We are facing an apocalyptic dissolution of all things. And the question becomes, to whom will we turn in the midst of this impending darkness? Cockburn is clear:

> oh, Satan, take thy cup away
> for i'll not drink your wine today
> i'll reach for the chalice of Light
> that stands on Jesus' table.

Where are we? We are standing in the falling dark of the last days, and there are before us two cups. Who are we? Battered and bruised lovers in a dangerous time. What's wrong? We keep reaching for the wrong cup. We keep falling for the temptation set before us to take the easy way out. What's the remedy? Reach for the chalice of light that stands on Jesus's table. Only in that choice can the celebration really begin.

# Betrayal and Shame

The chords are dark and weighty as the song begins. There is an ominous sense in the hall as the music fills the space. We can all feel it somewhere deep inside ourselves. And the opening line captures the feeling that has already taken hold in the audience: "There's a knot in my gut / As I gaze out today."[1] Yes, that is exactly it. A knot in our gut evoked almost immediately by those opening chords. A dis-ease born of anxiety and maybe guilt. There is something terribly, terribly wrong. But what is it? And where is it?

## The Beautiful Creatures Are Going Away

The artist continues, "There's a knot in my gut / As I gaze out today / On the planes of the city / All polychrome grey." Isn't that an oxymoron? Polychrome grey? Polychrome suggests a multiplicity of colors, but when you look at this city, somehow all of those colors seem to bleed into grey. More of a monotone than a polychrome. But "when the skin is peeled off it," when you peel back the polychrome grey skin of this city, "what is there to say?" Yes, that's the question. With this knot in our guts, with all of this "bad pressure coming down,"[2] bad pressure building up deep within us, what is there to say? And the singer answers by reaching for a falsetto that has never been his stock-in-trade. A falsetto that has him sing at a register so far beyond his normal voice that the words crack and strain, "The beautiful creatures are going away." The very vulnerability and fragility of this broken and oppressed creation is reflected in the artist's own vulnerability, his voice stretching to unattainable notes.

Bruce Cockburn is singing "Beautiful Creatures," and a hush falls over the audience that goes beyond the respect that they always show to this artist. This time, the hush has a different quality to it. This time, it is more like the meditative stillness of a sacred moment when a group of people face their own deep brokenness. When the skin is peeled off, when things are left bare for all to see, when we come before God in all of our broken complicity, what is there to say? Perhaps it is best to be still and say nothing. Perhaps this is a moment in which we need to look to our psalmist to sing the words that we cannot find for ourselves.

While the recorded version of "Beautiful Creatures" comes with full or-chestral accompaniment,[3] tonight it is just the singer and his guitar. There is something about the simple, solitary, sparse nature of this performance that intensifies and deepens the pathos of the song.

In "Broken Wheel," Cockburn asked, "This is my trouble / These were my fathers— / So how am I supposed to feel?"[4] Tonight he answers the question.

> Like a dam on a river
> My conscience is pressed
> By the weight of hard feelings
> Piled up in my breast
> The callous and vicious things
> Humans display
> The beautiful creatures are going away.

How is he supposed to feel? Like a dam about to burst, a dam about to burst into a flood of tears. "Look—see my tears— / they fill the whole night sky," he once sang.[5] And tonight anyone who has the eyes to see what the artist has seen will also have those eyes welling up with tears.

There is nothing self-righteous about this song. Cockburn tells us that *his* conscience is pressed, that there is a weight of hard feelings piled up in *his* breast. You have a sense from both the lyrics and the performance that he cannot absolve himself, and he will not allow us to absolve ourselves, from "the callous and vicious things / humans display." We are those humans.

This song names our brokenness and answers the question, what's wrong? with a disarming honesty. What's wrong? We are. What's wrong? We have proven ourselves to be callous and vicious creatures. What's wrong? The beau-tiful creatures are going away. Our callous and vicious way of life is driving away those beautiful creatures that we were called to love and care for. This is a song that mourns ecological despoliation. Species extinction isn't just a depressing statistic that leaves us numb or overwhelmed by too much infor-mation. No, if we are to be overwhelmed, then we must be overwhelmed by a grief that will break through our numbness. We must mourn the loss of these beautiful creatures. And so the artist follows the second chorus by holding a note for multiple measures, asking in that breaking, straining, painful, tear-invoking falsetto voice, "Why? Why?" We find ourselves catching our breath at the end of each question. If we are to ask this question with the intensity and honesty of this performance, then it needs to take something out of us, it needs to drain us of our breath. Maybe then we will begin to have some sense of what extinction is like.

In the final verse the artist brings his diagnosis of the human condition to a devastating conclusion.

> *From the stones of the fortress*
> *To the shapes in the air*
> *To the ache in the spirit*
> *We label despair*
> *We create what destroys*
> *Bind ourselves to betray*
> *The beautiful creatures are going away.*

What's wrong? "We create what destroys / Bind ourselves to betray." From the arrogant and self-protective structures of our culture to the emptiness of despair deep in our hearts, we are hell-bent on always creating what destroys. "Way out on the rim of the galaxy / the gifts of the Lord lie torn" precisely because our relationship with God, ourselves, and the rest of our creational kin has been imprisoned by a spirit of destruction. Once called to bless and to open up creation, we have been captivated by a spirit of cursing and closing down. And *captivated* is the right word. Cockburn tears the facade off our lives and tells us that we "*bind* ourselves to betray."[6] We are bound to betrayal. Through our own distorted volition, we bind ourselves to betrayal, allow ourselves to be held captive, taken as slaves, to betrayal. And because trust is at the very foundation of all life, because creation is rooted in covenant faithfulness, betrayal will always bring death. Betrayal unravels the very fabric of creation. No wonder the beautiful creatures are going away.

## A Most Horrid Blasphemy

So when Cockburn asks us, "if a tree falls in the forest does anybody hear?" he isn't just playing with the old philosophical quandary of whether a tree falling in the forest makes a sound if there isn't anyone present to hear it.[7] That is much too abstract and doesn't begin to address the reality of massive deforestation. The issue is whether anyone *can* really hear the cry of the forest that is being "hacked by parasitic greedhead scam." Can we hear the lament of the forest—that "ancient cord of coexistence"—as it is subjected to destruction, species extinction, and a thinning ozone layer, all for the sake of a "billion burgers worth of beef"?

We will hear the forest fall before the clear-cutting imperatives of a rapacious economy only if we first embrace that forest, indeed all of creation, as the generous gift of grace that it is. Hildegard of Bingen most evocatively put it this way:

> As the Creator loves His creation so creation loves the Creator. Creation, of course, was fashioned to be adored, to be showered, to be gifted with the love of the Creator. The entire world has been embraced by this kiss.[8]

Embraced by a kiss, creation is an ecstatic, generative response to the dancing, singing, calling love of the Creator. But what happens when creation is betrayed by a violent and exploitive kiss? What happens when the calling love of the Creator is drowned out by the roar of chainsaws and heavy machinery? What happens when love is replaced by violent greed? Blessing devolves into blasphemy.

Wendell Berry says that "our destruction of nature is not just bad stewardship, or stupid economics, or a betrayal of family responsibility; it is the most horrid blasphemy. It is flinging God's gifts into His face, as if they were of no worth beyond that assigned to them by our destruction of them."[9] Once you grasp the graced character of creation, once you have seen the Creator performing the creation-calling dance, and you have heard all of creation sing praise in response, then any defilement of creation will always be nothing less than blasphemy for you. If the entire world is indeed embraced by the divine kiss, then anything less will be sacrilege. The callous and vicious things that humans display to our creational kin are the most horrid blasphemy because they hold both the Creator and the creation in contempt. And in this song we hear a voice that is attuned to the lament of all creation. All of creation groans in travail, wails in labor pains, longing to be set free from this creation-denying force of betrayal and destruction.[10] No wonder the Torah says that the land itself will vomit out its inhabitants if they embrace betrayal and not faithfulness.[11] And we see such vomiting, such creational backlash and protest against human vicious exploitation and callous destruction, in the ecological crisis all around us.

Species extinction, global warming, smog alerts, water pollution, the clear-cutting of the rain forests, mountaintop removal, massive oil spills in the ocean, the loss of topsoil, the toxicity of much of agribusiness, and the depletion of the world's supply of potable water—it would take an incredible act of willful ignorance and denial to avert our gaze from the ecological crisis that we have inherited and are passing on to the next generations.[12] Such ecological devastation, sings Cockburn, is rooted in human callousness, violence, destruction, and betrayal. And here, Cockburn stands in the traditions of the prophets. A peaceable earth, called into being by the voice of the nova that is as gentle as the morning dew and founded upon the steadfast and faithful love of the Creator, is left gasping for breath at the hands of the Creator's disobedient image bearers.

We have seen in chapter 6 that the prophets understand ecological destruction as a direct consequence of human violence and sin. Because "there is no faithfulness or loyalty . . . in the land," proclaimed Hosea, "therefore the land mourns, and all who live in it languish; together with the wild animals and the birds of the air, even the fish of the sea are perishing."[13] Do you want to know the ultimate cause of species extinction? Then look no further than human infidelity. "The earth dries up and withers, the world languishes and withers; the heavens together with the earth. The earth lies polluted under its inhabitants," writes Isaiah. Why? Because "they have transgressed laws, violated the statutes, broken the everlasting covenant." That is why "a curse devours the earth." That is why "the earth is utterly broken." That is why "the earth is torn asunder."[14]

Covenant breaking always results in creational devastation precisely because God's covenant is always with all of creation. Our creational kin are not immune to our sin. The first time that we meet the word *covenant* in the Bible is directly after the Creator recognizes that there is nothing but an evil imagination in the human heart. And in an act of unspeakable grace the Creator decided to unite his already deeply broken heart with the deceitful and violent hearts of humans.[15] So after the deluge, after the flood that attempted to make a fresh start with this creation, God makes covenant with Noah. But that covenant is not just with Noah. That covenant is not limited to the human creature. Rather, we read that God says, "As for me, I am establishing my covenant with you and your descendants after you, and with *every living creature* that is with you, the birds, the domestic animals, and *every animal of the earth*."[16] Repeatedly in this text we read that the covenant is with *every living creature of all flesh*. And when the rainbow is set in the sky, we read, "I have set my bow in the clouds, and it shall be a sign of the covenant between me *and the earth*."[17] The earth that is the very foundation of all life is a party to the covenant. God makes covenant with the earth, and the rainbow is the sign of that covenant, the sign of God's faithfulness to all of creation, a sign of his promise to never again destroy the world by water.[18]

## Ain't It a Shame

But what happens if you see that rainbow sign in the midst of an environmental tragedy? In his post-Chernobyl blues song "Radium Rain," Cockburn has an ambivalent experience with a rainbow.

> *They're hosing down trucks at the border under*
> *a rainbow sign—*
> *the raindrops falling on my head burn into my*
> *  mind*
> *on a hillside in the distance there's a patch of*
> *green sunshine*
> *    ain't it a shame*
> *ain't it a shame*
> *about the radium rain*[19]

This is a rainbow of light refracted through the mist of no ordinary rain. This isn't even acid rain with its long-term environmental impact. No, this is radium rain. This is radioactive rain falling from the clouds after the meltdown of the Chernobyl nuclear reactor. No wonder these raindrops on the artist's head are burning into his mind. What does it mean when something as delightful as a spring shower is so toxic? What does it mean when the rainbow of covenantal faithfulness shines through that kind of rain? You see that patch of green sunshine where the sun has broken through the clouds, and all you can say is "shame." This radium rain is a matter of shame.

Of course the experts, the politicos, and the technocrats will all tell us that there is nothing to worry about. That was inferior Soviet technology. That could never happen here. But that is small comfort when you can't eat anything that grows in this radium rain and you better hold your breath when the cars go by.

There is a sense of impending collapse in this song. This radium rain is a portent of things to come. And in the midst of it all the artist has a vision of "a man on a roof with a blindfold on and a hand grenade in his fist." Notice the multifaceted precariousness of this situation. A man on a roof in the rain is scary enough. Add into the mix that this guy is blindfolded, and the level of danger rises considerably. Put a hand grenade in his fist, and we are facing a suicide bomber who threatens to destroy himself and all around him. This is our cultural and ecological situation. We are facing societal and environmental suicide. Wisely, the artist vacates the scene: "i walk stiff, with teeth clenched tight, filled with nostalgia for a clean wind's kiss." Longing for a moment of ecological homecoming, for a moment when a gentle misty wind is a kiss and not an attack, the artist, like the rest of us, tries to get away. And yet he must still sing his eco-blues song, "ain't it a shame . . . about the radium rain."

As he walks away, he sees a flock of birds.

> A flock of birds writes something on the sky in a
>     language i can't understand.
> God's graffiti—but it don't say why so much evil
>     seems to land on man
> when everyone I meet just wants to live and love
>     and get along as best they can
> ain't it a shame
> ain't it a shame
> about the radium rain

A flock of birds. God's graffiti. Not only is all of creation held in covenant with the Creator, but also all of creation is eloquent. This creation is not mute but speaks. Creation is revelatory. Just as the land can vomit out the inhabitants and creation can groan in travail, so also can creation speak—sometimes in praise, sometimes in sorrow—if we but have the ears to hear. This is, if you will, a creational glossolalia;

all of creation can speak in tongues, but we need to patiently learn the gift of interpretation. The birds write something on the sky, and the artist can't quite make out what they are saying. But he is pretty sure that they are not answering the question of "why so much evil seems to land on man." Maybe it is not their place to answer that question. Maybe that is our place. True enough, most folks just want to "get along as best they can," and yet there is this evil that seems to follow us everywhere we go.

The artist then launches into a blistering four-minute blues guitar solo that has all the emotional dynamics of a good cry. The solo reaches a wailing crescendo almost halfway through and then brings us ever more quietly to a concluding whimper. Four minutes of tears. Four minutes to come to grips with why so much evil does indeed "seem to land on man." Four minutes to share the grief of all creation. And perhaps four minutes to come to the sobering conclusion that we are the answer to our own question. Why does so much evil seem to land on man? Why do we have to live with this radium rain burning through our minds? Why are we faced with this violently suicidal situation? Maybe because "we create what destroys / bind ourselves to betray." That's why the beautiful creatures are going away. That's why we must live with the shame of this radium rain.

"Beautiful Creatures" and "Radium Rain" are songs of loss and deep pathos. But "too much pathos just makes you angry,"[20] and sometimes that anger overflows. I mean, what do you call the destruction of the world's rain forests? What words would you use to describe the breaking of this "ancient cord of coexistence," the demolition of the "climate control centre for the world?" How about, "green brain facing lobotomy"? How about, "hacked by parasitic greedhead scam"? When Cockburn sings "If a Tree Falls," we have moved beyond pathos to anger.[21]

> Cut and move on
> Cut and move on
> take out trees
> take out wildlife at a rate of a species every
>     single day
> take out people who've lived with this for 100,000
>     years—
> inject a billion burgers worth of beef—
> grain eaters—methane dispensers.

And so the question bears repeating, "if a tree falls in the forest does anybody hear?" Are we spiritually attuned enough to hear this wanton destruction as a "cortege rhythm of falling timber"? Do we notice that this is a funeral procession—the funeral of the forests and all that live therein, and also the funeral of our very civilization? If we cannot hear the forest fall, if we cannot hear the lament of creation through the deafening sound of the chainsaws, then we cannot begin to understand what is really wrong.

## The Trouble with Normal

Of course all of this is simply part of the normal course of things.[22] It is normal for human civilization to displace nature. It is normal for forests to be clear-cut in the name of progress. It is normal for an economy to grow without limits. It is normal for ecology to be sacrificed in the name of economy. All of this is normal. But the trouble with normal, Cockburn insists, is "it always gets worse."

> Callous men in business costume speak computerese
> Play pinball with the third world trying to keep it on its knees
> Their single crop starvation plans put sugar in your tea
> And the local third world's kept on reservations you don't see
> "It'll all go back to normal if we put our nation first"
> But the trouble with normal is it always gets worse.[23]

Agribusiness monocropping, the politics of panic with its preoccupation with national security, a moratorium of rights, the cultural genocide of the aboriginal peoples of the Americas, fashionable fascism—all of this, Cockburn insists, is nothing less than "the grinding devolution of the democratic dream."[24] The betrayal that has broken our relationship with God, reduced intimacy to sexual power games, and wreaked ecological havoc on the face of the earth also distorts our geopolitical lives and the socioeconomic structures within which we live.

"We create what destroys" and "bind ourselves to betray" because a prior binding has already happened—the binding of our imaginations.[25] Captive imaginations cannot conceive of life outside the constrictions of normalcy. But Cockburn takes it to be the artist's calling to see otherwise, to be able to see through the lies,[26] the reifications, the false sense of normality that will leave us numb, "paralyzed in the face of it all,"[27] with a defeated sense of resignation before the inevitable. In a recent interview Cockburn described his art in relation to political and economic forces this way: "State powers are interested in keeping us numb and asleep. We need to stay awake. Part of my job is to help people stay awake—and to help myself stay awake—by looking at these situations and writing songs about them. It's up to the listeners what they want to do about it, but I need to be a witness."[28]

What's wrong is that the forces of oppression have lulled us to sleep. Cockburn's art calls us to wake up. What's wrong is that violent repression dresses itself up as freedom and "they call it democracy."[29]

> padded with power here they come
> international loan sharks backed by the guns
> of market hungry military profiteers
> whose word is a swamp and whose brow is smeared
> with the blood of the poor

*who rob life of its quality*
*who render rage a necessity*
*by turning countries into labour camps*
*modern slavers in drag as champions of freedom*

*sinister cynical instrument*
*who makes the gun into a sacrament*
*the only response to this deification*
*of tyranny by so-called "developed" nations'*
*idolatry of ideology . . .*

*IMF dirty MF*
*takes away everything it can get*
*always making certain that there's one thing left*
*keep them on the hook with insupportable debt.*

With prophetic clarity, in this 1985 song Cockburn sees through what passes for democracy and development. In the tradition of the biblical prophets, Cockburn rails against the "deification / of tyranny by so-called 'developed' nations' / idolatry of ideology." The mournful guitar solo at the end of "Call It Democracy" brings to mind the cry of the poor who suffer under the oppression of the economic and political structures that go by the name "democracy."

Deification, idolatry, ideology—this is the making divine of what is a human construct, the idolatrous reification of ideology so that its constructed, particular, and self-interested character is disguised as simply the way things are. Ideology always invests the political and economic structures of oppression with divine power. This is always the strategy of empire, whether it be Babylon, Rome, or the Pax Americana. All empires present themselves as the benevolent bearers of the direction of history. And the present hegemony of Western, especially American, power is no different. "Modern slavers in drag as champions of freedom." Think of Reagan, Bush Sr. and Jr., Rumsfeld, Cheney, and their ideological grandfather, Milton Friedman—all of them in drag.

Cockburn's critique is harsh. This is an ideology that will "spend a buck to make a buck," but "you don't really give a flying f— about the people in misery." As a result of that line a Parental Advisory label gets slapped on the album. What kind of language is that for an artist who is supposedly a Christian? It is precisely the kind of language that we would expect from a prophetic voice. The prophets insist that idolatry is always a matter of "whoredom," or "harlotry." "The spirit of whoredom is within them," writes the prophet Hosea.[30] "A spirit of whoredom has led them astray, and they have played the whore, forsaking their God."[31] "You have played the whore. . . . You have loved a prostitute's pay on all threshing floors."[32] This is hard-hitting stuff. But if we were to translate that language into modern idiom in a way that would capture the offensiveness of this prophetic critique, we would say that idolatry is always a matter of "screwing around." If you get in bed with idols, the prophets would say, then you will always get screwed. Refusing to "know the Lord" always results in illegitimate copulation with idols.

No wonder Cockburn found it necessary to employ prophetic imagery to describe the neoliberal economics and imperial politics of the Reagan era.

> In the bar, in the senate, in the alley, in the study
> Pimping dreams of riches for everybody
> "Something for nothing, new lamps for old
> And the streets will be platinum, never mind gold"
> Well, hey, pass it on
> Misplaced your faith and the candy man's gone
> I hate to tell you but the candy man's gone.[33]

This secularized faith, with its technologically achieved eschatological hope, is a misplaced faith akin to the whoring after idolatry so graphically depicted throughout the prophetic literature.[34] While these pimped dreams have all the lasting power of a quick trick with a cheap hooker, they nonetheless wield a destructive power in our world. This kind of misplaced faith always results in violent oppression. Aboriginal peoples relegated to apartheid-style reservation systems,[35] Latin American refugees and shanty dwellers struggling against brutal dictatorships,[36] the proliferation of landmines that makes the land of home deadly,[37] and ecological despoliation that threatens to render this "bluegreen ball in black space" fundamentally hostile to human habitation[38]—these are the socioeconomic, geopolitical, and cultural-ecological realities of late-twentieth-century global capitalism.

What was true in the 1980s is only intensified in the twenty-first century.

> Brand new century private penitentiary
> Bank vault utopia padded for the few
> And its tumours for the masses, coughing for the masses
> Earphones for the masses and they all serve you
>
> Trickle down give /em the business
> Trickle down supposed to give us the goods
> Cups held out to catch a bit of the bounty
> Trickle down everywhere trickle down blood.[39]

This, Cockburn insists, is the captivity of our time; this is the spirit of our age, "the wind in which all must sway."[40] This is the spirit of global capitalism.

Global capitalism is the socioeconomic and geopolitical name given to the historical development of a borderless economic order ultimately ruled by transnational corporations. Under the guise of "trade liberalization," this is an economic order that moves vast sums of capital around the world every day in cyberspace and allows capital to invest in and exploit the human and natural resources of any nation if such investment and exploitation will increase the profit bottom line. Global capitalism, so defined, is a cultural force that "promises nothing less than the blossoming of a new civilization that will eventually bring an end to international conflict, resolve hitherto intractable problems like poverty and environmental degradation, and produce increased prosperity for all."[41] Cockburn believes that this is a hollow promise and an ideological cover for violence, oppression, and injustice. His appraisal comes to forceful expression in "Trickle Down":[42]

> *Take over takedown big bucks shakedown*
> *Schoolyard pusher offer anything-for-profit*
> *First got to privatize then you get to piratize*
> *Hooked on avarice—how do we get off it?*

This agenda of privatization, corporate takeovers, and trade liberalization is ultimately about transporting throughout the world a consumerist worldview wherein new markets will be available for our products because more and more people will be taken captive by the insatiability of avarice. Cockburn wants to help us kick the habit. Globalization "isn't just an aggressive stage in the history of capitalism . . . [but] a religious movement of previously unheard-of proportions," wherein "progress is its underlying myth, unlimited growth its foundational faith, the shopping mall . . . its place of worship, consumerism its overriding image, 'I'll have a Big Mac and fries' its ritual of initiation, and global consumerism its ultimate goal."[43] Therefore, Cockburn's art is self-consciously entering a spiritual battle zone, struggling with the principalities and powers of our age.

Here is the spiritual heart of our exile. It is not just that the forces of global capitalism render so many people socioeconomically, ecologically, and geopolitically homeless; but it is also that when such a home-destroying ideology dominates the spiritual landscape, when it creates such a world of sorrows, all sane people, all people with vision, will experience a profound homelessness.

What's wrong? Our bondage to betrayal and our penchant for destruction take on socioeconomic shape in structures of oppression. The violence of these political machinations and economic manipulations would serve to strip us of hope. But Cockburn has "seen the flame of hope among the hopeless / And that was truly the biggest heartbreak of all / That was the straw that broke me open."[44] Hopelessness is acquiescence to the empire, the powers of normalcy, and it is a luxury affordable only to those who can take their comfort from the empire. Cockburn's "hopeless," those who are victimized by the empire, those who are pawns in the moves of global capitalism, cannot, ironically, afford such a luxury. In the face of the death squads, there can be no postmodern ambiguity, no ethical undecidability. "If you think there's no difference between right and wrong," sings Cockburn, then "just go down to where the death squad lives." Because "without the could-be and the might-have-been / all you've got left is your fragile skin / and that ain't worth much down where the death squad lives."[45] Or, as he sings in his 1996 song "Night Train,"

> And in the absence of a vision there are nightmares
> And in the absence of compassion there is cancer
> Whose banner waves over palaces and mean streets
> And the rhythm of the night train is a mantra.[46]

What's wrong? In the absence of a vision there are nightmares, and we are sorely lacking an alternative vision. What's wrong? We are so bound to betrayal, we are so callous and vicious in our campaign of destruction, that we have no resources of compassion within us. What's wrong? We live in the falling dark. So what do you do with darkness?

# What Do
# You Do with
# Darkness?

Where are we? We are in a world of wonders, called into being through the extravagant love and ecstatic generative dance of the Lord of the starfields.

Who are we? We are humans, angel beasts, principal dancers in the dance of creation, called to bear the image of the Lord of the dance.

What's wrong? We live in the falling dark, subject to idolatry and ideology, perpetrating betrayal and violence. We live in a world of broken promises, misplaced faith, and distorted stewardship.

Here, in summary, is the way in which Christian faith answers the first three worldview questions. And we have seen that Bruce Cockburn's art proves to be profoundly fruitful in reawakening a Christian imagination. Cockburn offers us images, metaphors, and narratives, all embodied in the movement of sound and rhythm, that can help us both wake up to this tragedy and open our eyes to a different way of seeing. While Cockburn will remind us that "you've never seen everything," we realize nonetheless that through his art we've seen much. Sometimes too much. Sometimes he opens our eyes to things that we would prefer not to see. Things about our world and things about ourselves. That is, after all, the calling of the prophet. That *is* the ministry of the psalmist. Again, I find that Cockburn's richly evocative lyrics, carried by his evocative and compelling music, resonate with biblical faith in ways that suggest fresh meanings.

What's wrong? We live in the falling dark. And while there are moments when we can hear those "rumours of glory" whispering in the dark, the darkness seems to continue and deepen unabated. We share this experience with the biblical writers. They too lived in exile, under empire, and in the falling dark. So I find myself again drawn to weave together images borrowed from Cockburn with images borrowed from the Scriptures.

## Light in the Darkness

Exile is invariably described as a time of darkness. How can you see the light when you live under the imposing shadow of empire? Well, the prophet Isaiah had a vision of light.

> Arise, shine; for your light has come,
>    and the glory of the Lord has risen upon you.
> For darkness shall cover the earth,
>    and thick darkness the peoples;
> but the Lord will arise upon you,
>    and his glory will appear over you.[1]

So what happens when the light shines? What happens when those who have lived in the repressive shadow of empire come into the light? And what happens to those geopolitical forces of darkness? They too come into the light.

> Nations shall come to your light,
>    and kings to the brightness of your dawn.[2]

Isaiah's vision of homecoming goes beyond the joy of sons and daughters marching home to see an economic and geopolitical transformation. The wealth of the nations—gold and frankincense, lumber from Lebanon, flocks from Kedar—will all come flowing into that restored city. And even the ships of Tarshish, those enemy vessels that were used to exploit and attack the people, will return. But now they will carry your children home from exile and bring the silver and gold of the empire to be employed in the rebuilding project.

The vision gets crazier and crazier. In this vision of security and hospitality ("your gates shall always be open"[3]), the oppressor will become a servant, and the returned exiles will "suck the breasts of kings."[4] Kings that once sucked the life out of the people will now become a source of sustenance.

And then the prophet reaches a crescendo when he proclaims,

> I will appoint Peace as your overseer
>    and Righteousness as your taskmaster.

*Violence shall no more be heard in your land,*
*devastation or destruction within your borders;*
*you shall call your walls Salvation,*
*and your gates Praise.[5]*

A people who have been ruled by the violence of empire will be overseen by "Peace," and the cruel injustice of the empire's economics will be replaced by a righteous justice. A people who have known only violence are offered a vision in which the harsh cries of violence are no longer heard in the land. Instead of being walled in by imperial enslavement, "Salvation" is their wall, and the mournful lament in the gates is replaced with "Praise." The people who have lived in the falling dark have seen light.

We have seen in the last two chapters that the darkness is thick and pervasive. It sometimes looks like this darkness will indeed overcome the light. But Bruce Cockburn is a singer of songs of hope. So what happens when we allow the poetry of Isaiah and Bruce Cockburn to play off each other? Maybe it looks something like the following.[6]

### What Do You Do with Darkness?

*What do you do with darkness?*

*Be at home in it, yet be hungry for the dawn?*
*Kick at it until it bleeds daylight?*

*What do you do when you live in the falling dark?*

*Look for the crack where the light gets in?*
*Sing "I saw the light"?*
*"This little light of mine"?*

*Maybe all of these things.*

*But what do you do when the darkness is so pervasive,*
*so overpowering,*
*that it has captured your imagination?*

*What do you do when it is so dark that you simply can't imagine any light?*
*When there are no celestial horses,*
*no streams of beautiful lights in the night,*
*you can't get your night vision,*
*and there is no clarity of night.*

*What if across these fields of mourning*
*you can't see the light in the distance?*

*What do you do then?*

   *You suck the breasts of kings.*

*That's right—you suck the breasts of kings.*
   *Not queens, but kings.*

*In the falling dark*
*a light has come.*
*The darkness shall cover the earth,*
*and it is a thick darkness.*
*Thick with oppression,*
   *thick with displacement,*
   *thick with violence,*
   *thick with deceit,*
   *thick with the blood of the poor.*

*And against all of the evidence,*
   *against anything we can see in this thick darkness,*
   *a voice cries out,*
       *"Arise, shine; for your light has come,*
       *and the glory of Yahweh has risen upon you."*

*Where? Where is this light?*
*It's too dark, I can't see a damn thing.*
*But the voice continues,*
   *"Yes, it is dark,*
   *yes, it is a thick darkness,*
   *but Yahweh will arise upon you,*
   *and his glory shall appear over you."*

*Glory?*
*In the darkness?*

*Yahweh's glory?*
*Here?*

*I'm sorry, but Yahweh left town years ago,*
   *the glory has departed,*
   *the weight of glory has been replaced*
   *by an unbearable lightness,*
   *and that isn't the kind of light we are looking for.*

*But the voice continues.*
   *"Lift up your eyes and look around:*
   *your sons shall come from far away*
   *and your daughters shall be carried on nurses' arms."*

*There's a homecoming afoot,*
*the exiles are returning.*

*I got a dream and I'm not alone*
*Darkness dead and gone*
*All the people marching home*
*Kissing the rush of dawn*

*Santiago sunrise*
*See them marching home*
*See them rising like grass through cement*
*In the Santiago dawn*

*The darkness starts to dissipate.*
*I can almost see them.*
*I can almost see the displaced, the homeless,*
*the battered and abused . . .*
*I can almost see them coming home.*

*But the voice isn't finished.*
*Keep your eyes open*
*and in your night vision*
*you will see more amazing things.*

*Look over there . . . what's happening over there?*
*Are they ships?*
*Isn't that a naval fleet?*
*Aren't those ships of war?*
*What are they doing here?*
*They bring darkness and we're looking for light.*
*But wait, what's that I see on the decks?*
*It's the homecoming ones.*
*There's Martin and Oscar, Dorothy and Clare.*
*And who is with them?*
*What else do I see?*
*I see the very abundance of creation on these ships.*
*These ships that have plundered the nations*
*now return with what they have stolen.*
*It's almost as if it's the year of Jubilee.*

*And the voice says,*
*can you see it?*
*The glory is returning,*
*do you know what time it is?*
*It is no longer time for mourning,*
*but it is time for dancing.*

*It is no longer time for God's absence,*
  *it is glory time.*
*It is no longer time for darkness,*
  *the light is beginning to shine.*

*Darkness, dead and gone.*

*So I conclude that I must be sleeping.*
  *This must be a dream,*
  *and when I awake the disappointment will be too much for me.*
  *This is all impossible.*

*So the voice speaks again,*
  *If you can't see,*
  *then listen.*

*I'm doing a new thing,*
  *your gates shall always be open,*
  *they shall never be shut, not even in the night,*
  *so that the wealth of the nations will be able to come to you.*

  *The wealth of nations?*
  *The resources exploited by the powerful at the expense of the poor?*
  *The wealth of nations?*
  *A mere euphemism for the wealth of the elite?*
  *How can the wealth of nations be anything but a tool of oppression?*

*The voice replies,*
  *"You shall suck the milk of nations,*
  *you shall suck the breasts of kings."*

*The nations that have sucked the very lifeblood*
  *out of the poor,*
  *and out of the creation itself,*
  *shall become a source of sustenance?*
*Can I begin to imagine such a thing?*

*Not only that,*
  *you shall suck the breasts of kings.*

*As if the voice knew that this was all impossible to imagine,*
  *the voice put to us an even more impossible image;*
    *suck the breasts of kings.*
  *Life-giving sustenance,*
    *milk,*
    *from kings!*

*And in the impossibility of the image,*
*the light started to shine brighter.*

*And then the voice said that Peace shall be our overseer*
*and Righteousness will be our taskmaster.*
*Peace in a life that has been overseen by war,*
*Righteousness as our guide in a life that has known only injustice.*
*And so violence will no longer be heard in your land:*
*no longer will we hear the cry of children with empty stomachs,*
*no longer will we hear the moaning of a woman dying of AIDS,*
*no longer will we hear the violent shouts of family abuse,*
*no longer will we hear the deafening blast of the bombs,*
*no longer will violence be heard in our land,*
*because our walls shall be called salvation,*
*and our gates—those always open gates—shall be called praise.*

*Salvation,*
*the restoration of all things,*
*creation's groaning finished,*
*enmity gone,*
*life abundant,*
*a life suffused with justice and love,*
*care and hospitality.*
*Our walls shall be called "Salvation."*
*We will inhabit salvation,*
*Be at home in salvation.*

*If this is true, then no wonder our gates will be called "Praise."*
*Praise that breaks through the darkness.*
*Praise that gives thanks for the light.*
*Praise that rejoices in the glory.*
*A homemaking praise for a homecoming people.*

*What do you do with darkness?*
*Just beyond the range of normal sight,*
*just beyond the range of what we can see in the dark,*
*there's this glittering joker . . .*

*What do you do with darkness?*
*I was a dweller by a dark stream*
*a crying heart hooked on a dark dream,*
*in my convict soul I saw your love gleam,*
*and you showed me what you've done.*
*Jesus, thank you, joyous Son.*

## Praying in the Dark

What do you do in the dark? In "Postcards from Cambodia," Cockburn is faced with a darkness so deep and a brokenness so devastating that he has no recourse beyond prayer.

> *This is too big for anger,*
> *it's too big for blame.*
> *We stumble through history so*
> *humanly lame.*
> *So I bow down my head*
> *Say a prayer for us all*
> *That we don't fear the spirit*
> *when it comes to call.*[7]

And so I offer a prayer at the end of this chapter, at the end of this exploration of life "in the falling dark." This is a communal prayer that changes its shape to fit the changing needs of the community that is called to prayer. This particular prayer was written for Holy Week. Based on Cockburn's prayerful song "Dweller by a Dark Stream,"[8] the prayer is partially sung. A musical leader ("cantor") sings the verses of the song while the congregation sings the chorus as a response. A spoken prayer and times for silent and communal prayer are concluded with singing the last line of the chorus, "Jesus, thank you, joyous Son."[9]

*Leader*    Let us pray.

*Cantor*    It could have been me
put the thorns in your crown,
rooted as I am
in a violent ground.
How many times have I turned
your promise down,
still you pour out your love,
you pour out your love.

*People*    **I was a dweller by a dark stream**
**a crying heart hooked on a dark dream,**
**in my convict soul I saw your love gleam,**
**and you showed me what you've done.**
**Jesus, thank you, joyous Son.**

*Leader*    It was dark, Lord,
when you cried out.
It was dark,
as if all of creation was in mourning,

as if all of creation knew what you were doing on that cross,
as if all of creation knew what the people all missed.

*People*   **Jesus, thank you, joyous Son.**

*Cantor*   You entered a life like ours
to give us back our own.
You wanted us like you
as choosers not clones.
You offered up your flesh
and death was overthrown.
Now salvation is ours,
salvation is ours.

*People*   **I was a dweller by a dark stream**
**a crying heart hooked on a dark dream,**
**in my convict soul I saw your love gleam,**
**and you showed me what you've done.**
**Jesus, thank you, joyous Son.**

*Leader*   Jesus, forsaken one,
Jesus, who knows grief beyond all grief,
we pray for a world of grief,
a world of forsakenness.

[silent and spoken prayers for the world]

Come, Lord Jesus,
come Crucified One,
and set us free.

*People*   **Jesus, thank you, joyous Son.**

*Cantor*   So I'm walking this prison camp world.
I long for a glimpse of
the new world unfurled.
The chrysalis cracking
and moistened wings uncurl.
Like in the vision John saw,
the vision John saw.

*People*   **I was a dweller by a dark stream**
**a crying heart hooked on a dark dream,**
**in my convict soul I saw your love gleam,**
**and you showed me what you've done.**
**Jesus, thank you, joyous Son.**

*Leader*   It was dark, Lord,
dark in that cold grave.
And it got darker,
when that stone sealed your grave.
And it is still dark.
The darkness still threatens to overcome the light,
in the lives of the lonely,
the sick, the impoverished,
the frightened, the depressed.
And the stone is so heavy.
Who will roll away the stone?

[silent and spoken prayers for those in any kind of need]

Come, Lord Jesus,
come and break the bonds of darkness,
roll away the stone,
and set us free.

*People*   **Jesus, thank you, joyous Son.**

# Justice and Jesus

"The world demands to be described," I quoted Bono in the first chapter of this book. And so, "painters, poets, journalists, pornographers, and sitcom writers, by accident or design, are just following orders, whether from high or low, to describe the world we're in."[1] Whether our descriptions are debased or inspired, mundane or profound, we describe the world because we must. Such description is at the heart of human life in this world. But it is not simply that we are incurably world-describing, culture-forming animals. Rather, says Bono, we are "following orders." Describing the world is a calling, and that calling can come from sources that are either high or low. And artists have a particular role in fulfilling this human calling.

Recall, however, that Bono has also said that "as much as we need to describe the world we do live in, we need to dream up the kind of world we *want to live in.*" We paint our pictures, write our poetry, and compose our songs "above all *to glimpse another way of being.*"[2] This has something to do, I have suggested, with having a vision that is "just beyond the range of normal sight."

Consider the psalmist. Through impassioned, elegant, and often pained language, the psalmist describes the world in all of its beauty and broken-ness, its wonder and disappointment. Indeed, in the very act of description the psalmist evokes a world and invites those who sing these psalms to enter this world. While there is a profound sense in which the world is "given" as a reality prior to our description, it is also equally true that "there is no 'world' for us until we have named and languaged and storied whatever is. What we take to be the nature of things has been shaped by calling it so."[3] So, in Israel's

Psalms the singing community engages in an act of world construction that is often polemical and in tension with other worldviews.[4] This is very important if we are to understand human culture, not least the cultural act of songwriting. Humans are world makers. But we do not all construct the same world.

Consider Cockburn's specifically political songs. The world that he describes in songs like "People See through You," "Nicaragua," "Call It Democracy," "Rocket Launcher," "Stolen Land," "Trickle Down," and many, many others is decidedly different from the world inhabited by neoliberal politicians, economists, journalists, and your everyday North American consumer. Moreover, songs like "Creation Dream," "Starwheel," and "Lord of the Starfields" also invite us to live in a world some distance removed from a narrowly materialistic world of mute objects available for human economic exploitation. The world is first and foremost a "gift," not raw materials. So Cockburn engenders not only a different world but also a world in tension with other visions of life. In this way, the artist takes on the mantle of both psalmist and prophet. As we have seen, as a psalmist Cockburn offers us songs of lament and praise that describe and evoke a world of pained injustice and unspeakable beauty, a world that is "battered and bruised, yet lovely."[5] And as a prophet he proposes a vision of the world that tears the facade off the lies, the cover-ups, the injustices. In this way, Cockburn is an artist of prophetic critique.

But just as lament and praise must always go together for the psalmist, so also must prophetic critique always be coupled with a language that energizes prophetic hope. Offering a vision of another world in which we might live, prophets, psalmists, poets, and songwriters "are making available a world that does not yet exist beyond their imagination. . . . The poets want us to re-experience the present world under a different set of metaphors, and they want us to entertain an alternative world not yet visible."[6] Hence, critique must give way to hope.

Another way of saying this is that once you have described the world, identified the human vocation in this world, and named that which renders this world a site of brokenness, you need to go on and begin to address the redemption of this world. In other words, once you have answered the first three worldview questions—where are we? who are we? and what's wrong?—the fourth worldview question—what's the remedy?—cries out for response. If the artist does not move from prophetic critique to prophetic hope, if he or she does not move in some way from naming the problem to imaginatively suggesting a path of resolution and redemption, then the artist simply joins the ranks of "the singers of songs without hope" and will "need to take a hard look and start from scratch again."[7]

## Christendom and the "Postmodern Turn"

Bruce Cockburn is a singer of songs of hope. Indeed, the critique that he offers is the mirror side of his hope. It is precisely the gap between his envisioned hope and the reality that he confronts every day that gives birth to the most abrasive critique that we meet in his songs. And while that hope continues to evolve and change as the artist's experience widens and deepens, it is nonetheless clear that this is a hope rooted in Jesus Christ. And herein is a problem. As we have seen, while Cockburn has never shrunk back from naming his spirituality as Christian in origin and direction, and while we can see allusions to both the Bible and Jesus throughout his body of work, Cockburn nonetheless wears the name "Christian" uneasily. Too much that goes by the name of Christ is offensive and embarrassing and seems to be the opposite of the Jesus that Cockburn's music bears witness to. For example, in "Red Brother Red Sister" he sings of going to a powwow where he "felt the people's love / joy flow around." And it left him "crying just thinking about it / how they used my Saviour's name to keep you down."[8] Or more abrasively, in "Gospel of Bondage" Cockburn rails against the religious Right in America:

> You read the Bible in your special ways
> You're fond of quoting certain things it says—
> Mouth full of righteousness and wrath from above
> But when do we hear about forgiveness and love?[9]

Like so many of us, Bruce Cockburn bears the mantle of Christendom as a heavy burden on his shoulders. So when we begin to reflect on how Cockburn's hope is shaped by his understanding and experience of Jesus, we need to recognize the ambiguous relationship that he has with "Christianity."

This ambiguity, this wariness about presenting one's answer to the fourth worldview question with too much authoritative finality, is not unique to Christians, however. As legitimate as Christian embarrassment about our own violent past (and present) might be, there is a wider cultural sense of the danger of absolutism in addressing questions of worldview, religion, or ultimate perspectives. Some have called this the "postmodern turn."

Kenneth Gergen has written that "when convinced of the truth or right of a given worldview, a culture has only two significant options: totalitarian control of the opposition or annihilation of it."[10] Whether or not these are the only options, this has in fact been the legacy of much human history, not least the colonial history of the West over the last five hundred years.

Herein is the ethical heart of the postmodern problem with "Truth." Such uppercase "Truth" is necessarily exclusionary, arrogant, and violent. If one worldview, cultural perspective, or religion has the "Truth" and also has cultural, economic, and political power to back up that "Truth," then what will that culture do with those who do not share it? What will it do with the unenlightened, savage, barbarian, strange, infidel? You can see how this view of "Truth," this way of answering the fourth worldview question, this construal of the world and its future hope, not only marginalizes all other perspectives but also provides ideological legitimation for violence against the "other," against the "outsider." Gergen is right. The eradication of the other, either through control (and forced conversion is clearly a mechanism of such control) or annihilation of all such infidels (pagans, heathen, savages . . . take your pick), seems to be the prevalent option. It is no wonder, therefore, that postmodern philosopher Jean-François Lyotard tells us that modernity has given us "as much terror as we can take."[11] Renouncing the nostalgia for total and final worldviews because they seem to be inherently violent is a characteristic postmodern theme.[12]

Like many of us, Cockburn shares this postmodern sensibility. He may well have come to Christian faith as the foundation of his own vision of life, and he may well be open about employing Christian metaphors, narratives, images, and allusions throughout his lyrics, but he insists on bearing such witness with profound humility.

## What's Been Done in the Name of Jesus

Consider his 1981 reggae song "Justice." This song can be interpreted as a post-modern Christian reflection on the violent power of ideology. The first verse raises a series of rhetorical questions about the various ideologies on offer:

> What's been done in the name of Jesus
> What's been done in the name of Buddha
> What's been done in the name of Islam
> What's been done in the name of man
> What's been done in the name of liberation
> And in the name of civilization
> And in the name of race
> And in the name of peace
>> everybody
>> loves to see
>> justice done
>> on somebody else.[13]

Cataloging religions of both the East and the West, together with ideologies of secular humanism ("in the name of man"), Marxism ("in the name of liberation"), and the progress mythology ("in the name of civilization"), together with racism and even a falsely construed "peace," Cockburn discerns that terrible things are "done" in the name of these ideals. Invariably, these things are done to those who do not share that ideology and are seen to be obstacles or threats to the cultural and historical dominance of such ideologies.

But the artist begins self-critically with his own faith, "what's been done in the name of Jesus." We don't need to go as far back as the Crusades or the religious wars in Europe or even the Salem witch trials to cringe at what's been done and continues to be done in the name of Jesus.

In Canada, aboriginal children were forcibly removed from their homes and placed in church-administered residential schools to assimilate them into white culture. This was an act of cultural genocide, in the name of Jesus. "God hates fags" placards are waved outside of gay-affirming churches, and discriminatory legislation is passed against homosexual men and lesbians. All in the name of Jesus. Nationalistic ideology, especially in times of war, is legitimated in the name of Jesus. A rampantly consumeristic "prosperity gospel," wherein God wants us to be wealthy and to consume the earth's resources at an ever-escalating rate, is proclaimed in the name of Jesus. Indeed, ecological degradation is passed off as irrelevant in light of the coming apocalypse that will burn everything up anyway. All in the name of Jesus. No wonder Cockburn hesitates to call himself a Christian without some clear disclaimers. Anyone who dares to evoke Jesus in the light of all of this abuse must do so in humility and in repentance for all that has been done in his name.

Cockburn's point, however, like the postmodern critique of ideology, is even more radical than this. It isn't just that religions, worldviews, and other kinds of perspectives and ideals can sometimes be employed for exclusionary violence. Rather, the point is that *any* vision that makes large claims, *any* vision that purports to grasp the way things ultimately are, *any* ideal that claims universal finality, and *any* worldview that offers certain and absolute answers to the questions of where we are, who we are, what's wrong, and what is the remedy, will *necessarily* legitimate ideological marginalization and violence against outsiders. *Everybody* loves to see justice done, that is, justice meted out, on somebody else. Indeed, the punishment of the other for being the other is always construed as a matter of justice. Those folks are getting their "just desserts." No wonder George W. Bush's initial name for his post-9/11 antiterrorism campaign was "Operation Infinite Justice." The president and the majority of the American people wanted to see "justice done on somebody else." And characteristically, the president attributed to himself and to the ideology of America the moral authority to enact such "infinite justice." Worldviews that aspire to such totality tend to be totalitarian in character.[14]

So in the second verse, the artist asks, "Can you tell me how much bleeding / it takes to fill a word with meaning?" Our words, our slogans, our names, sings Cockburn, find their meaning, breath, and light in ideological violence. How much blood needs to be shed to give meaning to words like "freedom," "democracy," or "justice"? And "how much, how much death" will it take to give breath to phrases like "national security," "in God we trust," "Operation Infinite Justice," "support our troops," and "the free market"? And "how much, how much, how much flame / gives light to a name / for the hollow darkness / in which nations dress?" How many bombs must be dropped? How many people killed? How much environmental destruction? You see, without the flames of such violence, all that is left is the hollow darkness. There would appear to be no light available in such ideologies apart from the light of "the rockets' red glare, the bombs bursting in air," to cite the American national anthem.

The postmodern temptation in the face of such "justice" is to embrace a worldview that avoids all totalizing violence by affirming a "laidback pluralism" that will accept the legitimacy of all beliefs.[15] Sounds good compared to the alternative, but how good is this? While the affirmation of difference and plurality would seem to be preferable to the imposed hegemony of one worldview over all others, I wonder whether such a pluralism is achieved at the expense of taking any of these worldviews seriously. Indeed, I wonder whether such a postmodern pluralism really takes us much beyond the commodification of all of life that we have seen in the globalization of late capitalism. Peter Berger has said it well: "The pluralist situation is above all a market situation. In it, the religious institutions become marketing agencies and the religious traditions become consumer commodities."[16] We might add that all perspectives, all worldviews, all visions of life are reduced to commodities. Nicholas Boyle perceptively notes that "the belief that there is, not a single truth and a single world, but a multiplicity of mutually untranslatable perspectives, is strangely analogous to the belief that the market is a boundless medium within which perfect competition is possible between an infinite number of discrete commercial identities."[17] In such a construal of pluralism, "the moral world, like the material world, is supremely represented as a shopping mall: it is now open to us to stroll between the shelves and pick out, or opt for . . . whatever takes our fancy."[18]

Note, however, two consequences of such a postmodern pluralism. First, if all competing worldviews are no more than alternative visions of life that can be "bought into" and then discarded when they wear out or another perspective gains some market dominance, then isn't such a cultural reductionism its own form of violence? I mean, how seriously does one respect the otherness of an alternative perspective or take the time to listen intently to another voice when it is no more than a matter of personal consumerist whim which vision one adopts? Discerning spiritual truth takes more than comparative shopping and reading *Consumer Reports*.

But more importantly, if the metaphor of the shopping mall or the market is indeed apt in describing the postmodern situation, then how pluralistic is this? Note that it is one particular vision of life, that of liberal democratic capitalism, that sets the terms by which all other worldviews are understood. This is consumerism dressed up as choice. This kind of ideology looks suspiciously like Cockburn's "modern slavers in drag as champions of freedom."[19]

If we want to get beyond the violence of an ideologically imposed "justice," then neither self-enclosed ideologies nor the laidback pluralism of postmodernity will do. Neither perspective will engender any serious listening to other voices. The former fails to do so because these voices are illegitimate, and the latter because they are really not that important.

The question is, how can we break free of the ideologically self-justifying violence of worldviews that actually function as *world*views without losing ourselves in a promiscuous spirituality of belief consumerism? In the third verse of this song, Cockburn's answer would appear to be threefold.

First, we must acknowledge the truth of the postmodern critique. The third verse of "Justice" begins: "Everybody's seen the things they've seen / we all have to live with what we've been." We painfully know from history that the greater the ideal and the loftier the vision, the more devastating and brutal can be the reality. Whether we are talking about the Stalinist reality of the Marxist myth, the necessity of a growing gap between rich and poor in a capitalist economy, or the tragic emotional and sexual abuse that happens in the neat nuclear-family homes of the suburbs, we all have to live with what we've seen in the world around us and with what we have seen in our own broken and compromised lives. So the first step in breaking the grip of ideology on our lives is confessing our complicity in its self-protective violence and exclusion.

Second, exclusion must be replaced by the embrace of radical hospitality.[20] "When they say charity begins at home / they're not just talking about a toilet and a telephone." I take this to be a call to hospitality. There can be no real hearing and listening to the voice of another person without such hospitality. Hospitable embrace welcomes the other person and attends to, cares for, respects, and, indeed, loves the guest.

It is, however, not so easy to either acknowledge one's guilt or extend such hospitality. And if the iron grip of ideology is to be broken in our lives, then it won't happen in the cacophony of the postmodern mall. Rather, Cockburn sings that we have "got to search the silence of the soul's wild places." Here is the third requirement if ideology's grip is to be broken. We need to shut out the cacophony for a while, find a place where the deafening bombs of ideological violence cannot be heard, and be quiet in ourselves. And in such a meditative quietness we will come face-to-face with our complicity, our guilt, with what we know has been going on in our lives. And, if we are Christians, we will also face with shame the self-justifying and violent invocation of the name of Jesus.

Having shut out the words soaked in blood, the slogans of death, and false names born of ideological violence, the artist calls us to "search the silence of the soul's wild places / for a voice that can cross the spaces." We must listen for a voice that is different from all other voices. A voice that can bridge the spaces that these exclusionary "definitions we love create— / these names for heaven, hero, tribe and state."[21] This is a voice that deconstructs these ideologies, a voice that can smash these idols. It is a prophetic voice.

In the final verse of "Gospel of Bondage" we meet similar themes:

> *Sometimes you can hear the Spirit whispering to you,*
> *But if God stays silent, what else can you do*
> *Except listen to the silence? if you ever did you'd surely see*
> *That God won't be reduced to an ideology.*[22]

In the face of loud, belligerent, and arrogant voices, Cockburn counsels a more humble listening. Perhaps God's voice remains silent because the Holy One can't get a word in edgewise. Perhaps we are listening for the voice of one who "will not cry or lift up his voice, or make it heard in the street."[23] This requires a deep listening and a deep receptivity. But the artist is sure that if we listen to the silence, one thing will become clear. God won't be reduced to an ideology. And especially not ideologies constructed in God's name!

In the silence there is, nonetheless, a voice. But there is no point in there being such a voice if there is no listening. And here we see again the deep resonances between Cockburn's lyrics and the Scriptures of ancient Israel. "Hear, O Israel: The LORD is our God, the LORD alone."[24] "Shema Israel." "Listen, Israel." That is what it means to be Israel and to be the New Israel. Israel is a people constituted and characterized by listening to the voice "that can cross these spaces." The voice of God, heard for Israel in the Torah, made flesh for Christians in Jesus, is foundational for covenant people. If you forget that voice, if you stop listening, then you forget who you are and slip into a spiritual amnesia. This is a voice that calls for covenantal faithfulness in the face of the spiritual promiscuity that has become ideologically encoded in a postmodern culture of global capitalism.

What is remarkable about the account of hearing the voice of God during the exodus, however, is that the text makes a point of saying that the voice came only as a voice. "You heard the sound of words but saw no form; there was only a voice."[25] There was no form, just a voice. This is very important for biblical faith. If God could be rendered in a form, captured in a form, an image, then God could be domesticated and made docile. The voice would then behave itself and be employed to legitimate our own ideology as we confidently proclaim, "We have the voice on our side! See, there it is in the temple, in the theological tradition, in the religious language game that we play and the subculture that we erect."

Moses insists that the voice had no form. It is not fixed, final, controllable. It cannot be domesticated. Rather, the voice is dynamic, moving, pulsing, liberating, addressing, inviting, pleading, calling. And because the voice has no form, no image, it calls upon those who will listen to this voice to have no graven images, no idols. And that is why listening to this voice, which can cross the spaces of our ideological definitions, can liberate us from the destructive power of idolatry. You see, idolatry is at the very foundation of ideology.[26] And once we attempt to monopolize the voice through idolatry, then we lose the voice, because idols are deaf and dumb. They have nothing to say.[27]

That is why, after the idolatrous cacophony has been quelled, Cockburn calls us to search the silence, to hear the voice. Replacing the "idolatry of ideology"[28] with a humble listening to a "still small voice,"[29] perhaps we can hear an answer to the question that burns most deeply in our hearts: is there a remedy to the self-destructive violence at the heart of humanity? Perhaps in such listening we will meet a "justice" that is not about marginalizing and excluding, but about healing, a justice that restores and welcomes—perhaps even a true justice in the name of Jesus.

Justice must take flesh; it must be manifest in real lives in real time. The voice must take shape somewhere, in someone, and in some particular place. So, recognizing in candid honesty and humility all that has been done in the name of Jesus, we need nonetheless to return to Jesus. Not an ideological Jesus, not a Jesus who legitimates our idolatries, our graven images. But a Jesus who will manifest to us the very image of God, the image of who we are called to be as human lovers, dancers, and stewards. This voice that can cross the spaces of our ideological violence is a human voice, the voice of one who is the Son of Man as he is the Son of God. This is a voice with an accent that sounds like it comes from first-century Nazareth.

## "Jesus, Thank You, Joyous Son"

Jesus has been a constant companion from the very beginning of Bruce Cockburn's body of work. In the meditative "Thoughts on a Rainy Afternoon" on the debut album, we hear a prayer, "Jesus . . . Jesus don't let Toronto take my song away." And in the last verse of the song, recognizing the fragility of love ("like a moth's wing it's easily crushed") the artist prays, "Jesus . . . Jesus don't let tomorrow take my love away."[30] Somehow this artist's songs and deepest loves and longings are tied up with Jesus.

But this is not a Jesus easily available to us. This is not the Jesus of a smug and comfortable piety. No, if we are to meet the Jesus who will fulfill our deepest longings while overturning our self-justifying pieties, then we will have to wait. And we will have to recognize our own profound brokenness and blindness:

> he came from the mountain
> to walk among the wounded
> they couldn't see him
> but the snow did melt whenever he passed by.[31]

Haven't we met a figure like this somewhere else? Doesn't the arrival of one who brings the new life of spring after what seemed like an endless winter seem familiar to us? The "snow did melt whenever he passed by." Isn't that exactly what happened when Aslan returned to Narnia in C. S. Lewis's *The Lion, the Witch and the Wardrobe?*[32]

> he came behind winter
> his face was like the sun
> they wouldn't see it
> but he sang on the bank and made the waters run.

Notice the shift in verbs from the first to the second verse of "He Came from the Mountain." The artist recognizes both our inability to see this redemptive figure when he comes ("they *couldn't* see him") and our stubborn unwillingness to welcome redemption when it is on offer ("they *wouldn't* see him"). The final verse of the song suggests a resolution. Moving from "couldn't" to "wouldn't" to "could," the artist leaves us with the hope of renewed vision:

> he came to the lowlands
> he said we must have faces
> so we could see like him
> before our wings could ever come to fly.

This Aslan-like redeemer comes from the mountain to the lowlands, from the heights to the depths, and he comes to the wounded and the blind. He comes to those who cannot see the light of redemption when it is right before them, who refuse to welcome the spring that sets them free from the cold and comfortless darkness of an imposed winter.[33] And he speaks. This is the voice that can cross these spaces, and the voice says that "we must have faces / so we could see like him."

Voice and sight. Somehow the two must go together. We must hear before we can see. We must receive a revelatory word before we can acquire revelatory sight. And the word says, "we must have faces." Another allusion to C. S. Lewis. In his retelling of the Cupid and Psyche fable, Lewis reflects on the silence of the gods. Narrated by the ugly princess Orual, the story is a theodicy, a complaint against the capriciousness of the gods. But it is the very voicing of the complaint with depth and authenticity that occasions its own answer. The gods will not answer, the narrator tells us, until we finally come to the place where we truly say what we mean. And the metaphor that Lewis employs to capture this sense of authenticity is "till we have faces." How can the gods "meet us face to face till we have faces?"[34] How can our blindness be transformed into sight and our woundedness healed, our recalcitrant refusal to see the light be overcome, without the transparency of face-to-face encounter?

When we have faces, our own faces, the faces of authentic human life, then will we be able to "see like him," Cockburn writes. This is the promise on offer from the one who came from the mountain.[35] If we are to see like him, if we are to see "just beyond the range of normal sight,"[36] if we are to have night vision and see things as they really are, then we must have faces. Not the fragmented multiple personality disorder of the "Man of a Thousand Faces,"[37] but the true face of our humanity created in the image of God. "Now we see in a mirror, dimly," St. Paul writes, "but then we will see face to face."[38] Then all the pretense, the facades and the charades, will be gone. When we have faces, true faces, we will see as we are seen, we will open our wings and fly.

But not yet. There are still vestiges of winter, and the spring has not yet come in full force. We still hide behind multiple faces, are crippled by our woundedness, and struggle with our blindness. Nonetheless, the one who has come from the mountain has brought healing in his hands and spoken a word of promise that transforms despair into the hope that sings through the chorus of this song:

> in his world we wait
> in his hands our fate
> keep on climbing
> we shall see his gate
> in good time.

Here on this early album, Cockburn gives voice to a confident hope that is somehow tied up with Jesus. In "a world of pain and fire and steel,"[39] a world that is "battered and abused and lovely,"[40] the artist has a vision of transcendence. This is "his world." Our fate is "in his hands." And we wait with a longing yet confident hope. "We shall see his gate / in good time." Our vision may still be blurred. We may still be hiding behind a multiplicity of faces in our fear and our brokenness. But the one who has come from the mountain has brought good news. And in good time we will see his gate, that open gate to his coming kingdom, that gate of welcome and hospitality.

Such vision does not come easily, however. Sometimes you need to hit bottom before you can get a vision of hope. Sometimes you need to shout in the face of the gods before you can get an answer. Sometimes your journey needs to run aground in some harbor town where you lose the taste for being free. It is only then that you begin to get clarity about what really matters, catch a vision of all that is of lasting value in this world. Cockburn's "All the Diamonds in the World" is a testimony to Christian faith as beautiful as you will ever hear:

> all the diamonds in this world
> that mean anything to me
> are conjured up by wind and sunlight
> sparkling on the sea.[41]

We have moved from the mountain to the sea, from a primordial site of sacred encounter to a dangerous yet beautiful sea journey. And rather than taking the devil's advice to "drown yourself in jewels / like a thousand other fools" from the earlier song "Dialogue with the Devil,"[42] the artist confesses that the only jewels he needs are those refracted off the surface of a windswept sea. No "jewels on the Serpent's crown"[43] for this seafarer, even if the sea be populated by such serpents. But that doesn't take away from the danger of this journey.

> i ran aground in a harbour town
> lost the taste for being free.

This journey has run aground. There was something about this quest for freedom that led the pilgrim to a dead end, and he isn't so sure that he has the stomach to go on. As with all such quest narratives, there are obstacles, moments of confusion and disorientation, that bring into question the quest itself. And, as in all such narratives, there is a redemptive turn that gives the journey new hope and new direction:

> thank God He sent some gull-chased ship
> to carry me to sea.[44]

The journey is resumed through divine intervention. The quest that has run aground can begin anew. But this is no generic spiritual renewal. No, this redemptive turn has Christian particularity written all over it. The God who sent this gull-chased ship is the God of Jesus, the crucified one:

> two thousand years and half a world away
> dying trees still will grow greener when you pray.

The reference to the story of Jesus is clear. Two thousand years ago and half a world away from the life of a Canadian folksinger, something happened that continues to have healing power today. And perhaps there is a double meaning at work in the phrase "dying trees." On one level, Jesus is the crucified one, hung on a tree. The cross is a dying tree, a place for dying. This is a dying tree, yet on that tree death is defeated. Saint Paul says that "death has been swallowed up in victory."[45] This is a dying tree that gives way to resurrection, life defeating death.

But perhaps this suggests another meaning in these lines: "two thousand years and half a world away / dying trees still will grow greener when you pray." The events of two thousand years ago, the tragic events of passion week, are still powerfully transformative and liberating today, "when you pray." Prayer is necessary to set loose this redemptive power. And that could suggest that the "dying tree" is not just a reference to the cross of Jesus but perhaps also to the artist himself. He is the dying tree. Run aground in this harbor town, it seems like he has come to the end with no more taste for freedom, and maybe no more taste for life either. But dying trees can still "grow greener when you pray." Resurrection is on offer to all who will pray, to all who will ask. Cockburn later sings, "You offered up your flesh and death was overthrown / now salvation is ours, / salvation is ours." He has tasted that salvation. "Jesus, thank you, joyous Son."[46]

Salvation, however, is not arrival. Rather, salvation is setting out on the journey anew. The images of the last verse of this song all entail motion. On the move again on this gull-chased ship, the artist sees "silver scales flash bright and fade / in reeds along the shore." And in his renewed vision he sees something else: "like a pearl in a sea of liquid jade / His ship comes shining." The artist is on a God-sent ship (and interestingly a ship is one of the ancient Christian symbols of the church) and from that vantage point sees another ship—"His ship comes shining"—God's ship. And this ship is like a pearl. In one of his shortest parables Jesus said, "The kingdom of heaven is like a merchant in search of fine pearls; on finding one pearl of great value, he went and sold all that he had and bought it."[47] "Like a pearl in a sea of liquid jade / His ship comes shining." A pearl worth selling everything in order to acquire. A pearl worth more than anything in this world. And then Cockburn concludes this wonderful song with these rich images: "like a crystal swan in a sky of suns / His ship comes shining." This ship refracts the glory of all creation, refracts the stunning glory of God, refracts the rainbow glory of a thousand suns. Quite the song to offer on *Sun, Salt and Time* as an answer to the darkness of the preceding album, *Night Vision*. "God bless the children with visions of the Day," Cockburn sang at the end of *Night Vision*.[48] He now identifies himself in joyful humility with those very children.

We have seen throughout this book that images of Jesus are never far from Cockburn's lyrics. On the *Joy Will Find a Way* album that followed *Sun, Salt and Time*, we meet an evocative retelling of the story of Jesus in the three short verses of "A Life Story." Guitar, percussion, bass, and synthesizer combine in the opening two minutes of this song to evoke a sense of creation's birth, which is then identified in the first verse with the virgin birth. Cockburn sings:

> sky-wild
> far cry
> wings-slash-free
> Christ is born for you and me.

And then the song takes off with an infectious joy. The Christ child has been born for you and me, and that means this Christ must enter into the storms, chaos, and vulnerabilities of our lives.

> wind rush
> reed bend
> storm tossed sea
> Christ is nailed upon a tree.

There is that dying tree again. Playing with multiple allusions, the artist places the story of the cross in the context of the Spirit anointing both Jesus at his baptism and the church at Pentecost.[49] And yet we also meet the extreme fear and panic of the disciples caught in a storm on the Sea of Galilee.[50] All of this vulnerability and threat is taken up with Christ nailed upon a tree. The full force of evil—not just death, but evil itself, all that would break us and hold us captive—is set loose on the Christ on the cross. In this storm we see reeds bending and recall that Isaiah prophesied that the coming One would not break a bruised reed.[51] But on the cross we see that the Messiah is himself a bruised reed who is violently broken by the cosmic storm that is unleashed on him.

The guitar solo with full band rocking behind leaves us with the cross for a full minute and a half before the story is brought to its joyful and victorious conclusion:

> *mists part*
> *sun rise*
> *shining Key*
> *Christ is risen to lead us free.*

Christ is born, Christ has died, Christ is risen. There is the story. And it is a story of creation restored. The mists part as on that dawn of creation. The sun rises on the first day of the new creation. Resurrection is re-creation. In John's Gospel, the first witness to the resurrection is Mary Magdalene. She comes to a garden while it is still dark, and as the sun rises she meets the Son who has risen. And in that garden, echoing the beginning of the whole story in the Garden of Eden, Mary confuses Jesus with the gardener. It is an honest mistake. He is the Gardener of the new creation.[52]

Cockburn sees in this risen one a "shining Key." Jesus is the Key of David, says the book of Revelation: what he opens no one can shut, and what he shuts no one can open. Indeed, he holds the very keys of death and Hades in his hand.[53] And in this moment of resurrection, he opens those doors to set us free from all that will bind us to death, all that will bind us to sin, all that will bind us to idolatry and ideology. In this powerful six-minute song, with its three sparse verses, Cockburn sums up the heart of the Christian story and the most foundational Christian proclamation. In the Eucharist the gathered community confesses, "Christ has died, Christ is risen, Christ will come again." Cockburn's "Christ is born for you and me," "Christ is nailed upon a tree," "Christ is risen to lead us free" offers a similar threefold confession, adding the birth of Christ and leaving the return of Christ as a theme for other songs. While we will reflect further on themes of hope that are often associated with the return of Christ in the next chapter, we would do well to spend a little more time at the beginning of the story to conclude this chapter.

## "In the Cry of a Tiny Babe"

Bruce Cockburn seems to have a special attraction to the nativity stories of the birth of Jesus. For years he did a Christmas radio show in New York that culminated in the release of his 1993 album, *Christmas*. For those of us who have an allergic reaction to all Christmas albums released by popular artists, this may be the one exception. Lacking any hint of sweet sentimentality, this is an album that rings true. From the rollicking "Early on One Christmas Morn," "Mary Had a Baby," "Les Anges dans nos campagnes," and "Go Tell It on the Mountain" to the hauntingly meditative "Huron Carol" (with a lovely Hugh Marsh violin solo) and "It Came upon a Midnight Clear," the album invites the listener into the joy and the mystery of the Christmas story.

Cockburn's original song on the album, "Shepherds," beautifully narrates the story of the shepherds awakened in the night by a heavenly host described as "figures dancing in the sky / clothed with more colours than the world can contain."[54] Somehow this seems reminiscent of a crystal swan in a sky of suns refracting every color imaginable. And if we remember Cockburn calling us to "search the silence of the soul's wild places" in "Justice" or to "listen to the silence" in "Gospel of Bondage," then we might well want to sing "Gloria in the highest!" when we hear that "all the silences of the night / leap in song / like that of a river cascading / from the wild mountain to the slow human plain." The creation born of the Creator's song—*creatio per cantum*—now leaps into song again at the birth of the Savior. And then song of the night meets the cry of the day: "A child's cry sounds from far away / it's almost day / and in the brown-air town away below / three travelers reap a star harvest / and then go on their way again." The cry of a tiny babe, the cry of air first entering the lungs of this child of promise, tells us that it is almost day. So the three magi reap the harvest of their stargazing, greet the day born with this child, and go on their way. "Gloria! Gloria in the highest!"

In "Cry of a Tiny Babe" on the album *Nothing but a Burning Light*, we are offered another take on the nativity story. Here, Mary and Joseph have to deal with this pregnancy "without the help of a man" and the misunderstandings that such a thing might occasion between a betrothed couple. The song narrates the visit of the magi ("The child is born in the fullness of time / three wise astrologers take note of the signs / come to pay their respects to the fragile little king") and also highlights the fragility of this king's birth by telling the story of Herod's infanticide in Bethlehem:

> . . . *the governing body of the whole land*
> *is that of Herod, a paranoid man*
> *Who when he hears there's a baby born King of the Jews*
> *Sends death squads to kill all male children under two.*

From birth to the cross, this is a costly redemption that will face violent opposition. You see,

> . . . *it isn't to the palace that the Christ child comes*
> *But to shepherds and street people, hookers and bums.*

Perhaps they are the only ones who could receive such a king.

> *And the message is clear if you've got ears to hear*
> *That forgiveness is given for your guilt and fear*
> *It's a Christmas gift you don't have to buy*
> *There's a future shining in a baby's eyes*

*Like a stone on the surface of a still river*
*Driving the ripples on forever*
*Redemption rips through the surface of time*
*In the cry of a tiny babe.*

This birth, this incarnation, is like a stone dropped into a still river. The ripples radiate out from the point of contact with the water. But the ripples of this stone go on forever.[55] The stone that makes ripples on the surface of a still river is the redemption that rips through the surface of time.[56] Redemption isn't a natural evolutionary process. Redemption is an intervention in time, a radical entering into history to bring about the reversals of the kingdom of God. And it all happens in the cry of a tiny babe, the advent of a fragile little king.

# 13

# Waiting for a Miracle

Let's go back to where we started. Let's return to the Trailf Music Hall in Buffalo, New York, on March 20, 2007. Backstage with twenty of my students chatting with Bruce Cockburn, I became mindful of the time. While the students would be happy to stand there and converse with the artist until the early hours of the morning, I knew that Bruce and his crew had a long night and day ahead of them to get to their gig in Washington on the next evening. So I asked a concluding question: "What do you think, Bruce, are we still *in the falling dark*?" It had been more than thirty years since the album of that name had been released. Was 2007 as dark as 1976? In a post-9/11 culture under the administration of George W. Bush in the United States, in the light of Guantanamo Bay, the "war on terror," stunning inaction on global warming, and a whole host of other intractable problems at the beginning of the twenty-first century, are we still in the falling dark? Bruce thought for a moment and replied, "Yes, but it is darker." And then one of the students immediately added, "But 'joy will find a way.'" Bruce looked at him with a smile and said, "Yes, and that is the foundation of everything." And before he could say anything more, the young woman standing beside him (likely the youngest person in the house that night) said, "And we've got to 'kick at the darkness 'til it bleeds daylight.'" Bruce's smile got bigger as he gave her a playful punch on the shoulder and said, "You keep believing that." Our backstage audience with the artist was finished, and we left him with our gratitude.

## Working and Waiting

Joy will find a way, but you've got to kick at the darkness until it bleeds daylight. Between that confidence and that longing, hope is born. The 1974 song "Joy Will Find a Way" is a song about dying. It is a prayer that asks that we might have a good death at the completion of a good life:

> make me a bed of fond memories
> make me to lie down with a smile
> everything that rises afterwards falls
> and all that dies has first to live.[1]

Let me go to my deathbed with a good smile rooted in a life of fond memories. Let our lives be full of stories of wholeness and healing, of friendship and fellowship. There can be no mistaking that death is the culmination of life. All that is born, all that rises, afterward falls, and all that dies has first to live. This cycle of life and death is a natural process that need not be feared but embraced. And what makes it possible to embrace death is not just that it can be (we hope) at the end of a life full of fond memories but also that we know that it is not the end:

> as longing becomes love
> as night turns to day
> everything changes
> joy will find a way.

We are made for joy. Joy is woven into the very fabric of creation. What else would we expect of a world sung and danced into being by a Creator who seems to be overflowing with a cosmically infectious joy? This is perhaps the fondest memory of all. The end of all things will reflect the beginning. The joy that brought forth all of creation in that primordial shell-pink dawn will find a way to turn our darkness into light, the night of our death into the dawn of our resurrection.

Joy will find a way. Notice that the artist does not sing here that we will find a way for joy, or that we will somehow wrest joy out of the grip of sorrow. No, joy will find its own way. There is something wonderfully passive about this. Joy is received as a gift. Joy somehow finds its own way in our lives if we but wait for such joy and do not block its advent. The quiet confidence of this song bears witness to a deeply Christian orientation in Cockburn's spirituality. "Joy will find a way" is a foundational commitment for this artist. It is, as he said that evening backstage, "the foundation of everything."

And yet we've got to "kick at the darkness 'til it bleeds daylight." Here a confident orientation meets the pathos of disappointment and anger.

What do you do when longing does not become love? When the absence of communion remains absence and never enters into the presence of love? What do you do when the night is dark, long, and seemingly unending, with no sign of day on the horizon? What do you do when nothing changes, or at least it changes only in ways that make things worse, and "all joy has reached its eventide; the gladness of the earth is banished?"[2] What do you do when it seems like joy has lost its way?

There are three options available when the orientation of "joy will find a way" is confronted with the reality of a deeply broken inner and outer world. First, you could give up on joy. You could abandon a belief that "joy will find a way" as naive and self-delusional. But then you would be a singer "of songs without hope," and Cockburn would tell you "to take a hard look and start from scratch again."[3] Cockburn refuses to give up on joy.

Or, second, you could decide that joy is something to be grasped, controlled, and constructed. If joy has lost its way, if the darkness will not let go of its grasp, then maybe it is time to kick at some darkness, to grab a rocket launcher and show joy the way back home. You see, when those leaders who are "in drag as champions of freedom" "rob life of its quality," rob life of its joy, then doesn't all of this "render rage a necessity"? Don't we need to do something about this oppression? Aren't the destroyers of joy and the destroyers of this earth going to one day rise from their habitual feast to find themselves "staring down the throat of the beast / they call the revolution"?[4] Doesn't the absence of joy, the absence of justice, call for a militant response? There are times when Cockburn's songs seem to suggest such a stance.

But hope is found neither in abandonment nor in aggressive grasping. There is a third and more creative way to respond to the evidence stacked up against joy and hope. It is called "Waiting for a Miracle." In this 1988 song written in postrevolution Nicaragua, the artist paints a picture of people working to put their lives back together again after decades of a violent dictatorship. "Look at them working in the hot sun / the pilloried saints and the fallen ones."[5] Here the metaphor is not that of the darkness of night and the renewal of dawn, but of the unrelenting heat of the sun. These are "pilloried saints and the fallen ones." These are the ridiculed and broken, but they are saints. And in the heat of that day they are "working and waiting for the night to come / and waiting for a miracle." This longing for the relief of the night, a time to relax and to have respite from the oppressive heat, is taken up into larger hopes. They are "waiting for a miracle." More is at stake here than the end of a day's work in the rebuilding of Nicaragua.

The second verse ups the ante:

*Somewhere out there is a place that's cool*
*where peace and balance are the rule*
*working toward a future like some kind of mystic jewel*
*and waiting for a miracle.*

Here is a vision of shalom, a vision where peace and balance are the rule.[6] Life is restored to its wholeness, community flourishes, and all broken relationships are healed.[7] But how do we achieve such a life? How is this vision ever realized? Do we grasp at it and create such shalom? No. Do we just sit back and passively wait for it to happen? Not that, either. Rather, the artist puts together "working" and "waiting." This is an active, not a passive, hope. We work "toward a future like some kind of a mystic jewel." This future is "like a pearl in a sea of liquid jade,"[8] a pearl of great cost.[9] And such a future animates a life that works toward its realization. But unlike those who will autonomously grasp such a future, Cockburn recognizes that this jeweled future, this pearl in a sea of liquid jade, is received as a gift—"His ship comes shining."[10] Therefore we *work* and we *wait* for this miracle of shalom that is promised. We neither work as if it is up to us to make it happen nor passively sit and wait as if there is nothing for us to do. No, we work *and* we wait. We work in hopeful expectation of that future as we await its coming. Longing and confidence come together in working and waiting.[11]

Such working and waiting is also rooted in community. We are not alone in our longing for a better world. What confident hope we might have is grounded in a cloud of witnesses.

> You stand up proud
> you pretend you're strong
> in the hope that you can be
> like the ones who've cried
> like the ones who've died
> trying to set the angel in us free
> while they're waiting for a miracle

There is nothing easy about this working for a miracle. Sometimes you've got to put on a brave face and pretend you are strong when in fact you are on the edge of hopelessness. But that stance is rooted in memories that are perhaps more intense than the fond memories of "Joy Will Find a Way." These are the memories of those earlier pilloried saints. "Water of life is going to flow again / changed from the blood of heroes and knaves," wrote Cockburn in "Broken Wheel."[12] These are the martyrs; these are "the ones who've cried / the ones who've died / trying to set the angel in us free." These are the ones who have given their lives to working and waiting for the miracle of shalom. I don't know who Cockburn might be thinking of, but people like Dietrich Bonhoeffer, Oscar Romero, Steve Biko, Mahatma Gandhi, and Martin Luther King Jr. come to my mind. These are people who have cried and died in confident service of hope. They have seen a better land, they have been animated by a vision of shalom, and they have offered up their lives in a passionate longing to set us free for such a life.

This is no cheap hope on offer in Cockburn's song. No, this is a hope of confident longing. A hope of working and waiting:

*Struggle for a dollar, scuffle for a dime*
*step out from the past and try to hold the line*
*so how come history takes such a long, long time*
*When you're waiting for a miracle.*

In the struggle among the poorest of the poor for the daily resources to sustain life, in those who are working out there in the hot sun, in the lives of the ones who've cried and died for us, we see a hope that steps out from the tyranny of the past and tries to hold a new line.[13] No wonder Cockburn will later sing, "I've seen the flame of hope among the hopeless / And that was truly the biggest heartbreak of all / That was the straw that broke me open."[14] As we have seen, hopelessness is the luxury of the rich. Those who are really hopeless, those who have no resources to effect significant change in their social and economic situation, those "pilloried saints and the fallen ones," cannot afford this luxury. The lived hope that burns like a flame among the hopeless will not allow the oppressive structures of the past to have the final word. This is a hope that lives toward a future of shalom, a "mystic jewel," that is so appealing, so alluring, so wonderful, that it remains deeply impatient with a world of "pain and fire and steel"[15] and cries out, "so how come history takes such a long, long time / when you're waiting for a miracle?" You would be hard-pressed to find a more powerfully evocative expression of the pathos-filled hope that is at the heart of Christian faith. This is the kind of hope that we meet at the very end of the Bible, at the end of the book of Revelation, with its apocalyptic visions of both violent geo-historical collapse and a city of shalom: "Amen. Come, Lord Jesus!"[16] Come soon, because this history is taking such a long, long time.

## You've Never Seen Everything

Such a vision of longing and hope, working and waiting, absence and presence comes to an integrative expression in Cockburn's 2003 album, *You've Never Seen Everything*. While the title song would seem to be saying that you have never seen the depths of human depravity and brokenness, the chorus to the song puts the message of the whole album into perspective:

*Bad pressure coming down*
*Tears—what we really traffic in*
*ride the ribbon of shadow*
*Never feel the light falling around . . .*
*You've never seen everything.*[17]

You've never seen everything if you never feel the light falling all around. If all you can see is the bad pressure and the tears that we really traffic in, then your vision is still blurred. You haven't yet seen the flame of hope that fires up in the hearts of the hopeless. We find ourselves so overwhelmed by living "in the falling dark" that we are blind to the light: "all that glory shining around and we're all caught taking a dive."[18] As we saw in chapter 9, *You've Never Seen Everything* is an album preoccupied with seeing in the dark. "I can see in the dark, it's where I used to live," the artist sings.[19] But the album is crafted in such a way that this honest confrontation with the darkness is juxtaposed with the hope of light. "You've never seen everything" if all you can see is the dark. But you can't really see the light without confronting the darkness.

As we have seen, songs like "All Our Dark Tomorrows," "Trickle Down," and "Postcards from Cambodia" open our eyes to the darkness of the Bush administration, globalization, and genocide respectively. These songs do not allow us to avert our gaze. And the title track fixes our gaze on the darkness for a full nine minutes, with eerie music that matches the lyrics. "You've Never Seen Everything" is as painful a piece of music as Bruce Cockburn has ever written.[20] But this song appears on the album sandwiched between two songs of incredible beauty and hope.

The unspeakably beautiful song "Celestial Horses" was occasioned by an experience in a hot spring in the Rockies at the end of the 1970s. Facing the same kind of geopolitical tension that lay behind "Wondering Where the Lions Are," the artist has a mystical experience of hope as he soaks in that spring. As he watches the stars emerge ("here come those silver celestial horses") and basks in the "rays of the moon in the mountain air," he has a vision: "There's darkness in the canyon / But the Light comes pounding through / For me and for you." He knows that "Tomorrow may be a hissing blowtorch / Maybe a silken sky shaken by the wind." Tomorrow may bring with it nothing less than the blowtorch heat and earth-shaking wind of a nuclear holocaust as China and Russia continue to face off on their border. And the world may be in the "wake of those whispering horses"—whether the celestial horses of this evening or perhaps even the four horses of the apocalypse—but "there's always a pillar of cloud on the valley's rim." No matter how precarious our situation may be, there is always a pillar of cloud. There is always that pillar of cloud that led the Israelites when God liberated them from the imperial oppression of Egypt.[21] Yes, the situation is dangerous and the darkness seems overwhelming, but the artist has a vision of the presence of God in the midst of it all, a vision of an exodus of liberation. And this exodus path is to a promised land, a land of shalom that is on the other shore, on the other side of the Jordan River. This deeply biblical image that proved to be so powerfully liberating in the history of African slaves in the United States is now applied to a very different context with gentleness and subtlety:

> *Still river full of the depths of the candles*
> *Burning for the free ones riding on the other shore*
> *Even at the heart of these breathing shadows*
> *You can feel us gathering at the door.*

That other shore is the promised land. And there are folks who have already crossed that river. These are the "free ones riding on that other shore." For them the candles still burn. They are not in a place of darkness but of light. And as we face our own impending deaths, as we stand close to these breathing shadows, "you can feel us gathering at the door." The lions aren't "half as frightening as they were before"[22] once we can see that pillar of cloud, once we see that there may well be darkness in the valley, "but the Light comes pounding through / for me and for you." And it is important to see this Light before diving into the darkness of "You've Never Seen Everything."

Then, after giving us a visceral experience of a cosmic "bad pressure coming down" in "You've Never Seen Everything," the artist reminds us: "Don't Forget about Delight." Not bad advice after what he has just put us through in the previous song.

> *Amid the rumours and the expectations*
> *and all the stories dreamt and lived*
> *amid the clangour and the dislocation*
> *and things to fear and to forgive.*

In the wake of the stories of dislocation that the artist has just told us, stories of fear and stories that certainly require a considerable level of forgiveness because they are so violent, the artist calls us back to an even deeper memory.

> *Don't forget*
> *about delight*
> *Y know what I'm saying to you*
> *Don't forget*
> *about delight*
> *Y know*

Even in the midst of postmodern "post-ironic postulating" where "meaning feels like it's evaporating," and even when you find yourself "alone and stranded / with no friends to take your side," "don't forget about delight." In a world of "dark tomorrows," in a world "hooked on avarice," a world where "laughter is swallowed in expanding silence" and a "bad pressure is coming down," it is pretty hard to remember delight.[23] So the artist reminds us as he reminds himself. Dislocation, disappointment, meaninglessness, betrayal, and violence must all be confronted because they are devastatingly real in our lives. But they must never have the last word, or they will devour us and leave us without hope.

> *Spring birds peck among the pressed-down grasses*
> *Clouds like zeppelins cross the sky*
> *Anger drips and pools and then it passes*
> *And I say a prayer that I*
> *Don't forget*
> *about delight.*

Joy will find a way because joy is built into the very fabric of creation, and some-times, like Job, we need to be confronted by the beauty and wisdom of creation to help us put things in perspective, allow the anger to pass, and be brought back to delight.[24] We need to be quite literally grounded in the good ground of creation, the good earth in which the Creator delighted as he repeatedly pronounced that this is good, good, good, good, very good.[25] Don't forget this delight, because therein we will find hope.

*You've Never Seen Everything* is an album of such deep hope.[26] That "Celestial Horses" and "Don't Forget about Delight" bracket the title track is indicative of the vision of the album as a whole.

The album opens with two songs that come to us as the artist's state-of-his-soul report. We learn on the first track that this is a man who has been "Tried and Tested." A life of attentiveness, a life of having his eyes wide open, has its cost. Whether he is talking about the world around him in all of its political machinations, economic deception, and ecological despoliation or his own compromised and broken life, he has been "tried and tested." "By the planet's arc / By the falling dark." There we are again, in the falling dark. "By the weight of choice / By the still small voice." This is a life of responsibility, a life that cannot avoid that divine voice whispering through the cacophony.

In all of this, the artist confesses that he has been "pierced by beauty's blade and skinned by wind." This isn't the first time that Cockburn has reached for the image of piercing. In "Arrows of Light" he invited those arrows to come and "pierce my soul."[27] And in "Civilization and Its Discontents," after acknowledging that "even though I know who loves me I'm not that much less lost," we hear, "Pearl sky raining light like hail, come on and pierce me / Raining light like a vision of the holy grail, come on and pierce me."[28] Whether a joy-filled confession like "Arrows of Light" or an anguished appraisal of a culture of "blind fingers groping for the right track" in "Civilization and Its Discontents," the metaphor is the same—come and pierce me. In the falling dark we need to be pierced by light. And let there be no mistake, such a piercing is painful. But without being pierced by light, pierced by beauty and skinned by wind, we are lost.

Skinned by wind. Just as light is a ubiquitous metaphor in biblical faith, so also is wind. It is the wind, the breath of God, that hovers over the waters at the dawn of creation. It is this divine wind that is breathed into the human creature to bring life. It is this wind that comes and blows over Ezekiel's valley of dry bones and brings resurrection. And it is the wind of the Holy Spirit that blows through the early disciples on the day of Pentecost.[29] Wind and Spirit. Not surprisingly, Cockburn has employed the same metaphors in his songs. "Breath of the bright wind / make us one," he sings in "Arrows of Light." "It's the wind in the wings of a diving dove / You better listen for the laugh of love," he sings in "Listen for the Laugh."[30] If you want to break through the derisive, superficial, and deceptive laughter of our culture, then you need to listen for the laugh of love, the laugh that reverberates through "the wind in the wings of a diving dove." This is the laughter of the Spirit.[31]

In "Tried and Tested," the spiritual experience of this artist is neither sweet nor sentimental. He has been "pierced by beauty's blade and *skinned* by wind." No wonder he can sing on an earlier album:

> Sometimes a wind comes out of nowhere and
> Knocks you off your feet and look—see my tears—
> They fill the whole night sky
> The whole night sky.[32]

Skinned by wind, knocked off your feet by wind—this is no gentle breeze. Such encounters with the Spirit are precisely what has left the artist "tried and tested." Yet all of this is received as a deep gift.

> Pierced by beauty's blade and skinned by wind
> Begged for more—was given—begged again
> I'm still here
> I'm still here.

Pierced and skinned, the artist begs for more. This is not a spiritual masochism. This is a spirituality that understands hope is impossible without the Spirit and that an openness to the Spirit will always be intense, a matter of being tried and tested, while never predictable or under our control.

Openness is at the heart of it all. So, in the second song of the album, Cockburn acknowledges the lack of balance in his life, the anxiety that accompanies him every morning, and an endless hunger that permeates his soul. And yet he remains "open." Open to the light, open to intimacy, open to the gift of communion. But again, there can be no such openness without struggle. As Jacob wrestled with the angel for a blessing and ended up walking with a limp for the rest of his life because that struggle put his hipbone out of joint, so does Cockburn sing:

> I never live with balance
> I wanna feel you near me
> There's an aching in my hipbone
> Wanna let my heart drop open.[33]

Openness, whether to a lover, to the world, or to God, is costly.

This album bears witness to such a costly openness, a costly hope. In "Everywhere Dance" the artist sings that "we cry out for grace to lay truth bare," and the album as a whole seems to be the result. Whether in the anger and pain of "All Our Dark Tomorrows," "Trickle Down," "Postcards from Cambodia," and "You've Never Seen Everything" or in the pathos and longing of "Everywhere Dance" and "Put It in Your Heart," the album struggles toward hope. The struggle comes to its passionate denouement in "Wait No More."

Upon first hearing, it is easy to hear this song as an impatient longing for sexual intimacy—"it's no secret what I'm thinking of." But closer listening, especially in live performance, suggests that this song cannot be limited to sexual longing. In the vision that we meet in this song an ominous sense of the apocalyptic ("wild things are prowling—storm winds are howling tonight") is greeted by glimpses of redemption ("everything's transforming into pure crystals of light"). And it is clear that the artist wants to wait no more. He has been waiting a long time. "In his world we wait / in his hands our fate," he once sang.[34] The artist has been working and waiting for a miracle. Like the psalmists, he has been singing "how long" for so long that he is now burning with a spiritual impatience and longing that are overwhelming. But what is it that he is waiting for? The second verse provides an important clue:

> Sipping wine with angels in this torch-lit tavern by the sea
> What does it take for what's locked up inside to be free?
> Fold me into you, you know where I'm dying to be
> When my ship sets sail on that ocean of deep mystery.

A sea. A ship. Freedom. Doesn't this sound familiar?

> i ran aground in a harbour town
> lost the taste for being free
> thank God he sent some gull-chased ship
> to carry me to sea.[35]

Here we are again. By the sea with a deep sense of things being locked up and longing to be free. This song is an impassioned prayer. "Fold me into you, you know where I'm dying to be." Something like, "I want to be a particle of your light,"[36] this is a prayer for deep communion. It is indeed an erotic prayer, because it is born of eros, a love and a longing for the divine partner. We never run aground only once in life, and so the artist prays, "you know where I'm dying to be / when my ship sets sail on that ocean of deep mystery."[37] Let my ship set sail again. But you know that this journey can be resumed only if God sends some gull-chased ship to the rescue: "His ship comes shining."

"Wait No More" is a song of spiritual longing. It is a song that aches for the redemption of all things, the restoration of the shalom longed for in songs such as "Open," "Waiting for a Miracle," and "A Dream like Mine." The artist simply can't wait any longer for that day when we will "wake to remember how lovely we are." "The heart is a mirror; it throws back the blaze of love," he sings in the first verse. But now we see through a mirror dimly, then we will see face to face.[38] Then love will meet love.[39] Then, in the mirror of the divine lover looking back at us, we will remember how lovely we are and we will be restored to who we were always called to be.

Cockburn's art is a human attempt to glimpse into that mirror and hold it up for the rest of us. The album tells us that "you've never seen everything" and doesn't presume to fix that problem. Rather, the artist wants to help us see a little more, perhaps "just beyond the range of normal sight."[40] And it is clear that such vision, such hope, is a matter of the Spirit. In the final song of the album, "Messenger Wind," Cockburn describes himself as "one more voice in the human choir / rising like smoke from the mystical fire of the heart."[41] One more voice. But a voice indebted to the Spirit: "The wind that blows through everything / sweeps out the halls of my heart when I sing to you." The divine wind that animates all of creation animates this artist.[42] And his singing is a sweeping-out of the halls of his heart, an emptying of his heart for his listeners. This wind of the Spirit "carries the moon and the stars and the rain"; it "carries the seagulls and carries my shame away." This is a Spirit that carries all of creation, a cosmic Spirit of renewal and re-creation. And yet this Spirit also carries away the shame that we all bear. This Spirit "spins me around, stops me running away / from all the things I've been waiting to say, but don't." This is a Spirit that offers redemption, but not cheap escape. No more running. When the Spirit spins us around, we must engage the world with integrity and openness.

"Messenger Wind" is a dream, one that reveals to the artist the heart of his calling and offers a vision of life restored. And it is beautiful:

> Sun coming up paints the snow all around
> Rose on the roofs and the trees and the ground
> And the stream
> In my dream.

"Sun coming up paints the snow all around with rose light." The sun comes up yet again. A "shell-pink dawn," a "Santiago Dawn," the dawn of new creation. This insomniac artist has always been preoccupied with the dawn. And in this song he catches a glimpse of that dawn in a dream during a moment of blissful sleep.[43] All is painted in a rose light. Perhaps that is because finally that "Rose above the sky" has opened and the "Light behind the sun" has taken all.[44] Perhaps this rose light is reflected off of that Rose above the sky, that glittering joker, that joyous son. And the dream ends with this vision:

> Messenger wind swooping out of the sky
> Lights each tiny speck in the human kaleidoscope
> With hope.

Spirit, light, and hope. You won't have one without the others. Bruce Cockburn has offered us all three.

In a culture hooked on avarice and enamored of a shortsighted materialism, a culture that shows "unbelievable indifference" to "life / spirit / the future /

anything green / anything just,"[45] we are in desperate need of a "messenger wind swooping out of the sky." We are in desperate need of artists who can be messengers of the Spirit. We are in desperate need of artists like Bruce Cockburn, "child of the wind."[46]

In a culture that is still "in the falling dark," still running from the light, still hiding from the dawn, we need a "night vision," we need to learn how to "see in the dark."[47] We need artists who will allow the light to illuminate every dimension of our lives, "each tiny speck in the human kaleidoscope." Art cannot save us, but it can shed a light. It can open our eyes.

And in a culture "dancing arm in arm towards the looming end of days," a "world of sorrows" permeated by the "ache in the spirit we label despair," we are in desperate need of hope.[48]

Despair is the doorway to hope. Hope transcends sentimental optimism because it refuses to avert its gaze from the darkness, refuses to repress that ache in the spirit that we know as despair. Engaging the work of Bruce Cockburn, we have seen that this is a broken-wheeled world. We have seen the extremes of what humans can be. And we have heard a call to justice, to love, to fulfilling our calling as humans, creative and redemptive dancers in this dance of creation.

Where are we? In a world of wonders, called forth by love.

Who are we? We are angel beasts, rumors of glory, called to image the Creator God of love.

What's wrong? We live in the falling dark, a world of betrayal, idolatry, and ideology, hooked on avarice.

What's the remedy? We're given love and love must be returned. That love took on flesh in this glittering joker, dancing in the dragon's jaws.

In a culture of captivated imaginations we need liberation. In a culture of dehydrated imaginations we need fresh water. In a culture that has lost its imagination we need new dreams. Bruce Cockburn's art awakens such an imagination. And it is a Christian imagination.

Jesus, thank you, joyous Son.

# Discography

- *Bruce Cockburn*. Produced by Eugene Martynec. True North Records, 1970.

- *High Winds White Sky*. Produced by Eugene Martynec. True North Records, 1971.

- *Sunwheel Dance*. Produced by Eugene Martynec. True North Records, 1972.

- *Night Vision*. Produced by Eugene Martynec and Bruce Cockburn. True North Records, 1973.

- *Salt, Sun and Time*. Produced by Eugene Martynec and Bruce Cockburn. True North Records, 1974.

- *Joy Will Find a Way*. Produced by Eugene Martynec. True North Records, 1975.

- *In the Falling Dark*. Produced by Eugene Martynec. True North Records, 1976.

- *Circles in the Stream*. Produced by Eugene Martynec. True North Records, 1977.

- *Further Adventures Of*. Produced by Eugene Martynec. True North Records, 1978.

- *Dancing in the Dragon's Jaws*. Produced by Eugene Martynec. True North Records, 1979.

- *Humans*. Produced by Eugene Martynec. True North Records, 1980.

- *Mummy Dust*. Produced by Eugene Martynec. True North Records, 1981.

- *Inner City Front*. Produced by Bruce Cockburn. True North Records, 1981.

- *The Trouble with Normal*. Produced by Eugene Martynec. True North Records, 1983.

- *Stealing Fire*. Produced by Jon Goldsmith and Kerry Crawford. True North Records, 1984.

- *Rumours of Glory*. Compiled by Urlich Hetscher. Verklag "plane" GmbH, Dortmund, 1985. An album released in Germany including one previously unreleased song, "Yanquie Go Home" (since released on the deluxe edition of *Stealing Fire*).

- *World of Wonders*. Produced by Jon Goldsmith and Kerry Crawford. True North Records, 1986.

- *Waiting for a Miracle*. Produced by Jon Goldsmith and Bernie Finkelstein. True North Records, 1987.
- *Big Circumstance*. Produced by Jon Goldsmith. True North Records, 1988.
- *Bruce Cockburn Live*. Produced by Jon Goldsmith. True North Records, 1990.
- *Nothing but a Burning Light*. Produced by T-Bone Burnett. True North Records, 1991.
- *Christmas*. Produced by Bruce Cockburn. True North Records, 1993.
- *Dart to the Heart*. Produced by T-Bone Burnett. True North Records, 1994.
- *Charity of Night*. Produced by Bruce Cockburn and Colin Linden. True North Records, 1996.
- *You Pay Your Money and You Take Your Chance (Live)*. Produced by Bruce Cockburn and Colin Linden. True North Records, 1998.
- *Breakfast in New Orleans, Dinner in Timbuktu*. Produced by Bruce Cockburn and Colin Linden. True North Records, 1999.
- *Anything, Anywhere, Anytime: Singles*. Produced by Bruce Cockburn and Colin Linden. True North Records, 2002.
- *You've Never Seen Everything*. Produced by Bruce Cockburn and Colin Linden. True North Records, 2003.
- *Speechless: The Instrumental Bruce Cockburn*. Produced by Bruce Cockburn and Colin Linden. True North Records, 2005.
- *Life Short Call Now*. Produced by Jonathan Goldsmith. True North Records, 2006.
- *Slice of Life: Bruce Cockburn Live Solo*. Produced by Colin Linden. True North Records, 2009.
- *Small Source of Comfort*. Produced by Colin Linden. True North Records, 2011.

# Notes

## Chapter 1 God, Friendship, and Art

1. David Byrne's review of the show, *The Cockburn Project*, www.cockburnproject.net.

2. "To Fit in My Heart," *Life Short Call Now*.

3. The album itself concludes with an instrumental piece, "Nude Descending Staircase," alluding to the 1912 painting of the same name by Marcel Duchamp.

4. "Understanding Nothing," *Big Circumstance*.

5. Bruce Cockburn, interview by Sarah Hampton, "The Journey Is What I'm Interested In," *Globe and Mail*, Jan. 26, 2002, R3.

6. "Gospel of Bondage," *Big Circumstance*.

7. "Iris of the World," *Small Source of Comfort*.

8. In an interview with David Batstone, "Straight to the Heart: Bruce Cockburn's Songs of Subversion," *Sojourners*, September/October 1994, 25.

9. In this light, I find the title of my first article on Cockburn to have been a tad presumptuous. "The Christian Worldview of Bruce Cockburn: Prophetic Art in a Dangerous Time," *Toronto Journal of Theology* 5, no. 2 (1989): 170–87.

10. Cited in ibid.

11. *The Cockburn Project*, "Bruce Inducted into Canadian Music Hall of Fame," www.cockburnproject.net/news/20010305junos.html.

12. "The Gift," *Big Circumstance*. Similar themes are found in a very old song just recently recorded on *Small Source of Comfort*, "Gifts."

13. *Bono: In Conversation with Michka Assayas* (New York: Riverhead Books/Penguin, 2005), 26 (italics added).

14. Cited by Bill Flanagan, *U2 at the End of the World* (New York: Delacorte Press, 1995), 171.

15. On March 5, 2001. The Juno Awards are the Canadian equivalent to the Grammys in the United States.

16. Indeed, Bono has written an evocative introduction to the book of Psalms for *Selections from the Book of Psalms: Authorized King James Version* (New York: Grove, 1999).

17. Walter Brueggemann, *Abiding Astonishment: Psalms, Modernity and the Making of History* (Louisville: Westminster John Knox, 1991), 21. See also Brueggemann's *Israel's Praise: Doxology against Idolatry and Ideology* (Philadelphia: Fortress, 1988), and *The Message of the Psalms* (Minneapolis: Augsburg, 1984).

18. Ibid. Italics in original.

19. Brian J. Walsh, "Worldviews," in *The Complete Book of Everyday Christianity*, ed. Robert Banks and R. Paul Stevens (Downers Grove, IL: InterVarsity Press, 1997), 1136–37.

20. Charles Taylor's notion of a "social imaginary" that is carried in "images, stories, legends" and that both informs us of "how things usually go" and gives us an idea of how things "ought to go" by means of an implicit understanding is close to what I am getting at. *A Secular Age* (Cambridge, MA: Harvard University Press, 2007), 172–73.

21. On "lived narratives," see Christian Smith, *Moral, Believing Animals: Human Personhood and Culture* (Oxford: Oxford University Press, 2003), ch. 4.

22. Richard Middleton and I developed these four worldview questions in *The Transforming Vision: Shaping a Christian World View* (Downers Grove, IL: InterVarsity, 1984) and *Truth Is Stranger Than It Used to Be: Biblical Faith in a Postmodern Age* (Downers Grove, IL: InterVarsity, 1995).

## Chapter 2 Ecstatic Wonderings and Dangerous Kicking

1. "Wondering Where the Lions Are" has been covered by Steve Bell, *My Dinner with Bruce* (Signpost Music, 2006); Jimmy Buffett, *Hoot* (2006); Donavan Frankenreiter, *Recycled Recipes* (2007); Grace Griffith, *Minstrel Song* (Blix Street-Records, 2000); Bill Mallonee & Vigilantes of Love, *Roaring Lambs* (Squint Entertainment, 2000); Michael Occhipinti, *Creation Dream—The Songs of Bruce Cockburn* (True North, 2000); Leo Sayer, *World Radio* (Chrysalis, 1982); and B-Funn, *Kick at the Darkness: Songs of Bruce Cockburn* (Intrepid, 1991).

2. "Planet of the Clowns," *The Trouble with Normal.*

3. I began writing this chapter on February 16, 2009. My friend Robbin Burry died three days later, in the early evening of February 19. My prayer is that some kind of ecstasy now has a hold on her as she has passed into the arms of the Everlasting.

4. Paul Zollo, "Closer to the Light with Bruce Cockburn," *SongTalk* 4, no. 2 (1994). Accessed at http://cockburnproject.net/ as a comment on "Wondering Where the Lions Are."

5. Perhaps Erazim Kohak was getting at the same thing when he wrote, "Without the vision of eternity, there can be no tenable vision of history and no freedom, only a historicism which entraps humans in the order of time." *The Embers and the Stars: A Philosophical Inquiry into the Moral Sense of Nature* (Chicago: University of Chicago Press, 1984), 174.

6. Cited by Robert K. Johnston, *Reel Spirituality: Theology and Film in Dialogue* (Grand Rapids: Baker Academic, 2000), from the 1932 essay "Religion and Literature," in *Religion and Modern Literature: Essays in Theory and Criticism*, ed. G. B. Tennyson and Edward E. Ericson Jr. (Grand Rapids: Eerdmans, 1975), 21.

7. Bruce Cockburn, interview by Mike Rimmer, "Bruce Cockburn: Still Wondering Where the Lions Are," *Cross Rhythms* 77 (Oct. 30, 2003): accessed online at www.crossrhythms.co.uk /articles/music/Still_Wondering_Where_the_Lions_Are/8264/p1.

8. Howard Druckman, "The Quiet Man," *Nerve*, July 1986, 11.

9. Cockburn in Rimmer, "Still Wondering."

10. Ibid.

11. "Hills of Morning," *Dancing in the Dragon's Jaws*. This discussion is dependent on an earlier article that I coauthored with J. Richard Middleton, "Dancing in the Dragon's Jaws: Imaging God at the End of the Twentieth Century," *Crucible* 2, no. 3 (Spring 1992): 11–18.

12. "The Trouble with Normal," *The Trouble with Normal.*

13. Perhaps there is also here an allusion to the old Quaker hymn "The Lord of the Dance."

14. Luke 6:21, 25.

15. Psalm 30:11.

16. Isaiah 25:8; Jeremiah 31:13.

17. Genesis 1:2 (RSV).

18. Genesis 1:3.

19. This isn't to say that Cockburn never has escapist sentiments. Indeed, I think that some of Cockburn's songs that were most well received by Christians in the seventies were marred by a

dualistic spirituality of escape that is much too common in Christian piety, especially "evangelical" piety. I detect such a spirituality in songs such as "Can I Go with You?" (*Further Adventures Of*) and even the early favorite "Festival of Friends" (*In the Falling Dark*).

20. J. Richard Middleton documents both the anti-Babylonian rhetorical character of the opening chapters of Genesis and the role of Tiamat as the great sea monster that we meet in various biblical texts in his book *The Liberating Image: The Imago Dei in Genesis 1* (Grand Rapids: Brazos, 2005).

21. Paul Ricoeur calls this a "surplus of meaning" in the work that goes beyond what could be limited by the "intent" of the artist or author. *Interpretation Theory: Discourse and the Surplus of Meaning* (Fort Worth: Texas Christian University Press, 1976), chap. 2. See also his *Essays in Biblical Interpretation* (Philadelphia: Fortress, 1980).

22. Nicholas Lash and others have used this analogy for the interpretation of Scripture. See his classic essay "Performing the Scriptures," in *Theology on the Way to Emmaus* (London: SCM, 1986). My thanks to Steven Bouma-Prediger for the Ricoeur and Lash references.

23. A phrase often used by the late Ben Meyer when he taught biblical studies and interpretation at McMaster University.

24. Johnston, *Reel Spirituality*, 49. Also writing about theology and film, Craig Detweiler calls for a reversing of the hermeneutical flow and insists that the conversation must be driven by the films themselves, not the theology that the interpreter brings to the films. Such a hermeneutic wants to see "theology arising out of the art, rather than imposing it within the text." *Into the Dark: Seeing the Sacred in the Top Films of the 21st Century* (Grand Rapids: Baker Academic, 2008), 43. While I am in fundamental agreement with this prioritization of the artwork, it seems to me that the relation between art and interpreter is perhaps a little more dialectical than Detweiler's perspective would suggest. We do not want to impose a perspective or a theology on the art, but we can interpret art only as full human beings who are always experiencing art from some perspective, some fundamental assumptions, indeed some worldview. There is simply no way out of this hermeneutical circle.

25. Comments made in concert at Hastings Lake, Alberta, August 30, 1979. Transcribed by Doug Stacey and accessed as a comment on "Creation Dream" online at http://cockburnproject.net/songs&music/cd.html.

26. I have articulated my view of biblical authority in more depth in "Reimagining Biblical Authority," *Christian Scholar's Review* 26, no. 2 (Winter 1996): 206–20.

27. Walter Brueggemann, *Interpretation and Obedience* (Minneapolis: Fortress, 1991), 199.

28. Paul Ricoeur, *The Philosophy of Paul Ricoeur*, ed. Charles E. Reagan and David Steward (Boston: Beacon Press, 1979), esp. chaps. 15 and 16.

29. Walter Brueggemann, *The Prophetic Imagination*, 2nd ed. (Philadelphia: Fortress, 2001), 40.

30. See Walter Brueggemann, *Hopeful Imagination: Prophetic Voices in Exile* (Philadelphia: Fortress, 1986), 23–26.

31. C. S. Lewis, *The Personal Heresy*, cited in Leland Ryken, ed., *The Christian Imagination: The Practice of Faith in Literature and Writing*, rev. and expanded ed. (Colorado Springs: Shaw Books, 2002), 56. The noninclusive nature of Lewis's language reflects the era in which he wrote.

32. Bruce Cockburn, interview by Alex Varty, "Bruce Cockburn: Being Real," *Vancouver Free Press—Georgia Straight*, Feb. 12–26, 1986, 5.

33. Galatians 3:28.

34. "Maybe the Poet," *Stealing Fire*.

35. Brueggemann, *Prophetic Imagination*, 3 (italics in original).

36. Cockburn, in Rimmer, "Still Wondering."

37. "Trouble with Normal," *The Trouble with Normal*.

38. Brueggemann, *Prophetic Imagination*, 46.

39. "People See through You," *World of Wonders*.

40. "Waiting for a Miracle," *Waiting for a Miracle.*

41. Wassily Kandinsky, "Concerning the Spiritual in Art," in *Art, Creativity and the Sacred,* ed. Diane Apostolos-Cappadona (New York: Crossroad, 1986), 6.

42. Ibid.

43. David Dark, *Everyday Apocalypse: The Sacred Revealed in Radiohead, The Simpsons, and Other Pop Culture Icons* (Grand Rapids: Brazos, 2002), 12.

44. Ibid., 21. What Dark describes as apocalyptic art is functionally the same as what I am describing as prophetic art.

45. "Call It Democracy," *World of Wonders.* Whether Cockburn is always successful in such resistance to propagandizing is up for discussion. For example, a song like "The Gospel of Bondage" on *Big Circumstance* could be judged as propagandistic in tone, perhaps because it is an attack on right-wing Christian propaganda. Cockburn was right when he said, "If you're going to avoid letting your art degenerate into propaganda, you have to stay away from ideological guidelines in your art." But perhaps he isn't always successful in living up to this ideal. The Cockburn quote is from Druckman, "Quiet Man," 10.

46. "Lovers in a Dangerous Time," *Stealing Fire.* "Lovers" was a Top 40 hit for Cockburn in Canada and was named the eleventh-greatest Canadian song of all time on CBC's Radio One in 2005. It was also released on *Waiting for a Miracle and Anything, Anytime, Anywhere.* The song was covered by the Barenaked Ladies on the Cockburn tribute album *Kick at the Darkness* (Intrepid Records, 1991) and was that band's first Top 40 Canadian hit in 1992. Barenaked Ladies' "Lovers" was rereleased on *Disc One: All Their Greatest Hits* (Reprise Records, 2001), and a live version appears on the War Child benefit album, *Peace Songs* (Sony Music, 2003). Michael Occhipinti released a wonderful jazz instrumental rendition of the song on his album *Creation Dream: The Songs of Bruce Cockburn* (True North Records, 2000). Dan Fogelberg has also covered "Lovers" on *The Wild Places* (Epic/Full Moon, 1990).

47. J. T. Fraser, cited by Jeremy Rifkin, *Time Wars: The Primary Conflict of Human History* (New York: Touchstone Books, 1987), 59.

48. "Feast of Fools," *Further Adventures Of.*

49. Luke 9:25.

50. See Luke 6:20–26.

51. "Trouble with Normal."

52. "Isn't That What Friends Are For?" *Breakfast in New Orleans.*

53. Mary Jo Leddy, "We Beg to Differ," *Say to the Darkness* (Toronto: Lester and Orpen Dennys, 1990).

54. Leonard Cohen, "Anthem," *The Future* (Sony, 1992).

55. John 1:5.

56. Isaiah 60:1–3.

57. Specifically, John 15:1–17 and Jeremiah 29:1–14. This sermon was delivered at the wedding of Ericka Stephens and Andrew Rennie at Trinity Anglican Church in Cambridge, Ontario, on October 7, 2006.

## Chapter 3 Cockburn's Windows

1. From *An Experiment in Criticism*, cited in Leland Ryken, *The Christian Imagination: The Practice of Faith in Literature and Writing*, rev. and expanded (Colorado Springs: Shaw Books, 2002), 51.

2. "Going to the Country," *Bruce Cockburn.*

3. "Man of a Thousand Faces," *Bruce Cockburn.*

4. "All the Diamonds in the World," *Salt, Sun and Time.*

5. Ibid.

6. "Life's Mistress," *High Winds White Sky.*

7. "Up on the Hillside," *Sunwheel Dance.*

8. Matthew 28:16.

9. "God Bless the Children," *Night Vision.*

10. "All the Diamonds in the World," Sun, *Salt and Time.*

11. "Stained Glass," *Salt, Sun and Time.*

12. "Gavin's Woodpile," *In the Falling Dark.*

13. Cf. Romans 8:22.

14. "Lappish runes" is a reference to indigenous shamans in Lapland (the Arctic regions of Scandinavia) who covered their drums with striking magical symbols, which were then used as a means for divining the spirits.

15. In the 1960s the Dryden Paper Company dumped mercury into the Wabigoon River system in Northern Ontario, polluting the traditional fishing grounds of the Grassy Narrows Reserve and other First Nations communities. The result was an onslaught of Minimata disease in the community that continues to this day.

16. "Laughter," *Further Adventures Of.*

17. "You Get Bigger as You Go," *Humans.*

18. "How I Spent My Fall Vacation," *Humans.*

19. "Wanna Go Walking," *Inner City Front.*

20. "Sahara Gold," *Stealing Fire.*

21. "Peggy's Kitchen Wall," *Stealing Fire.*

22. "Gospel of Bondage," *Big Circumstance.*

23. "Waiting for a Miracle," *Waiting for a Miracle.*

24. Cf. 1 Corinthians 13:12.

25. Amos 5:24.

26. "Let the Bad Air Out," *Breakfast in New Orleans, Dinner in Timbuktu.*

27. "Call It Democracy," *World of Wonders.*

28. "Postcards from Cambodia," *You've Never Seen Everything.*

29. "Beautiful Creatures," *Life Short Call Now.*

30. "Postcards from Cambodia."

31. "Waiting for a Miracle."

## Chapter 4  Creation Dream

1. Esther Bowser, "May I Have This Dance? Dance Imagery and Covenant in Bruce Cockburn's *Dancing in the Dragon's Jaws*" (unpublished essay, University of Toronto, March 13, 2007), 1.

2. C. S. Lewis, *The Magician's Nephew* (London: Lions, 1980), 117.

3. Ibid., 116.

4. "Child of the Wind," *Nothing but a Burning Light.*

5. Norman Wirzba, *The Paradise of God: Renewing Religion in an Ecological Age* (Oxford: Oxford University Press, 2003), 111.

6. "Spring Song," *Bruce Cockburn.*

7. Italics added.

8. Whether this Fool is a reference to the first card in a deck of Tarot cards, or an early reference to Jesus, or both, doesn't really matter at this point. What seems significant is simply that this is not a renewal that we achieve on our own. We must search "beside the Fool." Recall that in "Man of a Thousand Faces" on this same album, Cockburn asks, "it's my turn but where's the guide?" This is an artist on a spiritual quest from the very beginning.

9. Similar themes of temporal circularity can be heard in "High Winds White Sky," *High Winds White Sky.*

10. "Keep It Open," *Bruce Cockburn.*

11. "Change Your Mind," *Bruce Cockburn.*

12. "Life Will Open," *Sunwheel Dance.*

13. Ibid.

14. "Fall," *Sunwheel Dance.*

15. "Mama Just Wants to Barrelhouse All Night Long," *Night Vision.*

16. "When the Sun Goes Nova," *Night Vision.*

17. "You Don't Have to Play the Horses," *Night Vision.*

18. "The Blues Got the World . . . ," *Night Vision.*

19. "God Bless the Children," *Night Vision.*

20. "Let Us Go Laughing," *High Winds White Sky.*

21. "Life's Mistress," *High Winds White Sky.*

22. Martin Wroe, "Bruce Cockburn," *Third Way* (Aug. 1987), 19.

23. C. S. Lewis, *The Lion, the Witch and the Wardrobe* (London: Fontana, 1950).

24. Ecclesiastes 1:2.

25. "Starwheel," *Joy Will Find a Way.*

26. On the ubiquity of metaphors of change in Cockburn's work, cf. "Change Your Mind," *Bruce Cockburn*; "Stained Glass," *Sun, Salt and Time*; "The Gift," *Big Circumstance*; "Mighty Trucks of Midnight," *Nothing but a Burning Light*; and "Life Short Call Now," *Life Short Call Now*, among others.

27. "Lord of the Starfields," *In the Falling Dark.*

28. Ecclesiastes 12:13.

29. Mark 12:28–34; Matthew 22:34–40. Cf. John 13:34–35.

30. Psalm 19:1–4.

31. "Lord of the Starfields."

32. Psalm 33:5.

33. The image of God as the "Ancient of Days" is found in the "night vision" of the prophet Daniel (7:9, 13, 22). The language of "beginning and end" is used with reference to Christ in Revelation 1:8, 17; 21:6; 22:13.

34. Perhaps "sower of life" is an allusion to the parable of the sower (Matthew 13:1–23; Mark 4:1–9; Luke 8:4–8) or to Genesis 2, where God plants a garden.

35. "Creation Dream," *Dancing in the Dragon's Jaws.* In a concert at Hastings Lake, Alberta, on August 30, 1979, Cockburn introduced this song as "a fictional rendering of creation. Not to be confused with Genesis." (From a transcript by Doug Stacey posted at The Cockburn Project, http://www.cockburnproject.net/.) I am struck, however, by how deeply this "creation dream" in fact resonates with the imagery and flow of Genesis 1.

36. Lewis, *Magician's Nephew*, 93.

37. "Hills of Morning," *Dancing in the Dragon's Jaws.*

38. "Mighty Trucks of Midnight," *Nothing But a Burning Light.*

39. "Outside a Broken Phone Booth with Money in My Hand," *Further Adventures Of.*

40. Wirzba, *Paradise of God*, 70. Wirzba also argues that if the ecological revolution is to be successful, it "must . . . include the expansion of our sympathies and the redirection of our desires in such a way that our loyalties to the biotic community become automatic, the spontaneous expression of how we feel" (111). Or, in Cockburn's terms, such an expansion of affection must become "basic as a breath."

41. Psalm 98:8.

42. Psalm 148.

43. Psalm 96:12; Luke 19:40.

44. "In the Falling Dark," *In the Falling Dark.*

45. On creation groaning in travail, see Romans 8:22–25. On creation as eloquent, see Albert Borgmann, *Crossing the Postmodern Divide* (Chicago: University of Chicago Press, 1992), 118. See also J. Richard Middleton and Brian J. Walsh, *Truth Is Stranger Than It Used to Be: Biblical Faith in a Postmodern Age* (Downers Grove, IL: InterVarsity Press, 1995), ch. 7; and Brian Walsh, Marianne Karsh, and Nik Ansell, "Trees, Forestry and the Responsiveness of Creation," *Cross Currents* 44, no. 2 (1994): 149–62.

46. "Everywhere Dance," *You've Never Seen Everything.*

47. "Understanding Nothing," *Big Circumstance.*

48. "World of Wonders," *World of Wonders.*

49. "Joy Will Find a Way," *Joy Will Find a Way.*

50. Genesis 9:8–17.

51. Bruce Cockburn, interview with Darren Hughes, "Strange Waters: A Conversation with Bruce Cockburn," *Beyond Magazine* 14 (2004), http://www.longpauses.com/blog/2008/10/strange-waters-conversation-with-bruce.html.

52. "Mystery," *Life Short Call Now.*

## Chapter 5 At Home in the Darkness, but Hungry for Dawn

1. Wendell Berry, *Remembering* (San Francisco: North Point Press, 1988).

2. This chapter is dependent on two of my earlier articles: "One Day I Shall Be Home" *Christianity and the Arts* 7.1 (Winter 2000): 28–32; and "'At Home in the Darkness, But Hungry for Dawn'—Global Homelessness and a Passion for Homecoming in the Music of Bruce Cockburn," *Cultural Encounters: A Journal for the Theology of Culture* 1.2 (Summer 2005): 75–88.

3. "Birmingham Shadows," *Charity of Night.*

4. "World of Wonders," *World of Wonders.*

5. "In the Falling Dark," *In the Falling Dark.*

6. Edward Said, "Reflections on Exile," in *Out There: Marginalization and Contemporary Cultures,* ed. Russell Ferguson, Martha Gever, Trinh T. Minh-ha, and Cornel West (New York: New Museum of Contemporary Art, 1990), 357.

7. For an extensive discussion of these themes, see Steven Bouma-Prediger and Brian J. Walsh, *Beyond Homelessness: Christian Faith in a Culture of Displacement* (Grand Rapids: Eerdmans, 2008).

8. "One Day I Walk," *High Winds White Sky.* This song has been covered by k.d. lang on her album *Hymns of the 49th Parallel* (Nonesuch Records, 2004); Anne Murray on *Snowbird* (Capital, 1970); Anne Murray and Glen Campbell, *Anne Murray and Glen Campbell* (EMI, 1999); New Glass Revival, *Commonwealth* (Flying Fish, 1981); The Rankins, *Uprooted* (Uni/Rounder, 1999); Tom Rush, *Ladies Love Outlaws* (Columbia, 1974); The Skydiggers, Various Artists, *Kick at the Darkness: Songs of Bruce Cockburn* (Intrepid, 1991).

9. Cockburn's understanding of himself as a nomad appears in "Birmingham Shadows"; "Use Me While You Can," *Breakfast in New Orleans, Dinner in Timbuktu;* and "Life Short Call Now," *Life Short Call Now*: "How many ways to say goodbye / Can one man fit in a nomad life?"

10. "Lord of the Starfields," *In the Falling Dark.*

11. "Shipwrecked at the Stable Door," *Big Circumstance.*

12. Kimberly Dovey, "Home and Homelessness," in *Home Environments,* ed. Irwin Altman and Carol Werner (New York: Plenum, 1985), 54.

13. "Dream like Mine," *Nothing but a Burning Light.*

14. Matthew 5:1–12; Luke 6:20–23.

15. "How I Spent My Fall Vacation," *Humans.*

16. "Joy Will Find a Way," *Joy Will Find a Way.*

17. "Loner," *Inner City Front.*

18. "Candy Man's Gone," *The Trouble with Normal.*

19. "Fascist Architecture," *Humans.*

20. *Stealing Fire.*

21. *World of Wonders.*

22. Ibid.

23. *Waiting for a Miracle.*

24. *Big Circumstance.*

25. The Year of Jubilee began on the Day of Atonement with the blowing of the trumpets. This was the fiftieth year, the Sabbath of Sabbaths in Israelite faith, in which all those who had lost their inherited homelands had them restored. See Leviticus 25.

26. See Isaiah 60–61.

27. "Great Big Love," *Nothing but a Burning Light*.

28. Matthew 11:28.

29. "Dweller by a Dark Stream," *Mummy Dust*.

30. "All Our Dark Tomorrows," *You've Never Seen Everything*.

31. Richard Middleton and I have written two reviews of this album: "On the Move Again," *re.generation quarterly* 3, no. 2 (Spring 1997): 40–41; and "Bruce Cockburn—Minstrel of a Prophetic Spirituality," *Catholic New Times* 21, no. 12 (Aug. 1997): 17.

32. The impossibility of escape is also a theme in "Night Train," "Get Up, Jonah," and "Pacing the Cage," on the same album.

33. "Birmingham Shadows," *Charity of Night*.

34. Indeed, the title track, "The Charity of Night," offers us three scenes, three painful memories, that constitute the "haunting hands of memory."

35. "Strange Waters," *Charity of Night*. This discussion is indebted to J. Richard Middleton's article "From Clenched Fist to the Open Hand: A Postmodern Reading of the Twenty-Third Psalm," in *The Strategic Smorgasbord of Post-Modernity: Literature and the Christian Critic*, ed. Deborah Bowen (Newcastle, UK: Cambridge Scholars Press, 2007), 307–25.

36. Psalm 23:1–3 (RSV).

37. "Pacing the Cage," *Charity of Night*.

38. "Going to the Country," *Bruce Cockburn*.

39. *World of Wonders*.

40. Deuteronomy 15:7, 11.

41. Psalm 23:2, 5, 6.

42. The metaphor of flight here might be an allusion to Isaiah 40:31: "But those who wait for the LORD shall renew their strength, they shall mount up with wings like eagles."

## Chapter 6   Creation Dreams and Ecological Nightmares

1. A version of this chapter has also appeared as "Creation Dreams and Ecological Nightmares," *Perspectives: A Journal of Reformed Thought* (February, 2011): 8–12. See also my article "Leave No Footprints," *Alternatives Journal* 37, no. 4 (June 2011): 23–25.

2. This chapter was first developed as a chapel talk at World Vision Canada and then as a sermon at Christ Church (Anglican) in Burritt's Rapids, Ontario, in the spring of 2009. At World Vision I was assisted in my presentation by the fine Toronto folk-jazz ensemble Hobson's Choice (http://www.hobsonschoicemusic.com), and at Christ Church the music was wonderfully led by the Cameron Strings (http://www.cameronstrings.ca). The significance of Burritt's Rapids won't be lost on any fans of the early songs of Bruce Cockburn, since many of them were composed when Cockburn lived in that town.

3. Genesis 1:1–4.

4. Jeremiah 4:23.

5. Genesis 1:9–12.

6. Isaiah 24:4–6, 11, 19.

7. Genesis 1:20–22.

8. Hosea 4:1–3.

9. Genesis 1:24–25.

10. Jeremiah 9:10.

11. Genesis 1:26–28, 30–31.

12. Jeremiah 4:23–26.

13. This is not the place for mounting a full biblical exposition against such heaven-focused pietism. I have argued for a creationally restorative worldview elsewhere, especially with J. Richard Middleton in *The Transforming Vision: Shaping a Christian World View* (Downers Grove, IL: InterVarsity, 1984), chaps. 3–5, and *Truth Is Stranger Than It Used to Be: Biblical Faith in a Postmodern Age* (Downers Grove, IL: InterVarsity, 1995), chaps. 5–7.

14. John 1:1–5.

15. Colossians 1:21–23. Italics added.

16. Sylvia Keesmaat and I have argued for a more creation-focused interpretation of Paul's Letter to the Colossians in *Colossians Remixed: Subverting the Empire* (Downers Grove, IL: InterVarsity Press, 2004), 112–13, 193–200.

## Chapter 7 Into a World of Dancers

1. "Creation Dream," "Hills of Morning," *Dancing in the Dragon's Jaws*; "Everywhere Dance," *You've Never Seen Everything*.

2. "Long Time Love Song," *Joy Will Find a Way*. See also "The Thirteenth Mountain," *Bruce Cockburn*; and "Life Will Open," *Sunwheel Dance*.

3. "Hills of Morning," *Dancing in the Dragon's Jaws*.

4. "Life Will Open."

5. The gender-exclusive language is intentional. Modernist notions of autonomy were both sexist and racist. Autonomy was a privilege of only the higher forms of the human species—white males. In the American Declaration of Independence, "we the people" did not include women, African slaves, or the aboriginal peoples of the Americas.

6. "Laughter," *Further Adventures Of*. Notice that Cockburn doesn't refer to the man "in" the world, but the man "of" the world. Echoing New Testament language of being "in but not of the world," it would appear that the implication is that this man is "worldly" in the biblical sense of having an imagination that cannot see beyond the range of normal sight.

7. "Life Will Open."

8. This has been the common perception in environmental ethics ever since the publication of Lynn White Jr.'s famous essay "The Historical Roots of Our Ecological Crisis," *Science* 155, no. 3767 (March 1967): 1203–7. It is important to note that White's argument against Christian complicity in the environmental crisis is historically well founded and that the only appropriate response of a Christian is to repent of the past sins of our religious tradition. That Christians have terribly misread their own Scriptures is something that I will attempt to show in the next few paragraphs. But White isn't to be faulted for telling the story of this misreading. Nor does a more ecologically friendly reading of the Bible erase our historical guilt. For helpful discussion of the ecological complaint against Christianity and for a compelling Christian ecological vision, see Steven Bouma-Prediger, *For the Beauty of the Earth: A Christian Vision for Creation Care*, 2nd ed. (Grand Rapids: Baker Academic, 2010).

9. For such a historical appraisal, see Paul Santmire, *The Travail of Nature: The Ambiguous Promise of Christian Theology* (Philadelphia: Fortress, 1985).

10. Genesis 1:28.

11. Again, this is not the place to offer a full and comprehensive interpretation of these texts with reference to original languages or ancient Near Eastern parallels. For such a study, see J. Richard Middleton's very fine book, *The Liberating Image: The Imago Dei in Genesis 1* (Grand Rapids: Brazos, 2005).

12. These paragraphs are dependent upon my earlier article with J. Richard Middleton, "Dancing in the Dragon's Jaws: Imaging God at the End of the Twentieth Century," *Crucible* 2, no. 3 (Spring 1992): 11–18.

13. Genesis 2:15.

14. Psalm 33:5; "Lord of the Starfields," *In the Falling Dark*.

15. "Starwheel," *Joy Will Find a Way*.

16. 1 Corinthians 13:4–5.

17. Norman Wirzba, *The Paradise of God: Renewing Religion in an Ecological Age* (Oxford: Oxford University Press, 2003), 140.

18. Colossians 1:15.

19. Philippians 2:6–8.

20. Harvey Cox, *Feast of Fools* (New York: Harper and Row, 1972).

21. Mark 9:35.

22. "Hills of Morning," *Dancing in the Dragon's Jaws*.

23. Perhaps a veiled reference to the Alex Colville painting of a looming train that graced the cover of Cockburn's 1973 album, *Night Vision*.

24. The final chapter of Harvey Cox's book *Feast of Fools* is called "Christ the Harlequin." Cockburn's indebtedness to Cox is acknowledged in the liner notes of the album.

25. The image of the river is rich in biblical meaning. In the Hebrew Scriptures, the River Jordan stands as that place of crossing from wilderness to promised land, from exile to homecoming, and the book of Revelation picks up these themes with the river of life. See Revelation 22:1–5.

26. "Spring Song," *Bruce Cockburn*.

27. "Put Our Hearts Together," *The Trouble with Normal*.

28. "Dancing in Paradise," *World of Wonders*.

29. "Berlin Tonight," *World of Wonders*.

30. "Wanna Go Walking," *Inner City Front*.

31. "One of the Best Ones," *Nothing but a Burning Light*.

32. "And We Dance," *Inner City Front*.

33. Ibid.

34. The number seven signifies completion or fullness in biblical symbolism, and the heart is the center of human life. The seven of hearts could, then, suggest that if you are to enter this dance, you must do so with full commitment, with your whole heart. I am indebted to Sylvia Keesmaat for this insight.

35. "No Footprints," *Dancing in the Dragon's Jaws*.

36. I am indebted to my student Esther Bowser for this interpretation. "May I Have This Dance? Dance Imagery and Covenant in Bruce Cockburn's *Dancing in the Dragon's Jaws*" (unpublished essay, University of Toronto, March 13, 2007).

37. "Gavin's Woodpile," *In the Falling Dark*.

38. Psalm 116:13; Jeremiah 31:4.

## Chapter 8  Humans

1. "Grim Travellers in Dawn Skies," *Humans*.

2. "You Get Bigger as You Go," *Humans*.

3. "No Footprints," *Dancing*.

4. "More Not More," *Humans*.

5. "Northern Lights," *Dancing*.

6. "The Rose above the Sky," *Humans*. Even the cover art bears witness to a significant shift in perspective between these two albums. While *Dragon's* is graced with a wonderfully colorful and allusive piece of art from the Canadian aboriginal artist Bill Morrissey, on the cover of *Humans* we meet a less than flattering photograph of a rather dazed-looking Bruce Cockburn. The rich and evocative visual symbolism and mythology of Morrissey meets the "what-you-see-is-what-you-get" world of broken humanity.

7. "You Get Bigger as You Go."

8. "Slow Down Fast," *Life Short Call Now*.

9. "What about the Bond," "Guerilla Betrayed," *Humans*.

10. A reference to Ingmar Bergman's 1957 film.

11. In the second verse of this song, Cockburn writes of an encounter with a young cop on a Roman street: "well don't shoot me man i'm a graceful slow dancer / i'm just a dream to you not real at all." He's still a dancer, but not quite real.

12. "Gavin's Woodpile," *In the Falling Dark*.

13. Psalm 88:3, 6, 8, 9, 17.

14. I am indebted to Richard Middleton for this insight into the nature of eros in Cockburn's work.

15. This depiction of psalms of orientation, disorientation, and reorientation is dependent upon Walter Brueggemann, *The Message of the Psalms* (Minneapolis: Augsburg, 1984), and Brueggemann, *The Psalms and the Life of Faith* (Minneapolis: Fortress, 1995).

16. "Creation Dream," *Dancing in the Dragon's Jaws*.

17. "Lord of the Starfields," *In the Falling Dark*.

18. Cf. the vision of the prophet Isaiah: "Is not this the fast that I choose: to loose the bonds of injustice, to undo the thongs of the yoke, to let the oppressed go free, and to break every yoke?" (Isaiah 58:6).

19. "Nick Cave's Love Song Lecture" (presented in Vienna, Sept. 25, 1999), http://everything2 .com/index.pl?node_id=800055.

20. "Whole Night Sky," *Charity of Night*.

21. Psalm 6:6–7a.

22. See Genesis 9:8–17.

23. Psalm 42:5, 9–10. For the psalmist's memories, see v. 4.

24. See, for example, Psalms 96 and 98.

25. Paul Ricoeur, *The Symbolism of Evil*, trans. Emerson Buchanan (Boston: Beacon Press, 1967).

26. Andy Whitman comments on this song: "Instead of pie in the sky we have a rose in the sky, an impossibly romantic, florid (quite literally) vision of beauty that goes on forever." "The Rose above the Sky," *Good Letters: The Image Blog*, Nov. 16, 2009, http://imagejournal.org /page/blog/the-rose-above-the-sky.

27. Gambling imagery can be found in numerous Cockburn songs. Cf. "You Don't Have to Play the Horses," *Night Vision*; "Starwheel," *Joy Will Find a Way*; "You Pay Your Money and You Take Your Chance," *Inner City Front*; "And We Dance," *Inner City Front*; "Put Our Hearts Together," *The Trouble with Normal*; and "The Gift," *Big Circumstance*.

28. Genesis 1:3; John 8:12.

29. Colossians 1:15–20, 27.

30. Psalm 8:5–8.

31. Similar tensions are noted in "Burden of the Angel/Beast," on *Dart to the Heart*. This song could also be seen as a meditation on Psalm 8: "Could be the famine / could be the feast / Could be the pusher / Could be the priest / Always ourselves we love the least / That's the burden of the angel/beast." Or we could say that we are "radiant angels" while also being "earthly slaves." "Loner," *Inner City Front*.

32. In "Great Big Love" on *Nothing but a Burning Light*, Cockburn sings, "Never had a lot of faith in human beings / But sometimes we manage to shine / Like a light on a hill beaming out to space / From somewhere hard to find."

## Chapter 9  Broken Wheel

1. Christian Smith, *Moral, Believing Animals: Human Personhood and Culture* (Oxford: Oxford University Press, 2003), 8.

2. Much of this discussion of "Broken Wheel" was first published in my coauthored article, with J. Richard Middleton, "Theology at the Rim of a Broken Wheel: Bruce Cockburn and Christian Faith in a Postmodern World," *Grail* 9, no. 2 (June 1993): 15–39.

3. Walter Brueggemann, *Hopeful Imagination: Prophetic Voices in Exile* (Philadelphia: Fortress, 1986), 41.

4. Isaiah 44:3; 55:1–2; 58:11.

5. John 4:7–15; 7:37–39; Revelation 21:6; 22:16–20.

6. Revelation 7:14; 12:11; 17:6.

7. Matthew 19:30; Mark 10:31; Luke 13:30.

8. Jeremiah 30:12–13.

9. John 9:1–12; cf. Mark 8:2–25.

10. I am indebted to my friend and former student Lisa Chisholm-Smith for this insight.

11. See Matthew 26:36–46. This is why many Christians observe Maundy Thursday, the eve of Good Friday, as a time of prayer and wakefulness.

12. Paul Ricoeur, *The Symbolism of Evil*, trans. Emerson Buchanan (Boston: Beacon Press, 1967), pt. 2.

13. "Put It in Your Heart," *You've Never Seen Everything*.

14. "Dweller by a Dark Stream," *Mummy Dust*.

15. Romans 7:17–21.

16. Romans 7:14.

17. "Trickle Down," *You've Never Seen Everything*.

18. Hosea 5:4.

19. "Night Train," *The Charity of Night*. Alcatraz is, of course, the infamous prison island in San Francisco Bay. St. Helena, Patmos, and the Château D'If are the islands where Napoleon, St. John, and the Count of Monte Cristo, respectively, were exiled and imprisoned.

20. "In the Falling Dark," *In the Falling Dark*.

21. "You've Never Seen Everything," *You've Never Seen Everything*.

22. I am indebted to my student West Livaudais for this analysis of the album art, from his brilliant essay "*You've Never Seen Everything*: Discerning with an Open Eye and an Open Heart" (unpublished essay, Wycliffe College, University of Toronto, Apr. 2007).

23. "All Our Dark Tomorrows," *You've Never Seen Everything*.

24. Jeremiah 17:9.

25. Genesis 6:5–6.

26. "Birmingham Shadows," *The Charity of Night*.

27. "Coldest Night of the Year," *Mummy Dust*.

28. "The Strong One," *Inner City Front*.

29. Genesis 3:7.

30. "Planet of the Clowns," *The Trouble with Normal*.

31. "You Pay Your Money and You Take Your Chance," *Inner City Front*.

32. Ibid.

33. "Coldest Night of the Year."

34. "Put Our Hearts Together," *The Trouble with Normal*.

35. "Sahara Gold" and "Making Contact" on *Stealing Fire*, and "Mango" on *Breakfast in New Orleans and Dinner in Timbuktu*, come to mind.

36. "Nick Cave's Love Song Lecture" (presented in Vienna, Sept. 25, 1999), http://everything2 .com/index.pl?node_id=800055.

37. *World of Wonders*.

38. Cockburn spoke of this sense of the absence of God in a number of interviews at this time. See Dan Oullette, "An Interview with Bruce Cockburn," *Radix*, Fall 1986, 28; Steve Rabey, "Bruce Cockburn's Social Gospel," *Contemporary Christian Music*, Oct. 1987, 33; and Steve Saint, "Bruce Cockburn: The U Interview," *U*, Apr./May 1987, 23.

39. Psalm 42:1–5.

40. "Dweller by a Dark Stream," *Mummy Dust*.

41. The stories of the temptation of Jesus are found in Matthew 4:1–11; Mark 1:12–13; and Luke 4:1–13.

42. From the album *Sunwheel Dance*.

43. All italics in these lyrics are added by the author.

44. Psalm 2:10–12a. See also 1 Samuel 10:1 and 1 Kings 19:18.

45. Matthew 26:48–49.

46. In the live version of the song on *Circles in the Stream,* the solo runs a full two minutes.

## Chapter 10 Betrayal and Shame

1. The scene is, again, The Trailf Music Hall in Buffalo, New York, but you can hear such a performance on the live album *Slice of Life*.

2. "You've Never Seen Everything," *You've Never Seen Everything*.

3. "Beautiful Creatures," *Life Short Call Now*.

4. "Broken Wheel," *Inner City Front*.

5. "The Whole Night Sky," *The Charity of Night*.

6. Italics added by author.

7. "If a Tree Falls," *Big Circumstance*.

8. Cited by Norman Wirzba, *The Paradise of God: Renewing Religion in an Ecological Age* (Oxford: Oxford University Press, 2003), 1.

9. Wendell Berry, *Sex, Economy, Freedom and Community* (New York: Pantheon, 1992), 98.

10. Romans 8:22.

11. See Leviticus 18:28; 20:22. I have addressed the question of creational responsiveness at greater length in an article jointly authored with Marianne Karsh and Nik Ansell, "Trees, Forestry and the Responsiveness of Creation," *Cross Currents* 44, no. 2 (Summer 1994): 149–62. This article is also included in *This Sacred Earth: Religion, Nature, Environment*, ed. Roger S. Gottlieb (New York: Routledge, 1995), 423–35.

12. Steven Bouma-Prediger and I have addressed our ecological homelessness at some length in *Beyond Homelessness: Christian Faith in a Culture of Dislocation* (Grand Rapids: Eerdmans, 2008), chap. 5. Bouma-Prediger's *For the Beauty of the Earth*, 2nd ed. (Grand Rapids: Baker Academic, 2010), offers a comprehensive Christian environmental perspective.

13. Hosea 4:1, 3.

14. Isaiah 24:4–6, 19.

15. Genesis 6:18.

16. Genesis 9:10.

17. Genesis 9:13.

18. I think that it is worth noting that the promise to never again destroy the world by water functions in this narrative as an implicit acknowledgment that God's plan to use the flood to cleanse the earth to start again was a failure. This is, if you will, a divine mistake. I have discussed this further in "From Shock and Awe to Shock and Grace: A Response to Naomi Klein's *The Shock Doctrine*," in *Globalization and the Gospel: Probing the Religious Foundations of Globalization,* ed. Michael W. Goheen and Erin Glanville (Vancouver: Regent College Publishing; Milton Keynes, UK: Paternoster, 2009), 141–60.

19. "Radium Rain," *Big Circumstance*.

20. "Civilization and Its Discontents," *The Trouble with Normal*.

21. "If a Tree Falls."

22. Much of this section was first published in my article "'At Home in the Darkness, but Hungry for Dawn'—Global Homelessness and a Passion for Homecoming in the Music of Bruce Cockburn," *Cultural Encounters* 1, no. 2 (Summer 2005): 75–88. See also my article, "One Day I shall be Home," *Christianity and the Arts* 7, no 1 (Winter 2000): 28–32.

23. "The Trouble with Normal," *The Trouble with Normal*.

24. Ibid.

25. "Beautiful Creatures," *Life Short Call Now.*

26. See "People See through You," *World of Wonders.*

27. "Gavin's Woodpile," *In the Falling Dark.*

28. Greg King, "In a Dangerous Time," *The Sun,* June 2004, www.thesunmagazine.org/_media/article/pdf/342_Cockburn.pdf.

29. "Call It Democracy," *World of Wonders.* "Call It Democracy" has been covered by Martyn Joseph, *Run for Cover* (PipeRecords, 2004).

30. Hosea 5:4.

31. Hosea 4:12.

32. Hosea 9:1.

33. "Candy Man's Gone," *The Trouble with Normal.*

34. In "Call It Democracy" Cockburn describes the local third world dictators who serve the interests of global capitalism as "open for business like a cheap bordello."

35. Cf. "Stolen Land," *Waiting for a Miracle,* and "Indian Wars," *Nothing but a Burning Light.*

36. Cf. "Rocket Launcher," "To Raise the Morning Star," "Dust and Diesel," and "Nicaragua," *Stealing Fire.*

37. Cf. "The Mines of Mozambique," *Charity of Night.*

38. "Planet of the Clowns," *The Trouble with Normal.*

39. "Trickle Down," *You've Never Seen Everything.*

40. "All Our Dark Tomorrows," *You've Never Seen Everything.*

41. Brian J. Walsh and Sylvia C. Keesmaat, *Colossians Remixed: Subverting the Empire* (Downers Grove, IL: InterVarsity, 2004), 28.

42. "Trickle Down." For an analysis of the recent history of global capitalism that is akin to Cockburn's critique, see Naomi Klein, *The Shock Doctrine: The Rise of Disaster Capitalism* (Toronto: Alfred A. Knopf Canada, 2007).

43. Walsh and Keesmaat, *Colossians Remixed,* 30.

44. "Last Night of the World," *Breakfast in New Orleans, Dinner in Timbuktu.*

45. "Where the Death Squad Lives," *Big Circumstance.*

46. "Night Train," *Charity of Night.*

## Chapter 11 What Do You Do with Darkness?

1. Isaiah 60:1–2.

2. Isaiah 60:3.

3. Isaiah 60:11.

4. Isaiah 60:16.

5. Isaiah 60:17b–18.

6. The sermon below was composed for a worship service celebrating the marriage of Meagan Crosby and Rob Shearer. Since Meagan and Rob are huge Cockburn fans (it was part of the attraction!), it seemed only appropriate to weave Cockburn lyrics (plus a few others) throughout the sermon. I won't footnote all the allusions but simply let the reader pick up on the references. You might find some Leonard Cohen and U2 echoes here and there as well.

7. "Postcards from Cambodia," *You've Never Seen Everything.*

8. "Dweller by a Dark Stream," *Mummy Dust.*

9. This prayer was composed for the Wine Before Breakfast worshiping community at the University of Toronto.

## Chapter 12 Justice and Jesus

1. *Bono: In Conversation with Michka Assayas* (New York: Riverhead Books/Penguin, 2005), 26.

2. Cited by Bill Flanagan, *U2 at the End of the World* (New York: Delacorte Press, 1995), 171.

3. Amos Wilder, "Story and Story-World," *Interpretation* 37 (1983): 361.

4. See Walter Brueggemann, *Israel's Praise: Doxology against Idolatry and Ideology* (Philadelphia: Fortress Press, 1988), esp. chap. 1.

5. "Planet of the Clowns," *The Trouble with Normal.*

6. Walter Brueggemann, *Hopeful Imagination: Prophetic Voices in Exile* (Philadelphia: Fortress, 1986), 24.

7. "Feast of Fools," *Further Adventures Of.*

8. "Red Brother Red Sister," first released on *Circles in the Stream.*

9. "Gospel of Bondage," *Big Circumstance.*

10. Kenneth Gergen, *The Saturated Self: Dilemmas of Identity in Contemporary Life* (New York: Basic Books, 1991), 252.

11. Jean-François Lyotard, *The Postmodern Condition: A Report on Knowledge*, trans. Geoff Bennington and Brian Massumi (Minneapolis: University of Minnesota Press, 1984), 81.

12. I have addressed postmodernity and Christian faith at greater length (with a liberal sprinkling of Cockburn quotes) in my book with J. Richard Middleton *Truth Is Stranger Than It Used to Be: Biblical Faith in a Postmodern Age* (Downers Grove, IL: InterVarsity, 1995).

13. "Justice," *Inner City Front.*

14. I have addressed the ideological propensity of worldviews at greater length in my article "Transformation: Dynamic Worldview or Repressive Ideology?" *Journal of Education and Christian Belief* 4, no. 2 (Autumn 2000): 101–14.

15. Terry Eagleton, "Awakening from Modernity," *Times Literary Supplement*, Feb. 20, 1987. Cited by David Harvey, *The Condition of Postmodernity: An Enquiry into the Origins of Cultural Change* (Oxford: Basil Blackwell, 1989), 9.

16. Peter Berger, *The Sacred Canopy: Elements of a Sociological Theory of Religion* (Garden City, NY: Doubleday, 1967), 138.

17. Nicholas Boyle, *Who Are We Now? Christian Humanism and the Global Market from Hegel to Heaney* (Edinburgh: T&T Clark, 1998), 152.

18. Ibid., 80.

19. "Call It Democracy," *World of Wonders.*

20. I highly recommend Miroslav Volf's remarkable book *Exclusion and Embrace: A Theological Exploration of Identity, Otherness and Reconciliation* (Nashville: Abingdon, 1996).

21. "Justice."

22. "Gospel of Bondage."

23. Isaiah 42:2.

24. Deuteronomy 6:4.

25. Deuteronomy 4:12.

26. A point strongly argued by Bob Goudzwaard in *Idols of Our Time* (Downers Grove, IL: InterVarsity, 1984). See also Bob Goudzwaard, Mark Vander Vennen, and David Van Heemst, *Hope in Troubled Times: A New Vision for Confronting Global Crises* (Grand Rapids: Baker Academic, 2007).

27. See Psalm 115.

28. "Call It Democracy," *World of Wonders.*

29. "Tried and Tested," *You've Never Seen Everything.*

30. "Thoughts on a Rainy Afternoon," *Bruce Cockburn.*

31. "He Came from the Mountain," *Sunwheel Dance.*

32. C. S. Lewis, *The Lion, the Witch and the Wardrobe* (London: Fontana, 1950).

33. "Always winter and never Christmas," says the faun, Mr. Tumnus. Ibid., 23.

34. C. S. Lewis, *Till We Have Faces: A Myth Retold* (New York: Time, 1966), 257.

35. In biblical faith, mountains function as sites of revelation and appearances of the divine. Moses meets God on Mount Sinai and receives the Torah (Exodus 19 and following); Elijah calls upon God in a contest with the prophets of Baal on Mount Carmel (1 Kings 18); the temple of the Lord is on Mount Zion; and Jesus preaches his most radical sermon on a mountain

(Matthew 5), is seen in a vision with Moses and Elijah on what is called the Mount of Transfiguration (Matthew 17:1–8), offers his final sermon on the Mount of Olives (Mark 13:1–37), and meets his disciples for their final commissioning after the resurrection on a mountain in Galilee (Matthew 28:16–20).

36. "Hills of Morning," *Dancing in the Dragon's Jaws.*

37. "Man of a Thousand Faces," *Bruce Cockburn.*

38. 1 Corinthians 13:12.

39. "Broken Wheel," *Inner City Front.*

40. "Planet of the Clowns," *The Trouble with Normal.*

41. "All the Diamonds in the World," *Sun, Salt and Time.*

42. *Sunwheel Dance.*

43. "Man of a Thousand Faces."

44. Note that the capitalization of "He," together with "His" later in the song, is intentional in the handwritten lyrics that accompanied the album.

45. 1 Corinthians 15:54.

46. "Dweller by a Dark Stream."

47. Matthew 13:45.

48. "God Bless the Children," *Night Vision.*

49. Matthew 3:13–17; Acts 2:1–4.

50. Mark 4:35–41.

51. Isaiah 42:3.

52. John 20:11–18.

53. Revelation 1:18; 3:7.

54. "Shepherds," *Christmas.* There are two versions of this song in the released Cockburn catalog. The first to be released was the version that appears on the Christmas album. This nearly three-minute song moves along at a good clip, with a tune that is easily singable. But on the released deluxe edition of *In the Falling Dark*, we are graced with a version of more than seven minutes that stretches the lyrics into a longer and more meditative piece infused with jazz sensibilities. While the lyrics are identical, they are two radically different songs.

55. Jesus likens himself to a stone that the builders rejected that ends up becoming the cornerstone (Matthew 21:42).

56. The image of a stone and ripples on the surface of a still river may well also be a visual allusion to the cover of Cockburn's 1977 live album, *Circles in the Stream.* The front cover of this album shows a hand with a stone in it, with ripples of water emanating below. Curiously, however, it appears that this stone has come *out* of the water and not been dropped in, almost as if the photograph has reversed the sequence of events. Perhaps the imagery here is that the songs themselves are like stones plucked out of a river, and in the very taking of the stones, the very offering of the songs, redemption ripples forth.

## Chapter 13  Waiting for a Miracle

1. "Joy Will Find a Way," *Joy Will Find a Way.*

2. Isaiah 24:11.

3. "Feast of Fools," *Further Adventures Of.*

4. "Call It Democracy," *World of Wonders.* In the book of Revelation we read that God will destroy "those who destroy the earth" (11:18).

5. "Waiting for a Miracle," *Waiting for a Miracle.*

6. Cf. "A Dream Like Mine," *Nothing but a Burning Light*: "Today I dream of how it used to be / Things were different before / The picture shifts to how it's going to be / Balance restored."

7. For further reflection on the biblical vision of shalom, see Steven Bouma-Prediger and Brian J. Walsh, *Beyond Homelessness: Christian Faith in a Culture of Displacement* (Grand

Rapids: Eerdmans, 2008), chap. 6; Nicholas Wolterstorff, *Until Justice and Peace Embrace* (Grand Rapids: Eerdmans, 1983).

8. "All the Diamonds in the World," *Salt, Sun and Time*.

9. Contrasted with the jewels identified with Satan in songs like "Man of a Thousand Faces," *Bruce Cockburn*, and "Dialogue with the Devil," *Sunwheel Dance*.

10. "All the Diamonds in the World."

11. I have also reflected on this song in relation to hope in my book *Subversive Christianity: Imaging God in a Dangerous Time* (Seattle: Alta Vista College Press, 1994), chap. 4.

12. "Broken Wheel," *Inner City Front*.

13. Cf. "Where the Death Squad Lives," *Big Circumstance*. "I've got friends trying to batter the system down / fighting the past till the future comes round." The concluding verse of this song picks up similar themes of hope:

> This world can be better than it is today.
> You can say i'm a dreamer but that's okay,
> without the could-be and the might-have-been
> all you've got left is your fragile skin
> and that ain't worth much down where the death squad lives.

14. "Last Night of the World," *Breakfast in New Orleans, Dinner in Timbuktu*.

15. "Broken Wheel," *Inner City Front*.

16. Revelation 22:20.

17. "You've Never Seen Everything," *You've Never Seen Everything*.

18. "In the Falling Dark," *In the Falling Dark*.

19. "All Our Dark Tomorrows," *You've Never Seen Everything*.

20. Perhaps rivaled for that dubious honor by "Beautiful Creatures," on *Life Short Call Now*.

21. Exodus 13:21–22.

22. "Wondering Where the Lions Are," *Dancing in the Dragon's Jaws*.

23. Lines from "All Our Dark Tomorrows," "Trickle Down," "Postcards from Cambodia," and "You've Never Seen Everything," respectively, on *You've Never Seen Everything*.

24. See Job 38–41. Steve Bouma-Prediger reflects on the healing power of creation in God's response to Job's complaints in *For the Beauty of the Earth: A Christian Vision of Creation Care*, 2nd ed. (Grand Rapids: Baker Academic, 2010), 93–98.

25. Genesis 1.

26. See my review of this album, "Hope in Exile: Messenger Wind Blows Through Bruce Cockburn," *Catholic New Times* (June 29, 2003): 16.

27. "Arrows of Light," *Joy Will Find a Way*.

28. "Civilization and Its Discontents," *The Trouble with Normal*.

29. Genesis 1:1; 2:7; Ezekiel 37:1–14; Acts 2:1–13.

30. *Dart to the Heart*.

31. In biblical imagery the Spirit appears as a dove at the baptism of Jesus (Matthew 3:16–17; Luke 3:22; John 1:32).

32. "The Whole Night Sky," *Charity of Night*.

33. "Open," *You've Never Seen Everything*. For Jacob wrestling with the angel, see Genesis 32:22–32.

34. "He Came from the Mountain," *Sunwheel Dance*.

35. "All the Diamonds," *Sun, Salt and Time*.

36. "Hills of Morning," *Dancing in the Dragon's Jaws*.

37. Indeed, sometimes we find ourselves "Shipwrecked at the Stable Door" singing "Big Circumstance has brought me here—wish it would send me home." *Big Circumstance*.

38. 1 Corinthians 13:12.

39. And "when you love love, then love loves you too." "Love Loves You Too," *Dart to the Heart*.

40. "Hills of Morning," *Dancing in the Dragon's Jaws*.

41. "Messenger Wind," *You've Never Seen Everything*.

42. "When you send forth your spirit, they are created; and you renew the face of the ground." Psalm 104:30.

43. In "To Raise a Morning Star," Cockburn sings of light rising from sleepers all around, "all those dreamers trying to light the sky." This collective light, this hope of these dreamers is "rising like lightning in the pregnant air / it's electric—i can feel its might / i can feel it crackling in my nails and hair / makes me feel like i'm dancing on feet of light," *Stealing Fire*. In "Messenger Wind" it would appear that Cockburn has now had such a dreaming experience of his own.

44. "The Rose above the Sky," *Humans*.

45. "You've Never Seen Everything."

46. "Child of the Wind," *Nothing but a Burning Light*.

47. "In the Falling Dark"; *Night Vision*; "All Our Dark Tomorrows."

48. "Slow Down Fast," "Beautiful Creatures," *Life Short Call Now*; "All Our Dark Tomorrows."

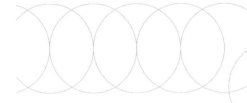

# Subject Index

# Song Index